ECONOMIC ISSUES, PROBLEMS AND PERSPECTIVES

CORPORATE AND INTERNATIONAL TAXATION: ANALYSES AND REFORMS

ECONOMIC ISSUES, PROBLEMS AND PERSPECTIVES

Additional books in this series can be found on Nova's website under the Series tab.

Additional E-books in this series can be found on Nova's website under the E-books tab.

ECONOMIC ISSUES, PROBLEMS AND PERSPECTIVES

CORPORATE AND INTERNATIONAL TAXATION: ANALYSES AND REFORMS

ALLISON S. GARNER
AND
DANIEL C. MURPHY
EDITORS

Nova Science Publishers, Inc.
New York

For permission to use material from this book please contact us:
Telephone 631-231-7269; Fax 631-231-8175
Web Site: http://www.novapublishers.com

Library of Congress Cataloging-in-Publication Data

Corporate and international taxation : analyses and reforms / editors, Allison S. Garner and Daniel C. Murphy.
p. cm.
Includes bibliographical references and index.
ISBN 978-1-61324-616-0 (hardcover : alk. paper) 1. Corporations--Taxation--United States. 2. International business enterprises--Taxation--United States. I. Garner, Allison S. II. Murphy, Daniel C.
HJ4653.C7C667 2011
336.24'30973--dc22

2011015364

Published by Nova Science Publishers, Inc. † New York

CONTENTS

PREFACE

The growing cost of brand-name prescription drugs can be a burden on patients, payers and providers of health care, particularly when price increases are large and occur suddenly. Controlling rising prescription drug prices helps to ensure that patients can afford medically necessary and sometimes life-saving medication, and to moderate costs for hospitals and third-party payers such as insurance plans and state and federal governments. This book examines prescription drug pricing costs and control concerns with a focus on extraordinary price increases for brand-name prescription drugs, as well as the characteristics and factors that contributed to this price increase.

Chapter 1- A striking feature of the modern U.S. economy is its growing openness—its increased integration with the rest of the world. The attention of tax policymakers has recently been focused on the growing participation of U.S. firms in the international economy and the increased pressure that engagement places on the U.S. system for taxing overseas business. Is the current U.S. tax system for taxing U.S. international business the appropriate one for the modern era of globalized business operations, or should its basic structure be reformed?

Chapter 2- At the beginning of the 111th Congress, economic stimulus proposals have dominated the legislative agenda, with a broad recognition that business tax incentives are among the policy options to consider. Two prominent proposals, H.R. 1 and S. 1, both titled the American Recovery and Reinvestment Act of 2009, were the focus of this debate. Both proposals include business tax incentives which would increase the after-tax rate of return on domestic investment and were subsequently enacted in P.L. 111-5. In contrast, little attention has been given to international policy options. An exception to this is a plan to reduce the tax rate on repatriated dividends that has received some consideration. Under such a plan, the U.S. tax that U.S. firms pay when their overseas operations remit ("repatriate") their foreign earnings as dividends to their U.S. parent corporations would be reduced. This provision was considered, but not adopted, as a floor amendment to a Senate version of the American Recovery and Reinvestment Act of 2009.

Chapter 3- H.R. 3970, introduced in the 110th Congress by then-Chairman Charles Rangel of the House Committee on Ways and Means, includes corporate tax revisions, trading a lower rate for a broader tax base as part of the revenue neutral reform package. S. 3018, introduced by Senators Ron Wyden and Judd Gregg in the 111th Congress, also provides for a lower corporate tax rate in exchange for a somewhat broader corporate tax base. Some discussions by economists in opinion pieces suggest there is an urgent need to lower the corporate tax rate, but not necessarily to broaden the tax base.

Chapter 4- In the early 2000s, reports indicated that an increasing number of U.S. firms have altered their structure by substituting a foreign parent corporation for a domestic one. Such "inversions" typically involved the creation of a new foreign corporation in a country with low tax rates (a "tax haven") that becomes the parent of the firm's foreign and U.S. component corporations. A chief motive for inversions was apparently savings by firms on their U.S. corporate income tax. One source of savings was tax on a firm's foreign income: the United States taxes corporations chartered in the United States on both U.S. and foreign income but taxes foreign-chartered corporations only on their U.S.-source income. An inversion can thus potentially reduce a firm's U.S. taxes on foreign income. Other tax savings apparently result from "earnings stripping," or the shifting of U.S.-source income from taxable U.S. components of the firm to the tax-exempt foreign parts.

Chapter 5- The federal government loses both individual and corporate income tax revenue from the shifting of profits and income into low-tax countries, often referred to as tax havens. The revenue losses from this tax avoidance and evasion are difficult to estimate, but some have suggested that the annual cost of offshore tax abuses may be around $100 billion per year. International tax avoidance can arise from large multinational corporations who shift profits into low-tax foreign subsidiaries or wealthy individual investors who set up secret bank accounts in tax haven countries.

Chapter 6- The term "international competitiveness" has long been an important part of tax policy debates and most recently has been prominent in discussions about fundamental U.S. tax reform. For example, in Executive Order 13369, President Bush stated that one goal of reform should be to "strengthen the competitiveness of the United States in the global market place." And in July 2007, the U.S. Treasury Department hosted a conference on business tax policy to explore ways in which the U.S. tax system might be reformed to enhance competitiveness. Yet despite its prominent use, the meaning of "competitiveness" is often vague, with its definition frequently depending on the perspective of the user. This report looks at competitiveness from three different perspectives: that of individual domestic firms, that of multinational corporations, and that of domestic labor. In each case, the report then applies economic analysis to the competitiveness concept, which adds clarity by identifying the specific ways in which taxes affect international trade and investment. With trade, tax burdens can affect what is traded, its overall level, and who benefits from trade, but they do not directly affect the trade balance. Further, it is the pattern of relative U.S. taxes within the domestic economy that matters for trade, not how a firm's taxes compare with those of its foreign competitors. With investment, taxes can affect the extent to which U.S. firms establish operations abroad and can affect economic efficiency and welfare as well as the distribution of income within the domestic economy and between the United States and foreign countries. This report was originally written by David L. Brumbaugh, Specialist in Public Finance. It explains basic economic principles.

In: Corporate and International Taxation
Editor: Allison S. Garner and Daniel C. Murphy
ISBN: 978-1-61324-616-0

Chapter 1

REFORM OF U.S. INTERNATIONAL TAXATION: ALTERNATIVES

Jane G. Gravelle

SUMMARY

A striking feature of the modern U.S. economy is its growing openness—its increased integration with the rest of the world. The attention of tax policymakers has recently been focused on the growing participation of U.S. firms in the international economy and the increased pressure that engagement places on the U.S. system for taxing overseas business. Is the current U.S. tax system for taxing U.S. international business the appropriate one for the modern era of globalized business operations, or should its basic structure be reformed?

The current U.S. system for taxing international business is a hybrid. In part the system is based on a residence principle, applying U.S. taxes on a worldwide basis to U.S. firms while granting foreign tax credits to alleviate double taxation. The system, however, also permits U.S. firms to defer foreign-source income indefinitely—a feature that approaches a territorial tax jurisdiction. In keeping with its mixed structure, the system produces a patchwork of economic effects that depend on the location of foreign investment and the circumstances of the firm. Broadly, the system poses a tax incentive to invest in countries with low-tax rates of their own and a disincentive to invest in high-tax countries. In theory, U.S. investment should be skewed towards low-tax countries and away from high-tax locations.

Evaluations of the current tax system vary, and so do prescriptions for reform. According to traditional economic analysis, world economic welfare is maximized by a system that applies the same tax burden to prospective (marginal) foreign and domestic investment so that taxes do not distort investment decisions. Such a system possesses "capital export neutrality," and could be accomplished by worldwide taxation applied to all foreign operations along with an unlimited foreign tax credit. In contrast, a system that maximizes national welfare—a system possessing "national neutrality"—would impose a higher tax burden on foreign investment, thus permitting an overall disincentive for foreign investment. Such a system would impose worldwide taxation, but would permit only a deduction, and not a credit, for foreign taxes.

A tax system based on territorial taxation would exempt overseas business investment from U.S. tax. In recent years, several proponents of territorial taxation have argued that changes in the world economy have rendered traditional prescriptions for international taxation obsolete, and instead prescribe territorial taxation as a means of maximizing both world and national economic welfare. For such a system to be neutral, however, capital would have to be completely immobile across locations. A case might be made that such a system is superior to the current hybrid system, but it is not clear that it is superior to other reforms, including not only a movement toward worldwide taxation by ending deferral, but also restricting deductions for costs associated with deferred income or restricting deferral and foreign tax credits for tax havens.

The increasingly global scope of U.S. business has a variety of dimensions. In trade, the overall level of exports plus imports has risen steadily and substantially in recent decades, increasing from 16% of U.S. gross domestic product (GDP) in 1976 to a 25% of GDP in 2009. Cross-border investment is growing even more dramatically. In 1976, the ratio of U.S. private assets to GDP was 0.20; by year end 2009 the ratio was 1.01.[1]

The bulk of the increase in "outbound" investment has been portfolio investment—investment in financial assets such as stocks and bonds without the active conduct of overseas business operations. But foreign direct investment by U.S. firms—actual foreign production by U.S.- owned companies—has increased too, rising from a ratio of 0.12 to 0.28 of GDP between 1976 and 2009. It is the taxation of U.S. business operations that has been the recent focus of policymakers, and that has raised the question of basic tax reform in the international sector: is the current U.S. tax system for taxing U.S. international business appropriate in this age of globalized business operations, or is reform needed?[2] Moreover, along with the increasing scope of international investment activities, there is an increasing opportunity for tax shelters that take advantage of low-tax foreign jurisdictions. How might revisions in the tax system exacerbate or address these tax shelter issues?

The current U.S. system is a "hybrid" construct, embodying a mix of opposing jurisdictional principles. Not surprisingly, the mixed system—in conjunction with foreign host-country taxes— poses a patchwork of incentive effects for U.S. firms and their global operations, in some cases taxing foreign operations favorably and posing an incentive to invest abroad, and in other cases imposing high tax burdens and posing a disincentive to overseas investment. In some cases, the system presents a rough tax neutrality towards overseas investment. It is perhaps the hybrid nature of the system that has led to calls for reform. Prescriptions for a "good" tax system vary, and the hybrid system satisfies none of them fully.

The report describes and assesses the principal prescriptions that have been offered for broad reform of the international system. The report begins with an overview of current law and of possible revisions. It then sets the framework for considering economic efficiency as well as tax shelter activities. Finally, it reviews alternative approaches to revision in light of those issues.

THE CURRENT SYSTEM AND POSSIBLE REVISIONS

The System's Structure

There are two alternative, conceptually "pure," principles on which countries base their tax in the international setting: residence and territory. Under a residence system, a country taxes its own residents (or domestically chartered "resident" corporations) on their worldwide income, regardless of its geographic source. Under a territorial or source-based system, a country taxes only income that is earned within its own borders.

In practice, no country uses a pure residence-based tax; historically, virtually all countries tax income foreign investors earn within their borders (although they may grant tax holidays in some cases as an inducement to investment). Some countries, however, do have an exclusively territorial or source-based tax.[3] The United States uses a system that taxes both income of foreign firms earned within its borders as well as the worldwide income of its U.S.-chartered firms.

Despite these nominal "residence" features, however, U.S. taxes do not apply to the foreign income of U.S.-owned corporations chartered abroad. As a result, a U.S. firm can indefinitely defer U.S. tax on its foreign income if it conducts its foreign operations through a foreign- chartered subsidiary corporation; U.S. taxes do not apply as long as the foreign subsidiary's income is reinvested overseas. With some exceptions, U.S. taxes apply only when the income is remitted to the U.S.-resident parent as dividends or other intra-firm payments such as interest and royalties. The deferral feature reduces the effective U.S. tax burden on foreign income and imparts an element of territoriality to the system; it also results in a dichotomous structure for taxing overseas business income: deferral in the case of foreign-subsidiary income and current taxation in the case of branches of U.S. chartered corporations. The bulk of active business investment by U.S. firms is through foreign-chartered subsidiaries.[4]

Along with deferral, another basic feature of the U.S. system is the foreign tax credit. While the United States taxes worldwide income on either a current or deferred basis, it also allows credits for foreign taxes paid on a dollar-for-dollar basis against U.S. taxes otherwise owed.[5] This treatment avoids the double-taxation that would otherwise apply and concedes the first right of taxation to the country of source. In effect, the United States gives the foreign host country the first opportunity to tax the income, and collects only what tax is left (up to its own rate) after the foreign host country collects its share.

When the foreign tax is higher than the U.S. tax, the credit is limited to the U.S. tax that would be due on the foreign income. The purpose of the limit is to protect the U.S. domestic tax base: without it, foreign countries could impose very high taxes without discouraging inbound U.S. investment, because the cost of the higher taxes would be shifted to the U.S. treasury. With the limitation, if foreign taxes exceed the U.S. tax that would be due, the excess foreign taxes cannot be credited. Foreign tax credits that exceed this limitation are termed "excess credits." Currently foreign tax credits are allowed on what is sometimes termed an "overall" basis, so that income and tax credits from all countries are combined. This treatment allows for "cross-crediting," where credits paid in excess of U.S. tax in one country may be used to offset U.S. tax in a country where the foreign tax is lower than the U.S. tax. To prevent abuse, tax credits are divided into "baskets" which separate passive income easily shifted to low-tax countries. Currently, there are two baskets, one for active income and one for passive income. About half of foreign-source active business income is earned by firms with overall excess credits.[6]

To address tax avoidance by shifting passive income into low-tax jurisdictions, Subpart F restricts the applicability of deferral in some situations. Subpart F provides that U.S. stockholders (e.g., parent firms) of foreign corporations are subject to current U.S. tax on certain types of subsidiary income, whether or not the income is repatriated. Only stockholders owning at least 10% of subsidiary stock and only subsidiaries that are at least 50% owned by 10% U.S. stockholders are subject to Subpart F. Countries that have territorial tax systems generally also have some type of anti-abuse provision to protect their tax base.

Tax deferral results in heightened importance for the system's rules for dividing income between related firms; the more income a firm can assign, for tax purposes, to a foreign subsidiary in a low-tax country, the lower its overall tax burden. The current system generally requires firms to set hypothetical "transfer prices," which are required to approximate the prices two firms would agree on if they conducted their transactions at arm's length. The system is complex and difficult to administer.

The foreign tax credit's limitation also places pressure on the system's rules for determining the source of income ("sourcing" rules). Because firms can only credit foreign taxes against the portion of taxable income attributable to foreign sources, taxpayers must assign both revenue and costs to either domestic or foreign sources. While the tax code contains rules for making such allocations, they are likewise complex and difficult to administer.

In sum, the United States taxes its resident corporations on their worldwide income, but permits indefinite deferral of active business income earned through foreign subsidiaries. Where U.S. taxes apply, foreign tax credits alleviate double taxation but are limited to offsetting U.S. tax on foreign income. Subpart F is designed to deny deferral to what is generally passive income.

Possible Revisions

Because the current U.S. tax system is a mix of a worldwide system and a territorial system, the fundamental tax reform issue is whether moving toward either "pure" system—a territorial or worldwide residence-based regime—would be an improvement. Moving toward a territorial system would involve permanently exempting most foreign-source active business income. (Most territorial proposals, however, would continue taxing passive income, as under current law's Subpart F.) Moving toward a worldwide tax would eliminate the deferral benefit and might also entail further restricting cross-crediting by increasing the number of baskets for the foreign tax credit limit. Some revisions that maintain the current system but tighten the rules for deductions include proposals to disallow certain deductions of the parent company (such as interest) that reflect the share of income that is deferred.

The report defers the discussion of the precise changes fundamental reform would entail. First, however, the report explains the tools economists have developed for evaluating the various international tax systems.

NEUTRALITY, EFFICIENCY, AND COMPETITIVENESS

The term competitiveness has often been invoked in the debate about U.S. policy in a global economy, including discussions of U.S. tax policy.[7] In economic analysis, however, it is not *countries* that are competitive, it is *companies* that are. A company generally thinks of itself as competitive if it can produce at the same cost as, or a lower cost than, other firms. But a country's firms cannot be competitive in all areas. Indeed, even if firms in a country are more productive than firms in all other countries in every respect, a country would still tend to produce those goods in which its relative advantage is greatest. The other countries need to produce goods with their resources as well. This notion is called comparative advantage, and it is an important concept in economic theory.[8]

When discussing national policy, including tax policy and its effect on the international allocation of capital, the issues are generally framed around issues of efficiency, neutrality, and optimal policies rather than notions of competitiveness. These terms can mean the same thing, or they can be slightly different. Neutrality generally refers to provisions that do not alter the allocation of investment from that which would occur without taxes. When markets are operating efficiently, a neutral tax policy will also be an efficient policy, since it will maintain the efficient allocation that would occur without taxes. Moreover, even when there are market imperfections, neutrality may still be the policy most likely to be efficient, given the difficulty in identifying and measuring market imperfections.

Optimal policy differs from efficiency in that it usually refers to a particular agent or actor choosing a policy that maximizes his or her own welfare. A country can also choose a policy that leads to the greatest welfare for its own citizens, even if that policy distorts the allocation of capital (is not neutral) and leads to less efficient worldwide production. The optimal policy from the perspective of a country, in other words, may not be the most efficient in terms of the worldwide allocation of capital, and may not be the optimal policy from the perspective of world economic welfare.

Economists have traditionally used three concepts to evaluate tax rules that apply to outbound investment. These concepts are referred to as neutrality concepts, although, as shown below, they are not always neutral in the sense of not distorting the allocation of investment. The concepts are capital export neutrality, capital import neutrality, and national neutrality. In order to evaluate the consequences of any multinational tax reform, it is crucial to understand these concepts, whether they are valid, and what they imply for policy. The concepts were developed when virtually all foreign investment took place as direct investment of multinational companies; virtually no foreign portfolio investment (ownership of foreign stock by U.S. citizens) existed. The growth in this portfolio investment has led to a new neutrality concept, referred to as capital ownership neutrality. We address these traditional and new concepts in turn.

Understanding Capital Export Neutrality, Capital Import Neutrality, and National Neutrality

Capital export neutrality requires a country to apply the same tax rate to its firms' investments, regardless of where they are located, and is embodied in a residence-based tax system. Capital import neutrality requires the same tax on firms with different nationalities that invest in a given location and is embodied in a territorial or source-based tax. National neutrality requires that the nation's total return on investment, including both that nation's taxes and its firms' profits, is equal in each jurisdiction, foreign and domestic. This form of neutrality is obtained by taxing foreign-source income and allowing a deduction for foreign taxes.

Some of these neutrality rules may also be rules for optimization. National neutrality is often described as optimal, but that outcome is only the case with perfectly mobile capital and no retaliation by foreign countries. There is also an optimizing rule for choosing the tax rate on inbound investment, which depends on how responsive that investment inflow is to the return.

Evaluating policy, discussed subsequently, is complicated because while some countries have territorial or source-based taxes, no country imposes a pure residence-based tax. While worldwide taxation as practiced in the United States and other countries has some attributes of a residence- based tax, it is a mixture of residence- and source-based tax. Tax is imposed on foreign firms operating within the United States, a source-based attribute. On outbound investment, the application of tax to repatriated income creates some resemblance to residence tax, but the foreign tax credit limitations cause it to depart from such a tax, and deferral provisions introduce an element of a source-based tax.

Because these concepts are so frequently misunderstood, it is useful to employ a simple illustrative example to explain them with the pure tax systems that are consistent with capital export neutrality and capital import neutrality. In these simple systems, national neutrality is the same as capital export neutrality, and its nuances will be discussed in the following section where more realistic tax systems are discussed. In this instance, it may be helpful to demonstrate the difference between residence-based and source-based taxes in achieving economic neutrality.

Consider a world beginning with no taxes, and assume that capital is perfectly substitutable across countries, implying that a firm will earn the same after-tax return in each location. The return is 10%. There are three countries: a high-tax country that imposes a 50% tax rate, a low-tax country that imposes a 25% tax rate, and a zero-tax country. All investment is made through the companies' direct operations, hence, there is no substitution of capital across firms and the capital owned by each country is fixed. The high and low-tax rate countries have capital which can be used to invest in their own country, or in the other two countries. To simplify, the zero-tax country is assumed to have only labor and no capital.

Table 1 shows the return to firms in the absence of any tax and with the two tax systems in place but before investment has shifted (which would alter the pre-tax return). Residence taxation, which produces capital export neutrality, has no effect on the allocation of investment by either country's firms because each firm still earns the same return in each location. Source-based taxation, however, will result in higher returns in the zero- and, to a lesser extent, low-tax countries. As a result, capital will flow out of the high-tax country, raising its return and lowering the wages of the workers in that country and into the zero-tax country, lowering its return and raising the wages of the workers in that country. The effect on the low-tax country depends on the size of that country and its labor force relative to the rest of the world. In addition to the effects on the return to capital and wages, output is produced inefficiently, which reduces world welfare.

Table 1. Illustration of the Effects of Residence- and Source-Based Taxation

Nationality of Firm	Return by Location of Investment (%)		
	High-Tax Country	Low-Tax Country	Zero-Tax Country
No Taxes			
High-Tax Country	10%	10%	10%
Low-Tax Country	10%	10%	10%
Residence Tax			
High-Tax Country	5%	5%	5%
Low-Tax Country	7.5%	7.5%	7.5%
Source-Based (Territorial) Tax			
High-Tax Country	5%	7.5%	10%
Low-Tax Country	5%	7.5%	10%

Note: The high-tax country has a 50% tax rate, while the low-tax country has a 25% tax rate.

Table 1 can also be used to show that the residence-based system is also consistent with national neutrality, but the source-based system is not. For the high-tax country, in each location it earns 5% in tax revenue and 5% in profits (for a total of 10%). Thus the total return to the nation is equated in each jurisdiction. The same is true of the low-tax country, although the total return is split into 2.5% taxes and 7.5% profits. The source-based system does not meet that standard. Even before investment shifts, the high-tax country, while earning 10% domestically and in the zero tax haven country, is earning only 7.5% in the low-tax country, since that country's government is collecting the tax. The same is true of the low-tax country with respect to investment taxed by the high-tax country.

National neutrality departs from capital export neutrality in the more complex, real world circumstances. It, in fact, requires that foreign-source income be taxed, and that any taxes imposed by the country of location be deducted (rather than the current rule of some countries, including the United States, that allow taxes to be credited). If foreign countries impose taxes, national neutrality does not lead to worldwide neutrality, since foreign investment is discouraged in countries that impose taxes.

National neutrality is really about optimal policy, which maximizes the welfare of the country's residents. It is an optimal policy if all capital is perfectly mobile; if not, it is actually optimal for a country to impose even more tax on outbound investment than is suggested by the neutrality standard.

In sum, according to these longstanding measures of neutrality and efficiency, capital export neutrality is appropriate for maximizing world output, national neutrality is appropriate for maximizing a nation's welfare, and capital import "neutrality" is not neutral at all.

Capital Ownership Neutrality

A new concept of neutrality has appeared in recent years. The term capital ownership neutrality (CON) is closely associated with Desai and Hines, professors, respectively, of business at Harvard and economics at the University of Michigan.[9] The term itself, however, appears to have been coined by Michael Devereaux,[10] a British economist. The underlying justification for the new standard's development, the growth of portfolio investment, was also discussed independently about the same time in a paper by Frisch.[11] Essentially, capital ownership neutrality is the same as capital import neutrality in that, under certain very restrictive assumptions, it is achieved by source-based taxation, and some of the earlier discussions viewed it as a resurrection of capital import neutrality.[12]

The issue of ownership neutrality developed because international investment markets changed. At the time the previous notions of neutral international tax systems were first developed— generally, the early 1960s—virtually all U.S. investment abroad was carried out through foreign direct investment by U.S. firms.[13] U.S. portfolio investors held almost no stock in foreign firms. Until the mid-1980s, the share of foreign stocks in U.S. residents' stock portfolios was less than 1%. Thus, it was reasonable to assume, as in the discussion above, that there was no substitution across the nationality of firms, but rather only across locations—that is, U.S. investors could not substitute investment abroad through foreign firms for investment in U.S. firms with foreign operations. Over time, however, the share of foreign stock owned by U.S. investors increased, and by the end of 2006, it was 22% of corporate equity owned by U.S. investors.[14] This increase did not occur smoothly: it increased in the latter part of the mid-1980s to about 6%, leveled out for a number of years, then again rose around 1993 and 1994 to about 11%, where it stayed until around 2001, and then rose again.

A closer look at the CON concept indicates that, to make the argument that capital ownership neutrality (and therefore source-based taxation) should be the guiding principle for an efficient and neutral tax system, three requirements are needed. First, firms are assumed not to substitute operations in one location for those in another—capital is completely immobile across locations. Second, firms must differ in their productivity—that is, some firms are more efficient than others—and there must be substitution across portfolios that results in firms being shut out of lines-of-business that they could run more efficiently. Third, there must be no mechanisms available to obtain the benefits of productive efficiency—short of owning the productive capital assets. For example, relatively inefficient firms cannot rent efficient technologies or hire efficient managers away from efficient firms.

If only the first requirement is met (immobility across locations), any system of taxing investment abroad would be neutral because the particular distortion—allocation of investment across locations—is simply assumed away. It doesn't matter if overseas operations are taxed higher or lower than domestic investment, because investment has no reason to move. Residence taxation would be efficient as well as source-based taxation, because the national affiliation of firms would not matter to productivity (although residence taxation would not be optimal for the high- tax country which would have no revenues).[15]

If the two remaining assumptions also apply—productivity differs and no mechanisms exist to boost efficiency—it can be shown that residence-based taxation is inefficient while source-based taxation produces efficiency. For example, returning to Table 1, suppose some firms in each country are particularly productive and can earn 12% before tax rather than 10%. With residence- based taxation, the after-tax return of the high-tax country's productive firms, which would yield an after-tax return of 6%, would not be enough for these firms to operate and, if the only way to realize the higher return is to own the capital, the higher pre-tax yields of these more efficient firms would not be realized. With source-based taxation, the efficient firms in each country would operate and displace the less efficient ones.

In the more realistic tax systems where countries also tax capital income in their own location, the high-tax country's especially productive firms would still operate in their own country. That is, by taxing income within its borders, a high-tax country that is attempting to practice capital export neutrality with a worldwide tax still faces neutral ground in its home country. Thus, any distortion arising in practice from the current system would involve foreign firms and the solution of exempting foreign-source income from tax is the solution consistent with capital ownership neutrality.

Consider each of the restrictions in turn. The first is the assumption that capital is immobile across locations; as noted above, there is considerable evidence that it is not and, indeed, that it is quite elastic. So at best, it would be a question of picking which type of distortion is worse. As long as capital is mobile across jurisdictions, "capital ownership neutrality" is not neutral. At most, the model shows that there is no way to achieve neutrality and that one is in a second-best world.

The second restriction requires a high, perhaps perfect, degree of substitution in portfolios of different types of stocks that would lead to the exclusion of stock of high-tax countries. There is considerable evidence to suggest that such perfect substitution is not the case. It has long been known that there is a significant home bias in the holding of both portfolio and direct assets. Despite global securities markets, American residents continue to hold 80% of their stock portfolios in stock of U.S. firms. If portfolio investment were perfectly substitutable, the U.S. share would be expected to be closer to the share of total assets. The U.S. accounts for about a third of total fixed investment of the OECD countries.[16]

The fact that the portfolio share has grown does not in itself provide evidence of a significant elasticity; rather, it may reflect a variety of technical and institutional changes that make holding foreign stocks more feasible. Moreover, the portfolio shares are consistent with the notion that the holdings that do exist are not so much due to tax differences but to a general desire to diversify assets across countries to reduce cyclical risk. Two-thirds of investment is in other countries with similar tax rates. At the end of 2005, the two largest shares were for the U.K. (16%) and Japan (15%). While the U.K., with a 30% corporate rate, has a lower statutory rate than the U.S. (39% including state taxes), Japan has a rate of 41%. The next two largest claimants with 7% and 6% have rates of 35% and 35%.[17] There are significant shares in two tax havens, Bermuda (5%) and the Cayman Islands (3%). According to the Department of Treasury, however, the Bermuda investments are largely former U.S. firms that have moved their location to avoid U.S. tax (a phenomenon called inversion, which was subsequently addressed with legislative restrictions), and the Cayman Islands investments are in offshore financial centers (again likely a tax avoidance issue rather than direct production issue).[18]

An imperfect portfolio substitution elasticity also suggests that the phenomenon of eliminating efficient firms is less likely to happen. Firms that are especially productive and efficient will earn higher returns than other firms in similar circumstances of nationality and location, and they would be expected to be retained in both domestic and foreign investors' portfolios. Any firms whose size is contracted by portfolio shifts due to tax rates are more likely to be the marginal firms that have a normal level of productivity.

Finally, this model assumes that there are no other ways to enjoy the additional productivity of more efficient firms. In effect, the model begins with the assumption of productive advantages without defining in formal terms—so that the effects can be modeled—the source of the productivity.

For example, if the greater productivity of the firm is due to the employment of managers with greater skills, then that productivity arises at a cost, and these management skills embodied in the individuals resident in a given country should be free to move to their highest use, and allocated efficiently. Since they add a surplus value, they would not be driven out of the market, and worldwide efficiency requires a capital export neutrality approach to labor resources as well as capital.

If the asset is uniquely tied to the firm—such as a value through a trademark, intangible R&D, or even a management set-up—the model does not allow for the fact that ownership of the productive assets and ownership of the intangible asset can, in most cases, be separated. Trademarks and patents can be franchised and sold. Or, if the intangible cannot be separately sold (for example, if the R&D could be easily copied and thus is not patented but kept secret), there are ways for the firm to operate without ownership of the capital assets, such as factories, machinery, and equipment, that give rise to normal products. These assets could be leased by the firm with the intangible asset. Moreover, if the asset is not closely tied to management, the firm could arrange for contract manufacturing, a technique commonly used to shift profits. These techniques may be less than perfect if there are principal-agent costs,[19] but this effect is of questionable importance.

In light of the many ways in which the efficiency costs of capital ownership non-neutrality are unlikely to be significant compared to location distortions, it seems questionable to use meeting this standard of neutrality to evaluate tax reform changes and questionable to see source-based taxation as an efficient international tax regime.

ASSESSING THE EXISTING TAX SYSTEM

The above examples illustrate the various traditional concepts of neutrality and how they are embodied in basic tax structures. However, as described at the report's outset, the U.S. tax system is a hybrid—neither a pure territorial or residence-based system. Accordingly, it presents a patchwork of incentive effects, sometimes posing an incentive to invest abroad and, in other situations, presenting either a disincentive or tax neutrality. We look in this section at the existing system's principal incentive effects.

First, in some cases the U.S. system resembles residence-based taxation—it taxes foreign branch income on a current basis while allowing a foreign tax credit. Even where current taxation applies, however, the U.S. system departs from pure residence taxation by placing a limit on its foreign tax credit. If pure residence-based means taxing income of residents at the same rate, regardless of where it is earned, an unlimited foreign tax credit would be required. Under such a credit, when the foreign tax is lower than the home country tax, the home country would collect a residual, equating the total tax imposed to that on its domestic investment. When the foreign country's tax is higher, the home country would have to refund the excess so that, again, the tax on the foreign investment would be the same as the tax on domestic investment. In practice, however, an unlimited foreign tax credit is not feasible because of its potential threat to the home country tax base (here, that of the United States). Without a limit, countries host to foreign investment could simply raise their taxes on inbound investment without limit and without fear of driving foreign investors away. The foreign investors could simply credit their high foreign taxes against their home-country tax bill. The U.S. thus limits its foreign tax credit to offsetting U.S. taxes on foreign (and not domestic) income.

The incentive effects of a worldwide system with a limited credit depend on exactly how the credit is limited. If the limit applies separately for each country (a "per-country" limit), the system would achieve neutrality on outbound investment with respect to low tax-rate countries, but not high tax-rate countries. If taxes can be averaged across countries—that is, if a firm calculates a single limit aggregated across countries, the neutrality consequences are less clear. In that case, the excess credits from the investment in a high-tax country can be used to offset tax due on investments in the low-tax country (can be "cross credited"). For example, assume profits were $100 in a high-tax location with a 50% rate and $100 in the no-tax location, with the home country tax rate 25%. With no cross crediting, a firm from the 25% tax rate country uses the foreign tax of $50 to wipe out the home country tax of $25, with only the tax of $50 applying, while the firm would pay a home country tax of $25 on the income earned in the zero tax jurisdiction. The total tax is $75. With cross crediting, the total foreign-source income is $200, the total foreign tax paid is $50 (in the high-tax country, on $100 of profit), and the total home- country tax due is also $50 (25% of $200 of income in both countries). All foreign tax is credited and the total tax is $50.

Cross crediting, as allowed in the U.S. tax system, can therefore reduce the disincentive to invest in high-tax countries if the firm already has investment in the zero tax country, because the excess credits have a value. Similarly, it can increase the incentive to invest in the zero tax country if the country already has investment in the high-tax country, since excess credits can effectively remove any residual tax in the zero tax country. In either case, foreign investment is encouraged relative to domestic investment. In practice, the U.S. tax system permits extensive cross crediting; it does not require a per-country limitation, although it does require firms to calculate separate limits for passive and active business income.

Second, the U.S. tax system departs from residence-based taxation in its use of deferral. As described above, U.S. taxes generally do not apply to the foreign business income of foreign- chartered subsidiaries. This feature of the tax system introduces elements of a territorial or source-based taxation into the system, and also introduces a distortion in firms' decisions of whether to return profits to the United States or reinvest them abroad. Moreover the interaction of deferral with cross crediting provides some scope for firms to choose the times and places of repatriation to minimize tax liability. In general, the availability of deferral—like the territorial taxation it at least approaches—poses an incentive for U.S. firms to invest in low-tax countries. Also, once capital has been invested abroad, the provision encourages firms to retain their earnings overseas rather than returning them to the United States.

This mixture of treatments also provides methods for avoiding tax apart from the direct effects on investment allocation. Deferral provides an incentive to artificially shift profits to low-tax jurisdictions. Since firms can choose between branch operations and investment via foreign- chartered subsidiaries, they can use a branch form when operations are starting up and typically lose money to allow losses to be deducted from the U.S. worldwide income tax, and then shift to a subsidiary form when the operation becomes profitable.

In sum, the current system poses a patchwork of incentive effects that is in keeping with its hybrid nature. Where current taxation applies—for example, to branch income—there is a disincentive to invest in high-tax countries, and either an incentive or neutrality towards investment in low-tax countries, depending on whether the investing firm can use cross-crediting of foreign taxes. Where deferral is available, the system poses an incentive to invest in low-tax countries. The system also provides mechanisms for artificially sheltering income from tax.

TERRITORIAL TAXATION: THE DIVIDEND EXEMPTION PROPOSAL

The preceding sections showed why the theoretical argument that territorial taxation is optimal is difficult to defend. Some have argued, however, that while territorial taxation may not be the most efficient system in a perfect world, it is nonetheless superior to the hybrid, patchwork system that is the current U.S. system—a "second best" argument. A territorial tax was recently proposed by the National Commission on Fiscal Responsibility and Reform, although the specific details were not provided.[20] To best understand this argument for territorial taxation, it is helpful to examine the specific version proposed in a 2001 American Enterprise Institute monograph by economists Harry Grubert and John Mutti. A similar plan was set forth in 2005 by President Bush's advisory commission on tax reform.[21]

Grubert and Mutti described their proposal as a "dividend exemption" system, thus focusing on the chief modification their plan would make to the current regime: it would exempt from U.S. taxes dividends repatriated to U.S. parents from foreign subsidiary corporations, thus moving from current law's deferral for foreign income to a permanent exemption. More generally, an exemption system can be viewed as a territorial tax system whose application is restricted to active business investment abroad, but that continues to tax portfolio investment of firms (such as interest, royalties, and similar income) on a current basis.

Several additional features of the plan are important to the advantages it might have over the current system. First, the plan would not permit foreign tax credits to be claimed for foreign taxes paid with respect to repatriated earnings. The repatriations, after all, would be exempt from U.S. tax, thus obviating the need for relief from double taxation. Second, deductions allocable to tax- exempt foreign-source income would be disallowed. Here, the reasoning is that the purpose of deductions is to remove items of cost from the tax base; since overseas income would no longer be in the U.S. tax base, removal of associated costs would not be necessary. Importantly, this would mean that a portion of debt incurred by a U.S. parent corporation would not be deductible—the portion assumed to be used in financing tax-exempt foreign subsidiaries.

As described in the preceding sections, the capital import neutrality and capital ownership neutrality standards both recommend adoption of territorial taxation, but traditional economic theory is skeptical of the theoretical justification of the two standards. Grubert and Mutti argue, however, that even if CIN and CON are rejected on theoretical grounds, an exemption system is superior to the current hybrid system in terms of several important factors: efficiency, simplicity, and the raising of tax revenue.

First, efficiency: Grubert and Mutti argue that current law's application of tax to repatriated foreign earnings encourages wasteful and inefficient behavior on the part of corporations in devising methods of repatriating foreign earnings without paying U.S. tax. Under an exemption system, such wasteful planning would be unnecessary. Also, since foreign tax credits would no longer be applicable, cross-crediting of excess foreign tax credits would no longer shield investment in low-tax foreign locations from U.S. tax, and the artificial diversion of technology- exploiting investment to low-tax locations would no longer occur. [22]

Nevertheless, elimination of these sources of inefficiency alone would not be sufficient to make an exemption system less wasteful than current law. If elimination of tax on repatriations were the only feature of an exemption system, the system would likely increase inefficiency by encouraging added investment in low-tax countries. Rather, the crucial element to an exemption system's purported superiority is its elimination of interest deductions for overseas investment. The inclusion of this provision would actually result in an increase in the average tax burden for overseas investment, thus generating an efficiency gain from an improved allocation of investment away from low-tax overseas locations and into the domestic economy.[23]

An exemption system may also increase tax revenue. The Grubert and Mutti analysis concludes that the system would generate $7.7 billion annually in added U.S. revenue.[24] (Their estimate is based on 1994 data, so it would likely be larger in the current economy.) More recently, the Joint Committee on Taxation has estimated the revenue gain at about $6 billion per year.[25] As with the efficiency gains, however, the increase in tax revenues is crucially dependent on denial of deductions for costs allocated to tax-exempt foreign income. Without the new restrictions, an exemption system would likely reduce tax revenue. The Joint Committee on Taxation has estimated that current law's deferral reduces revenues by approximately $6 billion.[26] By the same token, an exemption system would lose tax revenue compared to the current system if the current system were to deny deductions to deferred income.

In the area of simplicity, proponents of an exemption system emphasize its reduction in the need for tax planning. It should be noted, however, that tax complexity—and its accompanying difficulties for tax administration—exist when entities or activities are taxed according to different rules. Under an exemption system, foreign subsidiary corporations would be tax exempt as under current law, and since the exemption would be permanent rather than temporary, its import for firms' tax planners would be magnified. Accordingly, the tax system's transfer pricing rules for allocating income among U.S. parent firms and their foreign subsidiaries would become more important; more pressure would apply to rules that are inherently difficult to enforce. The same would be true for the distinction between active and passive income, since active income would be permanently exempt and passive-investment income would be taxed on a current basis. Firms would have an even greater incentive to move from branch to subsidiary operations for start-up firms.

In a recent article critical of territorial tax proposals, Kleinbard pointed out analyses by Grubert and others that emphasized the growth in the importance of royalties as a share of repatriated earnings for multinationals, suggesting that the exploitation of intangible assets by multinationals in foreign locations is increasing. However, where the Grubert and Mutti analysis sees this as an important reason to adopt an exemption system—cross-crediting of foreign taxes would no longer pose an incentive to low-tax investment under an exemption system—Kleinbard sees it as a liability. The growth of intangibles, argues Kleinbard, would place enormous pressure on the administration of transfer prices.[27]

Proponents of an exemption system concede that it is not perfect, but argue that it is at least superior to the highly imperfect system now in existence. Even this defense, however, has its shortcomings: the most economically attractive aspects of the exemption proposals could, in principle, be adopted piecemeal, and its most distortionary aspects could be left behind. Specifically, more restrictive rules for deducting interest and other costs could be adopted without exempting dividend repatriations from U.S. tax. Such plans could enhance economic efficiency more than would the full-blown exemption systems.

Even with these criticisms of the Mutti/Grubert exemption plan, perhaps the most severe is this: why accept second best? The report next examines what moving towards a residence-based system would look like, in practice.

A Residence-Based System in Practice

The capital export neutrality standard recommends a system that would be based on residence— that is, a system that taxes the income of home-country firms, regardless of where it is earned. The present section looks at the shape a residence-based system would likely take.

Current law's deferral system would be repealed under a residence-based system, and U.S. taxation would apply on a current basis to the income of foreign subsidiaries, whether or not the income is repatriated. If it were not for foreign taxes, deferral's repeal would move the system to the brink of capital export neutrality (except for the portfolio investment concern): the tax burden on foreign investment would roughly equal the tax rate on domestic investment. Foreign taxes, however, complicate matters and make pure capital export neutrality difficult to achieve, in practice. The problem arises when a foreign host country's tax rate exceeds the U.S. domestic tax rate. In such cases, pure capital export neutrality would require an unlimited foreign tax credit. Foreign taxes would offset U.S. taxes on domestic as well as foreign income—only by this mechanism could the high foreign tax burden be brought into line with taxes on domestic investment. Yet, as noted in the preceding section on the existing tax system, an unlimited foreign tax credit is impractical: foreign governments could, in effect, draw on the U.S. Treasury by raising taxes on U.S. investors, *ad infinitum*.

Advocates of a residence-based system have in some cases advocated a more restrictive form of the foreign tax credit limitation that would place more limits on "cross crediting" than does current law's two-part limit. For example, at various times in the past, the United States has required firms to calculate their limitation on a country-by-country basis (a so-called "per- country" limitation), under which taxes paid to one country could not be credited against U.S. tax on income from another country.[28] The Wyden-Gregg Tax Reform Act , S. 3018, introduced in the 111th Congress would, in the context of a general corporate reform that would broaden the base and reduce the rate, eliminate deferral and institute a per country foreign tax credit limit. An alternative or additional approach to restricting cross crediting was implemented by the Tax Reform Act of 1986 (P.L. 99-514), which, instead of requiring separate limits for each country, specified a variety of different types of income for which separate limits ("baskets") were required. The American Jobs Creation Act of 2004 (AJCA; P.L. 108-3 57), however, reduced the number of separate limits to current law's two.[29] Note, however, that a more restrictive foreign tax credit limitation would not necessarily move a residence-based system closer to pure capital export neutrality. As noted above, while cross crediting may pose an incentive to invest in low-tax countries, it also mitigates the disincentive to invest in high-tax countries.

Capital export neutrality requires equal tax burdens on foreign and domestic investment. There are several features of the current system that favor domestic over foreign investment, and whose modification would move the current system in the direction of capital export neutrality. The most important of these is the 9% tax deduction for domestic production enacted in 2004 by AJCA. Other tax benefits that are restricted to domestic investment are the Section 179 "expensing" allowance for machines and equipment and the research and experimentation tax credit.

As noted above, Grubert and Altshuler revisited the topic of international tax reform in 2006. In their analysis, they compared the exemption system with what they termed a "burden neutral" worldwide taxation system. In constructing this latter system, they couple elimination of deferral with a reduction in the statutory U.S. tax rate that applies to foreign earnings—thus using the added tax revenue from deferral's repeal to, in effect, "purchase" a cut in the tax rate. The goal of the exchange is to not damage what they term the "competitive position" of U.S. multinationals. As a consequence of the countervailing changes, the burden on investment in a range of low-tax countries would increase; the burden of a range of income that is repatriated under current law would fall, but the overall burden on overseas investment would be unchanged.

Grubert and Altshuler note that the overall advantage of their burden-neutral worldwide proposal over current law depends on outcomes which are, as yet, unknown: how many firms would be in an excess credit position under the plan and what the burden-neutral tax rate would be. They also caution that the plan would have another weakness: foreign countries would have an incentive to raise their tax rates in the face of current U.S. taxation because inbound U.S. investment would be less sensitive to the foreign rates.[30] They further note that their plan's reduction of tax rates at the corporate level would shift more of the overall U.S. tax burden on corporations from the corporate to the shareholder level—a virtue in the modern world where capital is increasingly mobile since shareholder-level taxes are generally imposed on a residence basis and thus achieve allocative efficiency.

PRESIDENT OBAMA'S PROPOSALS TO RESTRICT DEFERRAL AND CROSS-CREDITING

It is also possible to move toward further restrictions on deferral without eliminating it entirely. One such proposal, contained in H.R. 3970, the tax reform proposal introduced by Chairman Rangel of the Ways and Means Committee, would disallow certain deductions of parent company costs (the most important being interest) that reflect the share of income that is deferred. This provisions, projected to raise revenue of $106 billion over 10 years, would make investment in low-tax countries much less attractive.[31] The revenue from this provision and other changes were to be used to lower the corporate statutory tax rate.

This proposal also included a foreign tax credit pooling proposal, which would allow a share of foreign tax credits equal to the share of income repatriated. This provision limits the ability of firms to repatriate income from high tax countries and use excess foreign tax credits to shield income from low tax countries from the foreign tax credit. President Obama proposed these changes, along with others, in his FY20 10 and FY20 11 budget proposals.[32] (The allocation of deductions, however, excluded research and development expenditures).

The deferral provision was projected to raise $3.3 billion in FY2013 and $25.6 billion over 10 years and the foreign credit and the foreign tax credit pooling provision was projected to raise $3.2 billion in FY2013 and $32 billion over 10 years.

Another provision (contained in the FY2010 proposals, but not in the FY2011 outline) would eliminate "check-the-box," a provision that allows firms to elect to treat subsidiaries as separate entities or disregarded entities. These regulations permit firms to avoid current taxation on certain income that would be subject to Subpart F anti-abuse rules (such as interest on loans from a subsidiary in a low tax country to a related subsidiary in a high tax country). This provision was originally projected to raise $86 billion over 10 years.

A provision in the FY2011 proposal would treat excess income from intangibles as Subpart F income and assigns them to a separate foreign tax credit basket. This provision is projected to raise $1.6 billion in FY2013, and $15.5 billion over 10 years. It may have been a substitute for "check-the-box" revisions.

The proposals also included a provision that would disallow foreign tax credits when the associated income is not received, as can occur with an arrangement termed a "reverse hybrids." This provision was adopted in 2010 (P.L. 111-226). P.L. 111-226 contained a number of provisions that were directed at perceived abuses of the foreign tax credit. Several other more limited proposals were included in the President's budget proposals.[33]

TAX HAVENS: ISSUES AND POLICY OPTIONS

The topic of "tax havens" has been a focus of recent international tax policy discussions. (This topic is treated in more detail in another CRS report.)[34]Tax havens do not fit neatly into the traditional CEN/CMN/NN evaluation framework outlined above—perhaps because the tax haven issue involves as much artificial shifting of income and investment as it does questions about how investment is actually allocated. To the extent tax havens abet the shifting of income from its true geographic source to low-tax jurisdictions (the havens themselves), they raise questions about protecting the U.S. Treasury from revenue losses. They also raise questions about tax fairness (not all taxpayers are in position to reduce their U.S. taxes by using tax havens). And to the extent tax havens reduce the tax burden on investment that truly occurs overseas, they also raise the same questions about economic efficiency and neutrality addressed by the traditional framework outlined above.

"Tax haven" is not a precisely defined term, but in most usages it refers to a country—in many cases small ones—where non-residents can save taxes by conducting various investments, transactions, and activities. Attributes that make a country a successful tax haven include low or non-existent tax rates applicable to foreigners; strict bank and financial secrecy laws; and a highly developed communications, financial, and legal infrastructure.

At the heart of the tax haven issue is the discrepancy between real economic activity and what is only apparent. Much of the economic activity that appears to occur in tax havens actually occurs elsewhere, and is only associated with particular tax haven countries because of sometimes spurious relationships between the person or firm conducting the activity and the tax-haven country. Thus, for example, much (or even most) of the income reported by U.S.-controlled subsidiaries chartered in tax havens may well have its true economic location either in some other foreign country or even in the United States itself. In several small tax haven locations, income of U.S.-controlled foreign subsidiaries are many times larger than GDP. In Bermuda and the Cayman Islands, this income was respectively, over six times and over five times.[35]

In part, U.S. firms may find tax havens useful tax-saving mechanisms because of particular aspects of the U.S. tax structure. Here, no illegal tax evasion or even transfer-price manipulation may be necessary to obtain tax savings. An example is the technique sometimes termed a corporate "inversion" reorganization, under which the overall parent of a corporate group shifts from a U.S.-chartered entity to a foreign corporation organized in an offshore tax haven. The rearrangement can potentially reduce or eliminate U.S. tax that would otherwise be due when foreign income is repatriated.[36]

U.S. firms can also use tax havens to shift income out of foreign countries where there are corporate income taxes to the zero-tax environment many tax havens offer. Short of outright tax evasion, techniques for shifting income include manipulation of transfer prices affixed to intrafirm sales and other transfers, and the structuring of intrafirm lending and interest charges so as to shift income out of high-tax countries to tax havens (sometimes called "earnings stripping").

Transfer price manipulation can also theoretically be used to shift what is actually U.S.-source income to offshore tax-haven subsidiary corporations.

Along with income shifting and expatriation by corporations, tax havens in some cases apparently abet the outright evasion of taxes, in some cases by U.S. citizens. For example, income from illegal activity in the United States can be shielded from U.S. authorities if a tax haven offers sufficient bank secrecy. Or, taxes on legally generated U.S. income are apparently evaded in some cases by depositing the income in secrecy-protected foreign bank accounts.[37] The focus of this report, however, is the activities of multinational firms, so its concern with tax havens is more with legal (albeit what some might term "abusive") income shifting rather than outright tax evasion.

In part, the ability of firms to divert income from other foreign locations to tax havens has implications for the real location of investment: just because a tax haven is not the true source of income does not make the associated tax savings any less real for the underlying investment, wherever it may be located. We can interpret the effect of tax havens on actual investment in terms of the efficiency framework outlined in previous sections of the report. First, regarding the allocation of investment between the United States and foreign locations, existing data indicate that the United States is a relatively "high tax" country, even if tax havens are omitted from the calculation.[38] Thus, much of the income shifted to tax havens is likely shifted from countries whose taxes are lower than U.S. taxes to begin with. As a result, it is likely that tax havens on balance magnify the distorting effects of deferral, thus further diverting U.S. investment to foreign locations and, in turn, reducing economic efficiency and U.S. national welfare. This efficiency effect, however, may be mitigated by a reduction in the tax-induced distortion of location decisions across foreign countries.[39]

Along with efficiency effects, tax havens reduce tax revenue collections by capital-exporting countries. In the case of U.S. firms' use of tax havens, the revenue loss can accrue both to the United States (in the case of income shifted from domestic sources) and other countries (in the case of income shifted from other countries with higher taxes). Tax havens likewise have the potential of damaging perceptions of tax fairness when public reports appear of large firms and wealthy individuals using tax havens to avoid or evade substantial taxes.[40] Accordingly, a policy question is how tax evasion, or what might be termed "abusive" tax avoidance through tax havens, can be reduced.

One possible approach to tax havens is multilateral (that is, multi-country) action. The concept here is that tax havens flourish in part because of a lack of coordination in tax-administration between non-haven countries and that efforts to suppress tax-haven activities cannot be successful without solidarity among non-haven countries.[41] One prominent multilateral effort has been the Organization for Economic Cooperation and Development's (OECD's) "harmful tax practices project," initiated in 1996. The focus of the OECD's project has been to identify tax havens and to induce them to increase their "transparency" (presumably reduce secrecy about financial transactions) and to increase the number and scope of exchange of tax information agreements with tax havens.[42]

A unilateral approach was proposed by the Clinton Administration with its FY2001 budget proposal. The basis of the plan was to be a list of jurisdictions identified by the Treasury Department as tax havens. Foreign tax credits and the deferral benefit would be restricted for taxpayers using the identified tax havens.[43] More narrow unilateral approaches proposed in the past have primarily involved increasing information reporting requirements.

Several legislative proposals, including proposals in President Obama's budget, have been made to address evasion and avoidance. Some provisions were adopted in the Hire Act in 2010 (P.L. 111-147).[44]

General Reforms of the Corporate Tax and Implications for International Tax Treatment

Despite increasing globalization of the U.S. economy, foreign direct investment remains a small share of the U.S.-owned capital stock. For that reason, it would perhaps not be appropriate for international concerns to dominate the formulation of corporate tax policy. Nevertheless, there are specific forms of corporate tax revisions that might have important consequences for international taxation.

Under the current U.S. system, taxes on corporate profits at the individual level (dividends and capital gains) tend to be collected (due to tax treaties) on a residence basis. If taxes at the individual level could be increased and taxes at the corporate level decreased, the tax would shift towards a residence-based system without any other changes and without any additional concerns about portfolio substitution. In 2003, relief for double taxation was provided by reducing the tax rate on corporate dividends from the ordinary tax rate to 15% for those in brackets above the 15% rate, and to 5% for others. The 5% rate is now scheduled to fall to zero.

Using 2004 figures, where data on qualified dividends are available, the 35% corporate tax rate could have been rolled back to a 31% rate, or even less, for the same revenue cost if a corporate rate reduction rather than reductions in the individual level tax had occurred.[45] There are many other potential changes that could raise revenue to permit a further lowering of the corporate rate. At the individual level, these might include higher capital gains tax rates, accrual taxation of gains on corporate stock, and limits or modest taxes on retirement savings (which would benefit from corporate rate reductions). At the corporate level, a number of base broadening provisions might be considered. It could be feasible to lower the corporate tax rate to 25% with relatively modest changes in tax rules.[46]

A lower U.S. corporate tax is desirable if one believes that the most serious distortion in the international tax system is the tendency of capital to flow to low-tax foreign jurisdictions because of deferral. Such a proposition is a reasonable one, as the United States is generally a high-tax country. Lower corporate tax rates are also responsive to concerns that portfolio substitution disfavors U.S. owned firms.

While international concerns should not necessarily dominate the issues surrounding corporate tax policy,[47] they do suggest the economic desirability of certain types of corporate tax reforms that would improve economic efficiency in the international area.

ACKNOWLEDGMENTS

This report was originally written with David Brumbaugh.

End Notes

[1] Data on trade, U.S. assets abroad, and foreign assets in the United States are from the website of the U.S. Department of Commerce, Bureau of Economic Analysis, at http://www.bea.gov. The fixed assets data were adjusted to include estimated stocks of inventory and intangible capital.

[2] Interest in international reform comes from a variety of sources. For example, the President's executive order (E.O. 13369) establishing his advisory panel on tax reform cited international competitiveness concerns as one principal reason for considering tax reform; the panel's final report included a fundamental change in the structure of the U.S. international system as part of one of its reform options. See President's Advisory Panel on Federal Tax Reform, *Simple, Fair, and Pro-Growth: Proposals to Fix America's Tax System* (Washington, November 2005). In Congress, in June 2006, the House Ways and Means Committee's Subcommittee on Select Revenue Measures held a hearing on international tax reform. The topic is also receiving attention in the academic and professional world: the *National Tax Journal* published a four-article forum on international tax reform in its December 2001 issue.

[3] President Bush's Advisory Panel on Tax Reform published a list of countries that use a territorial system either by statute or treaty. The territorial countries are: Australia, Austria, Belgium, Canada, Denmark, Finland, France, Germany, Greece, Hungary, Iceland, Italy, Luxembourg, Netherlands, Norway, Portugal, Slovak Republic, Spain, Sweden, Switzerland, and Turkey. The following countries tax foreign-source income at some point and rely on foreign tax credits to relieve double taxation: Czech Republic, Iceland, Japan, Korea, Mexico, New Zealand, Poland, the United Kingdom, and the United States. President's Advisory Panel on Federal Tax Reform, *Simple, Fair, and Pro- Growth: Proposals to Fix America's Tax System* (Washington, November 2005), p. 243.

[4] According to IRS data for 2006, before-tax earnings and profits of foreign subsidiaries was $509 billion while branch gross income was $145 billion. The data are posted on the IRS website at http://www.irs.gov/pub/irs-soi/06it01cf.xls, http://www.irs.gov/pub/irs-soi/06it01mi.xls.

[5] U.S. parent firms are permitted to claim foreign tax credits for foreign taxes paid by their foreign-chartered subsidiaries. Such "indirect" credits can be claimed by the parent when the foreign-source income is remitted as dividends.

[6] Rosanne Altshuler and Harry Grubert, *Corporate Taxes in the World Economy: Reforming the Taxation of Cross-Border Income*, unpublished paper presented at the James A. Baker II Institute for Public Policy conference on tax reform, April 27-28, 2006, p. 43.

[7] For a more detailed discussion of this concept see CRS Report RS22445, *Taxes and International Competitiveness*, by Donald J. Marples.

[8] Comparative advantage is not a technical or unfamiliar concept; it is a common, everyday occurrence. A lawyer may be able to do his or her paralegal employee's work more efficiently, but that activity is not the best use of his or her time. A lawyer has an absolute advantage in both law practice and paralegal work, but a comparative advantage in practicing law.

[9] Mihir Desai and James Hines, Evaluating International Tax Reform, *National Tax Journal*, vol. 56, September 2003.

[10] Michael P. Devereux, "Capital Export Neutrality, Capital Import Neutrality, Capital Ownership Neutrality, and All That," Unpublished Paper, June 11, 1990.

[11] Daniel J. Frisch, "The Economics of International Tax Policy: Some Old and New Approaches," *Tax Notes*, April 30, 1990.

[12] Frisch, in "The Economics of International Tax Policy: Some Old and New Approaches," states, "In short, a major element of the CIN view would seem to possess a grain of truth," (p. 590) referring to the capital import neutrality framework. Devereux, in "Capital Export Neutrality, Capital Import Neutrality, Capital Ownership Neutrality, and All That," indicated that he originally attempted to redefine capital import neutrality to cover the capital ownership neutrality concept.

[13] The concepts were first developed by Peggy Musgrave. See, for example, her *United States Taxation of Foreign Investment Income: Issues and Arguments* (Cambridge MA: Harvard Law School, 1969), pp. 108-121.

[14] Calculated by reducing U.S. corporate equity issues by foreign stock holdings in the United States determining U.S. holdings of foreign stocks as a share. Data on corporate equities can be found in the Board of Governors of the Federal Reserve Flow of Funds Accounts, Table L213, which can be found at http://www.federalreserve.gov/releases/Z1/ Current/. Historical series can also be found in the National Income and Product Accounts at http://www.bea.gov/ national/nipaweb/Ni_FedBeaSna/TableView.asp?SelectedTable=5&FirstYear=1998&LastYear=2005&Freq=Year.

[15] This optimality issue has also been addressed with the notion of National Ownership Neutrality, which indicates that it is both efficient and optimal to have source-based taxation.

[16] Congressional Budget Office, *Corporate Tax Rates: International Comparisons*, November, 2005.

[17] Data are from tax rates cited in Congressional Budget Office. *Corporate Tax Rates: International Comparisons, November, 2005,* and portfolio share data are from U.S. Department of Treasury *Report on U.S. Portfolio Holdings of Foreign Securities*.

[18] U.S. Department of Treasury, *Report on U.S. Portfolio Holdings of Foreign Securities*.

[19] Principal-agent costs occur when the objectives of the two parties are not identical. For example, the contract manufacturer (the agent) may want to increase the scale of the operation rather than maximizing profits for the firm authorizing the manufacturing (the principal).

[20] National Commission on Fiscal Responsibility and Reform, The Moment of Truth., Washington, D.C., The White House, December 2010.

[21] Harry Grubert and John Mutti, *Taxing International Business Income: Dividend Exemption versus the Current System* (Washington: American Enterprise Institute, 2001), 67 pp; President's Advisory Panel on Tax Reform, *Simple, Fair, and Pro-Growth: Proposals to Fix America's Tax System* (Washington, 1985), pp. 239-244.

[22] Ibid., p. 11. Note, however, that cross-crediting also reduces current law's inefficient disincentive to invest in high- tax countries on the part of firms without excess credits, a feature not considered by the Grubert/Mutti analysis. Because income earned by firms with a deficit of credits outweighs that of firms with excess credits, it is plausible that an exemption system's loss of this easing of inefficiency would outweigh the gains from reduced investment in low-tax countries.

[23] Writing more recently, Grubert and his co-author Rosanne Altshuler note that if an exemption system is actively considered by policymakers, its adoption with its full panoply of deduction restrictions intact would be problematic. Rosanne Altshuler and Harry Grubert, *Corporate Taxes in the World Economy: Reforming the Taxation of Cross- Border Income*, unpublished paper presented at the James A. Baker II Inst. for Public Policy conference on tax reform, April 27-28, 2006, p. 4.

[24] Harry Grubert and John Mutti, *Taxing International Business Income*, p. 38.

[25] Report in U.S. Congressional Budget Office, *Budget Options* (Washington, February 2007), p. 319.

[26] Joint Committee on Taxation, *Estimates of Federal Tax Expenditures 2006-2010*, JCS-2-06, April 25, 2006.

[27] Edward D. Klienbard, "Throw Territorial Taxation from the Train," *Tax Notes,* February 5, 2007, pp. 552-553.

[28] From 1954 to 1961, taxpayers were required to use a per-country limitation. For a synopsis of changes in limitation policy, see Thomas Horst, "The Overall vs. the Per-Country Limitation on the U.S. Foreign Tax Credit," in U.S. Department of the Treasury, Office of Tax Analysis, *1978 Compendium of Tax Research* (Washington: GPO, 1978), pp. 213-214.

[29] The purest form of a separate limitation would require a separate limitation to be calculated for each investment a firm makes. Clearly, however, such a policy would present considerable administrative difficulties.

[30] Rosanne Altshuler and Harry Grubert, *Corporate Taxes in the World Economy: Reforming the Taxation of Cross-Border Income*, p. 17.

[31] The provisions of H.R. 3970 are discussed in CRS Report RL34249, *The Tax Reduction and Reform Act of 2007: An Overview*, by Jane G. Gravelle. The bill also contains a provision that repeals a planned liberalization of interest allocation rules for purposes of the foreign tax credit limit. This provision is discussed in CRS Report RL34494, *The Foreign Tax Credit's Interest Allocation Rules*, by Jane G. Gravelle and Donald J. Marples.

[32] U.S. Department of Treasury. General Explanations of the Administration's Fiscal Year 2010 Revenue Proposals (Green Book), Washington, DC, May 2009. General Explanations of the Administration's Fiscal Year 2011 Revenue Proposals (Green Book), Washington, DC, February, 2010.

[33] See CRS Report R40623, *Tax Havens: International Tax Avoidance and Evasion*, by Jane G. Gravelle, for a summary of these enacted and proposed revisions.

[34] CRS Report R40623, *Tax Havens: International Tax Avoidance and Evasion*, by Jane G. Gravelle.

[35] Ibid., see Table 4.

[36] For more information, see CRS Report RL31444, *Firms That Incorporate Abroad for Tax Purposes: Corporate "Inversions" and "Expatriation"*, by Donald J. Marples.

[37] For a discussion of tax havens and illegal activities, see Martin A. Sullivan, "Sex, Drugs, and Tax Evasion," *Tax Notes*, June 18, 2007, pp. 1098-1100.

[38] 2002 Internal Revenue Service data on U.S.-controlled foreign subsidiaries show that subsidiaries pay, on average, a lower percentage of their pre-tax earnings in tax than do firms in the United States. This is true even for developed countries such as the United Kingdom and Canada.

[39] That tax havens actually stimulate investment in nearby higher-tax countries is argued in Mihir A. Desai, C. Fritz Foley, and James R. Hines, Jr., "Do Tax Havens Divert Economic Activity?" *Economics Letters*, vol. 90, 2006, pp. 219-224.

[40] Senate Finance Committee Chairman Max Baucus, for example, has observed that when tax havens are used for tax evasion "the honest American taxpayers who work hard, and do not have the ability to engage in offshore activity, are left holding the bill." Sen. Max Baucus, Hearing Statement Regarding Offshore Tax Evasion, May 3, 2007. Available as Finance Committee news release on the committee's website at

[41] To illustrate, imagine a situation where country A has exchange of information agreements both with country B and tax haven H. Country B, however, has no exchange agreement with the tax haven. Conceivably, would-be taxpayers from country A could channel tax-saving tax haven transactions through country B.

[42] Jeffrey Owens, Director, OECD Centre for Tax Policy and Administration, "OECD's Work in Counteracting the Use of Tax Havens to Evade Taxes," unpublished paper presented at the American Enterprise Institute, December 11, 2006. Some U.S. critics of the OECD criticized what they saw as the initiative's underlying premise that low taxes are suspect. It was indeed partly on this basis that the Bush administration persuaded the OECD to focus on transparency and exchange of information rather than efforts to persuade targeted countries to change their tax practices towards non-residents. See Hon. Paul O'Neill, Secretary of the Treasury, testimony before the Senate Committee on Governmental Affairs, Permanent Subcommittee on Investigations, July 18, 2001. Available at the committee's website, at http://hsgac.senate.gov/071801_psioneil.htm.

[43] For a description of the proposal, see U.S. Congress, Joint Committee on Taxation, *Description of Revenue Proposals Contained in the President's Fiscal Year 2001 Budget Proposals* (Washington: GPO, 2000), pp. 500-509.

[44] See CRS Report R40623, *Tax Havens: International Tax Avoidance and Evasion*, by Jane G. Gravelle for descriptions.

[45] In 2004, taxable qualified dividends for individual income taxes were $104 billion according to the Statistics of Income data. Assuming a 15% rate differential, rolling back the provision for dividends would have raised revenues by $15.6 billion. The gain from raising the capital gains tax rate back to 20% depends on the behavioral response—how much individuals reduce their realizations, given tax increases. Based on the realization responses the Joint Tax Committee used in the past, and the Congressional Budget Office baseline, the gain for capital gains would be $9.2 billion. If the realizations response were based on the response used by the Congressional Budget Office in projecting the baseline, it would raise $12.7 billion. There is some evidence that even that response is too large as discussed in CRS Report R41364, *Capital Gains Tax Options: Behavioral Responses and Revenues*, by Jane G. Gravelle If the revenue gain is to be used to reduce the corporate tax and raise after-tax profits, they need to be grossed up by (1-t) where t is the effective individual tax rate on an additional dollar of corporate after-tax profits. The estimate assumes an average tax rate of 25% and that half of the income goes to non-taxable recipients such as pension funds, for an overall rate of 12.5%. Corporate tax revenues were $189 billion in FY2004, but this value was unusually low because of bonus depreciation. Adjusting for bonus depreciation brings the revenue to $236 billion. (For a discussion, see CRS Report RL33672, *Revenue Feedback from the 2001-2004 Tax Cuts*, by Jane G. Gravelle.) The revenue gains divided by the gross-up factor and then by corporate tax receipts indicate the percentage reduction in the corporate tax (12% and 13.5% respectively), which are then multiplied by the 35% rate to determine the percentage point reduction.

[46] Taxing capital gains at full rates would have raised, for 2004, $7 billion to $20 billion, or even more, allowing a rate decrease of one to three percentage points. Accrual taxation would yield dramatically larger revenues. Two examples of corporate base broadeners include the production activities deduction for domestic manufacturing and certain industries, and the title passage rule, which is a rule allowing an arbitrary allocation of income from U.S. exports to be assigned to foreign-source income for purposes of the foreign tax credit limit (effectively an export subsidy). According to tax expenditure estimates, the production activities

deduction (which is being phased in) will reach a cost of $10 billion by FY20 10. The title passage rule costs about $6 billion. These two corporate provisions should permit a three percentage point reduction, bringing the rate to between 27% and 28%.

[47] Two reasons to provide relief at the individual level are (1) to focus tax cuts on marginal investment, which is more likely to be taxable investment to individuals rather than investment in pension funds and retirement accounts; and (2) to reduce the distortion that capital gains taxes impose on the willingness to realize gains and adjust assets. This latter distortion, however, would be improved if an accrual basis capital gains tax on corporate stock were adopted. Such a move would also raise a great deal of revenue that could be used to lower corporate tax rates. Doing so would also end concerns about using corporations with lower tax rates to shelter income.

In: Corporate and International Taxation
Editor: Allison S. Garner and Daniel C. Murphy
ISBN: 978-1-61324-616-0

Chapter 2

TAX CUTS ON REPATRIATION EARNINGS AS ECONOMIC STIMULUS: AN ECONOMIC ANALYSIS

Donald J. Marples and Jane G. Gravelle

SUMMARY

At the beginning of the 111th Congress, economic stimulus proposals have dominated the legislative agenda, with a broad recognition that business tax incentives are among the policy options to consider. Two prominent proposals, H.R. 1 and S. 1, both titled the American Recovery and Reinvestment Act of 2009, were the focus of this debate. Both proposals include business tax incentives which would increase the after-tax rate of return on domestic investment and were subsequently enacted in P.L. 111-5. In contrast, little attention has been given to international policy options. An exception to this is a plan to reduce the tax rate on repatriated dividends that has received some consideration. Under such a plan, the U.S. tax that U.S. firms pay when their overseas operations remit ("repatriate") their foreign earnings as dividends to their U.S. parent corporations would be reduced. This provision was considered, but not adopted, as a floor amendment to a Senate version of the American Recovery and Reinvestment Act of 2009.

A conceptually similar proposal was enacted as part of the American Jobs Creation Act (P.L. 108-357). The provision provided a temporary reduced rate for repatriated earnings, with the condition that the repatriated earnings be used for domestic investment. While empirical evidence is clear that this provision resulted in a significant increase in repatriated earnings, empirical evidence is unable to show a corresponding increase in domestic investment or employment.

Viewed in the current debate on how to most efficiently stimulate the economy, economic theory suggests that the simulative effect of a temporary tax cut for repatriations may be partially offset by exchange rate adjustments that would reduce net exports. In addition, how businesses use repatriated earnings will impact the stimulative effect of a tax cut for repatriations. For example, repatriated earnings will have a larger stimulative effect if they are used to increase current investment. A smaller stimulative effect will result, in contrast, if the repatriated earnings are used to shore up "cash-flow" issues.

The legislative agenda at the start of the 111th Congress has been dominated by efforts aimed at stimulating the U.S. economy. Two prominent proposals, H.R. 1 and S. 1, both titled the American Recovery and Reinvestment Act of 2009, were the focus of this debate. Both proposals include business tax incentives which would increase the after-tax rate of return on some domestic investment and were subsequently enacted in P.L. 111-5. In contrast, little attention has been given to international policy options. One international option that has received some consideration is a plan to reduce a tax cut for repatriated dividends. Under this option, the U.S. tax that a U.S. parent corporation pays when its overseas operations repatriate foreign earnings to its U.S. parent, as dividends, would be reduced. This provision was considered, but not adopted, as a floor amendment to a Senate version of the American Recovery and Reinvestment Act of 2009. The business community has continued to suggest another repatriation holiday.[1]

A conceptually similar proposal was enacted as part of the American Jobs Creation Act (P.L. 108-357). The provision provided a temporary reduced rate for repatriated earnings, with the condition that the repatriated earnings be used for domestic investment. While empirical evidence is clear that this provision resulted in a significant increase in repatriated earnings, empirical evidence is unable to show a corresponding increase in domestic investment or employment by firms that utilized the repatriation provisions.

In the context of the current debate on stimulus, the use of the repatriations and not the magnitude of repatriations stimulated are likely to be the key to the proposal's effect on U.S. economic growth. This follows from two points. First, even if sizeable repatriations occur, the rate of return on U.S. investment will be unaffected by the repatriations. Assuming firms are not liquidity- constrained, it is possible that the bulk of the repatriations will be used as dividends to stockholders or used to pay down corporate debt. This scenario is especially likely for large firms.[2] Second, when the repatriations occur, those that are denominated in foreign currencies will be converted to dollars. The corresponding increase in the demand for dollars may drive up the price of the dollar in world currency markets. As a result, U.S. net exports may decline from levels that would otherwise occur, and the stimulative impact of the repatriations on the U.S. economy would be lessened.

THE U.S. INTERNATIONAL TAX SYSTEM

The United States bases its jurisdiction to tax international income on residence. As a result, U.S.- chartered corporations are taxed on their worldwide income, but foreign corporations are taxed only on their U.S.-source income. Accordingly, a U.S. firm with overseas operations can indefinitely postpone its U.S. tax on its foreign income by operating through a foreign subsidiary. Using the same principle, U.S. taxes are deferred as long as its foreign earnings remain in the control of its foreign subsidiary and are reinvested abroad. The U.S. firm pays taxes on its overseas earnings only when they are paid to the U.S. parent corporation as intra-firm dividends or other income.

Another prominent feature of the U.S. tax system is the foreign tax credit. The foreign tax credit is designed to alleviate double taxation where U.S. and foreign governments' tax jurisdictions overlap—that is the U.S. firm pays taxes at the higher of the U.S. or foreign tax rate. With respect to repatriated dividends, U.S. firms can claim foreign tax credits for foreign taxes paid by their subsidiaries on the earnings used to pay the repatriated dividends. The ability to defer U.S. tax, thus, poses an incentive for U.S. firms to invest abroad in countries with low tax rates. Proposals to cut taxes on repatriations are based on the premise that even this deferred tax on intra-firm dividends discourages repatriations and encourages firms to reinvest foreign earnings abroad and that a cut in the tax would stimulate repatriations.

REPATRIATED EARNINGS PROVISIONS IN THE AMERICAN JOBS CREATION ACT

The repatriated earnings provision included in the American Jobs Creation Act (P.L. 108-357) reduced the taxes due on repatriated earnings. In particular, the provision provided a deduction equal to 85% of the increase in foreign-source earnings repatriated. For a firm paying taxes at the 35% corporate tax rate, this reduced the tax rate on repatriated earnings to the equivalent of 5.25%.

The act required firms to adopt domestic investment plans for qualifying repatriations and limited the maximum deduction allowed. The maximum allowable deduction was set equal to the greater of $500 million or the amount of earnings shown to be permanently reinvested outside the United States in a firm's books of accounts certified before June 30, 2003.

The deduction was designed and intended to be available for one year. At the taxpayer's option, the year would be the first tax year beginning on or after the date of enactment of P.L. 108-357 or the last tax year beginning before that date. The conference report for the act stated the "conferees emphasize that this is a temporary economic stimulus measure, and that there is no intent to make this measure permanent, or to 'extend' or enact it again in the future."[3]

IMPACTS OF A REDUCTION IN THE TAX ON REPATRIATED EARNINGS

A number of researchers have studied the impact of the reduction in the tax on repatriated earnings that came out of the American Jobs Creation Act. The studies have generally focused on two particular responses: the level of repatriations and the impact on economic growth. In short, the studies generally conclude that the reduction in the tax rate on repatriated earnings led to a sharp increase in the level of repatriated earnings, but that the repatriations did not increase domestic investment or employment. They further conclude that much of the repatriations were returned to shareholders through stock repurchases.

Impact on Repatriated Earnings

The impact of a reduction in the tax on repatriated earnings depends on whether the reduction is permanent or temporary. As mentioned above, the provision enacted in P.L. 108-357 was envisioned as being a temporary and one-time reduction.

A permanent reduction in the tax on repatriated earnings is not likely to result in an increase in repatriations. According to the "new view" of dividends, once a firm invests equity capital in a foreign subsidiary, the payment of home-country taxes is inevitable.[4] Given this inevitability, once the capital is abroad, repatriation taxes have no impact on the firm's decision whether to repatriate foreign earnings in the present or to instead reinvest them abroad. Instead, repatriations will follow a life-cycle model, unaffected by repatriation taxes, where young foreign subsidiaries will receive capital from their U.S. parent so long as there are profitable foreign investment opportunities, followed by a period of self-financing of foreign investment by the foreign subsidiary, and ending with a period of repatriations made by mature foreign subsidiaries.

In contrast, a temporary reduction in the tax on repatriated earnings is likely to result in an increase in repatriations in the short-run. Note that the long-run result, above, depended upon the tax on repatriated earnings being the same in the present and the future. This no longer holds for a temporary reduction, and thus repatriation taxes may affect the level of repatriations. This is not to say that all firms will increase repatriations in response to the tax reduction. It is expected that a young firm's repatriation decisions would still be unaffected by repatriation taxes, as long as the reduction expires prior to the firm intending to repatriate profits. In addition, any short-term increase in repatriations may be offset by a decrease in repatriations in later years. This is especially likely to occur if corporations view a temporary rate reduction as likely to recur.

The actual pattern of repatriations observed after enactment of the American Jobs Creation Act validated the short-run economic prediction. According to the Internal Revenue Service, 843 of the roughly 9,700 eligible corporations took advantage of the deduction.[5] This sub-set of eligible corporations repatriated $312 billion in qualified earnings and created total deductions of $265 billion. Using the most recent year of data available, the data suggest that approximately one-third of all offshore earnings were repatriated in the tax year after enactment. As way of comparison, base dividends for the same corporations total approximately $34 billion and suggest a normal repatriation rate of little more than 4%. Thus, not controlling for other factors, the rate reduction resulted in a greater-than-eight-fold increase in repatriations.

The IRS study of the provision, cited above, provided information on the recipients. The benefits of the repatriation provision are not evenly spread across industries. The pharmaceutical and medicine industry accounted for $99 billion in repatriations or 32% of the total. The computer and electronic equipment industry accounted for $58 billion or 18% of the total. Thus these two industries accounted for half of the repatriations. Most of the dividends were repatriated from low tax countries or tax havens.

The benefits were also highly concentrated in a few firms. According to a recent study, five firms (Pfizer, Merck, Hewlett-Packard, Johnson & Johnson, and IBM) are responsible for $88 billion, over a quarter (28%) of total repatriations.[6] The top 10 firms (adding Schering-Plough, Du Pont, Bristol-Myers Squibb, Eli Lilly, and PepsiCo) accounted for 42%. The top 15 (adding Procter and Gamble, Intel, Coca-Cola, Altria, and Motorola), accounted for over half (52%).

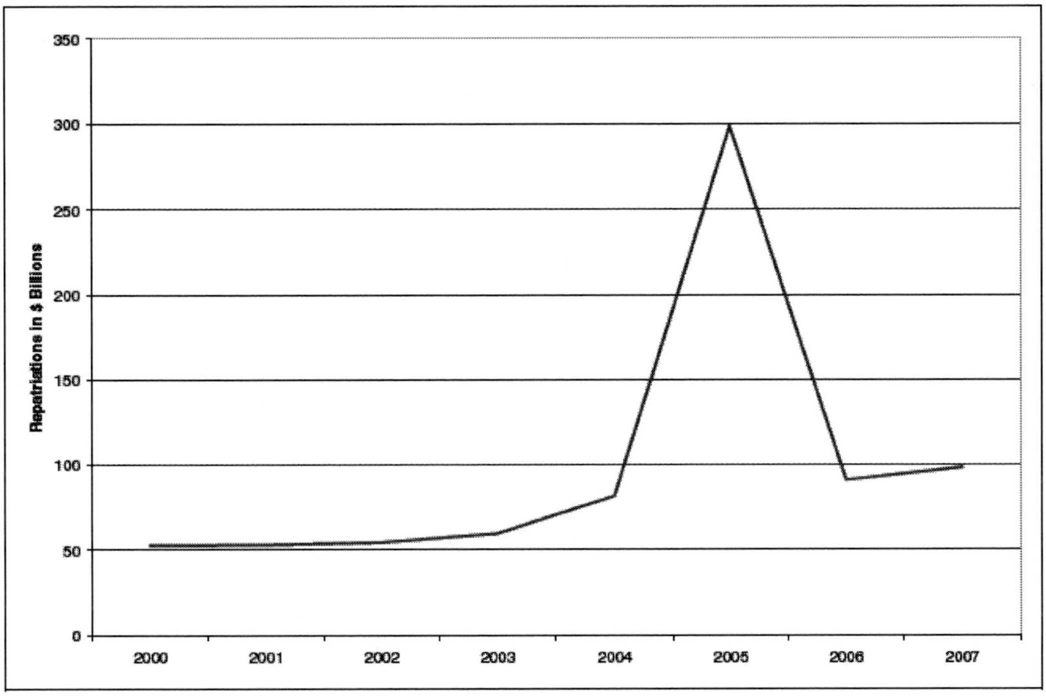

Source: Bureau of Economic Analysis, International Transactions, Table 7a.

Figure 1. Repatriations by U.S. Multinational Corporations, 2000-2007.

Using an alternative measure of repatriations also shows a large "spike" in repatriations resulting from the American Jobs Creation Act. As seen in Figure 1, U.S. multinationals increased their repatriations by approximately 266% from the prior year.

The empirical evidence also suggests that corporations expect the temporary rate reduction to recur. According to several researchers, unrepatriated earnings have rapidly grown since 2005.[7] In fact, since the last repatriation rate reduction, unrepatriated earnings for all corporations have grown by 72% to $958 billion and by 81% to $639 billion for firms that repatriated under the American Jobs Creation Act.

Impact on Economic Growth

Given the empirical evidence that a temporary reduction in taxes on repatriated earnings leads to an increase in repatriated earnings, how does this affect economic growth? Two factors that will impact the answer are how the repatriated earning are used and the role of flexible exchange rates. Simply put, the more the repatriated earnings are used to shore up a corporation's balance sheet or paid to shareholders the less the simulative effect of the repatriations. On top of that, flexible exchange rates will likely further depress the simulative impact of the repatriations.

Use of Repatriated Earnings and Economic Stimulus

Fiscal policy, such as a reduction in the tax rate on repatriated earnings, boosts economic activity by increasing the short-run demand for goods and services. Put bluntly, the earning must be spent, in order to stimulate the economy. With this in mind, the American Jobs Creation Act required that corporations have an approved plan to reinvest the repatriated earnings prior to claiming the 85% deduction. The main criticism of the reinvestment plan provision was that it allowed an overly generous range of reinvestment options—all but executive compensation and stock repurchase programs—and that it was not explicitly linked to specific uses. Proponents of the reinvestment plan argue that the range of options allowed reflects a recognition of the fungibility of money.

Economic theory finds that changes in the after-tax cost of new investment are most likely to induce new investment. In contrast, incentives which increase after-tax profits (and benefit mainly cash-flow) without changing the incentive for new investment do not generally induce much new hiring or production, because these types of incentives do not alter the conditions of the pre-incentive investment equilibrium.

Two studies have attempted to quantify the impact of cash-flow incentives. According to the Sinai study, instituting repatriation provisions similar to those in the American Jobs Creation Act would improve the net cash-flow of participating companies by approximately $535 billion in 2009. The Congressional Budget Office (CBO) estimates that the stimulative impact (or multiplier) of a specific cash-flow proposal, for loss carrybacks, at between 0 and 40 cents of GDP per tax dollar not received.[8] This range of the stimulative effect for loss carrybacks should likely be viewed as an upper-bound estimate for the cash-flow effect of a repatriation rate reduction. This follows from the observation that corporations with current losses—and thus having losses to carryback— are more likely to be cash constrained and able to benefit from a cash-flow provision than the relatively large multination corporations that are likely to have a better cash-flow position. (By contrast, CBO sets the multiplier for federal spending at 1 to 2.5, for transfer payments at 0.8 to 2.2, and for individual tax cuts at 0.5 to 1.7.)[9]

Which category of incentive a reduction in the tax on repatriated earnings belongs in depends upon the degree to which repatriated earnings change the incentive for new investment. This in turn depends upon the degree to which the reinvestment plan compels investment. Given a weak focus of the reinvestment plan, economic theory suggests that it is likely that a reduction in the tax on repatriated earnings falls into the less stimulative category.[10]

Empirical analyses of the stimulative effects of the repatriation provisions in the American Jobs Creation Act also suggests a limited stimulative impact from the provisions. They conclude that much of the repatriated earnings were used for cash-flow purposes and little evidence exists that new investment was spurred.

Several analysts have used public data sources, such as annual reports and press releases, to report the subsequent actions of participants in the American Jobs Creation Act, primarily firms that repatriated but also reduced employment, a sign that the scale of domestic operations was not increasing. In Table 1 we summarize selected information from these reports for these firms. Taken together, the firms identified in Table 1 account for nearly one-third of all repatriations under the American Jobs Creation Act. In general, two trends emerge from these analyses: (1) corporations that utilized the repatriation provisions were unable to expand domestic operations and (2) corporations in several industries appear to have increased their rate of repatriations after the expiration of the repatriation provisions. These event studies, while informative, are not able to imply any causal relationship between use of the repatriation provisions and subsequent firm responses, since they are unable to compare the response with an alternative response in the absence of utilization of the repatriation provisions. They also cannot be generalized to other firms.

Building upon the event study literature, a series of empirical econometric studies have concluded that the American Jobs Creation Act repatriation provisions did not increase domestic economic activity. Dharmapala et al. find that repatriations had a small and statistically insignificant impact both on domestic capital expenditures and employment.[11] Clemons and Kinney, similarly, are unable to find evidence that investment expenditures increased in corporations that utilized the repatriation provisions of the JOBS Act. [12] In summary, these studies both found the repatriation provisions to be an ineffective means of increasing economic growth.

Table 1. Selected Information on 12 Corporations that Utilized the Repatriation Provisions in the American Jobs Creation Act.

Company	JOBS Act Repatriation Amount ($Billions)	Jobs Lost in 2005-2006	Pre-JOBS Act Accumulation of Foreign Earnings (two years, $ Billions)	Post-JOBS Act Accumulated Foreign Earnings ($ Billions)
Pfizer	37	10,000	67	101
CitiGroup	3.2	n/a	9	35.8
Merck	15.9	7,000	33	29.7
Hewlett-Packard	14.5	14,500	28.9	23.7
Proctor & Gamble	10.7	unspecified # lost	24.7	54
IBM	9.5	n/a	34.7	33
PepsiCo	7.5	200-250	16.3	25.5
Motorola	4.4	unspecified # lost	13.7	8.1
Honeywell	2.7	2,000	5.5	7
Ford	0.9	30,000-40,000	n/a	n/a
National Semiconductor	0.5	5 percent of workforce	n/a	n/a
Colgate-Palmolive	0.8	4,000	n/a	n/a

Sources: Columns 2 and 3: Lee A. Sheppard and Martin A. Sullivan, "Multinationals Accumulate to Repatriate," Tax Notes, January 19, 2009, pp. 295-298; and various media reports; Column 4: Sheppard and Sullivan .

There is some empirical evidence, however, that the repatriations were used to return money to shareholders though stock repurchase programs.[13] Dharmapala et al. found that a $1 increase in repatriations increased stock repurchases by $0.91, a use prohibited under the American Jobs Creation Act. (Note that because of the fungibility of money, firms that use part of the repatriation to repurchase shares may not violate the law). Clemmons and Kinney also concluded that the only significant increase in expenditures for participating corporations was on stock repurchases. Another study found similar results, estimating that 20% of the repatriation was used for stock repurchases.[14]

In contrast to these empirical studies, the simulations conducted in the Sinai study find that a temporary reduction in the tax on repatriated earnings would increase domestic economic activity in the 2009-20 13 time period.[15] According to the simulation results, the reduction in the tax on repatriated earnings would increase gross domestic product (GDP) by an average of $62 billion per year, and business capital spending and research and development by an average of $7 billion per year. The study also finds an increase in employment that peaks at 614,000 additional jobs in 2011.

Exchange Rate Adjustments and Economic Stimulus

The stimulative effect of the reduced tax rate on repatriated earnings is expected to be muted by the international system of flexible exchange rates and, subsequently, by trade. This effect will occur, because as foreign denominated earnings of foreign subsidiaries are repatriated they are also converted to U.S. dollars. This result increases the demand for dollars which leads to an appreciation, or increase, in the price of the dollar in foreign exchange markets. This stronger dollar makes U.S.-made exports more expensive and foreign imports less expensive. As a result, U.S. exports would temporarily decline, further straining the economy and at least partially offsetting any stimulative effect of the repatriated earnings.

End Notes

[1] John Chambers and Safra Catz, "The Overseas Profits Elephant in the Room," *Wall Street Journal*, October 20, 2010, http://online.wsj.com/article/SB10001424052748704469004575533880328930598.html#articleTabs%3 Darticle.

[2] See CRS Report RS21 126, *Tax Cuts and Economic Stimulus: How Effective Are the Alternatives?*, by Jane G. Gravelle, for a more detailed discussion.

[3] U.S. Congress, Conference Committees, 2004, *American Jobs Creation Act of 2004*, conference report to accompany H.R. 4520, H.Rept. 108-755, 108th Cong., 2nd sess. (Washington: GPO, 2004), p. 314.

[4] Jane Gravelle, "Federal Corporate Income Tax," in *The Encyclopedia of Taxation and Tax Policy*, ed. Joseph J. Cordes, Robert D. Ebel, and Jane G. Gravelle (Washington, DC: The Urban Institute, 1999), p. 175.

[5] Melissa Redmiles, *The One-Time Recieved Dividends Deduction*, Internal Revenue Service, Statistics of Income Bulletin, Washington, DC, Spring 2008, http://www.irs.gov/pub/irs-soi/08codivdeductbul.pdf.

[6] Rodney P. Mock and Andreas Simon, "Permanently Reinvested Earnings: Priceless," *Tax Notes*, November 17, 2008, pp. 835-848.

[7] Allen Sinai, Macro Economic Effects of Reducing the Effective Tax Rate on Repatriated Foreign Subsidiary Earnings in a Credit- and Liquidity-Constrained Environment, Decisions Economics, Inc, Economic Studies Series, Dec. 11, 2008, http://www.accf.org/media and Lee A. Shepard and Martin A. Sullivan, "Multinationals Accumulate to Repatriate," Tax Notes, January 19, 2009, pp. 295-298. Thomas J. Brennan, "What Happens After a Holiday? Long-Term Effects of the Repatriation Provision of the AJCA," Northwestern Journal of Law and Social Policy, vol. 5, Spring 2010, http://www.law.northwestern. edu/journals/njlsp/v5/n1/1/.

[8] U.S. Congress, House Committee on the Budget, *The State of the Economy and Issues in Developing an Effective Policy Response*, The Economic Outlook and Budget Challenges, 111th Cong., 1st sess., January 27, 2009.

[9] The CBO multipliers are similar to those used by other forecasters. See CRS Report R40 104, *Economic Stimulus: Issues and Policies*, by Jane G. Gravelle, Thomas L. Hungerford, and Marc Labonte for a complete discussion on multiplier effects.

[10] Dhammika Dharmapala, C. Fritz Foley, and Kristin J. Forbes, "The Unintended Consequences of the Homeland Investment Act: Implications for Financial Constraints, Governance, and International Tax Policy," unpublished working paper, September 2008; Roy Clemons and Michael R. Kinney," An Analysis of the Tax Holiday for Repatriations Under the Jobs Act," *Tax Notes*, August 25, 2008, pp. 759-768; and Jennifer Blouin and Linda Krull, "Bringing it Home: A Study of the Incentives Surrounding the Repatriations of Foreign Earnings Under the Jobs Creation Act of 2004," Unpublished Working Paper, Wharton School and University of Oregon, July 2008.

[11] Dhammika Dharmapala, C. Fritz Foley, and Kristin J. Forbes, "The Unintended Consequences of the Homeland Investment Act: Implications for Financial Constraints, Governance, and International Tax Policy," unpublished working paper, September 2008.

[12] Roy Clemons and Michael R. Kinney, "An Analysis of the Tax Holiday for Repatriations Under the Jobs Act," *Tax Notes*, August 25, 2008, pp. 759-768.

[13] In addition to stock repurchases, increasing dividends are a way of returning money to shareholders. Given the temporary nature of the repatriation provisions, however, stock repurchases would be the expected vehicle to return money to shareholders, since they represent less of a commitment to ongoing distributions.

[14] Jennifer Blouin and Linda Krull, "Bringing it Home: A Study of the Incentives Surrounding the Repatriations of Foreign Earnings Under the Jobs Creation Act of 2004," Unpublished Working Paper, Wharton School and University of Oregon, July 2008.

[15]Allen Sinai, *Macro Economic Effects of Reducing the Effective Tax Rate on Repatriated Foreign Subsidiary Earnings in a Credit- and Liquidity-Constrained Environment,* Decisions Economics, Inc, Economic Studies Series, Dec. 11, 2008, http://www.accf.org/media

In: Corporate and International Taxation
Editor: Allison S. Garner and Daniel C. Murphy
ISBN: 978-1-61324-616-0

Chapter 3

CORPORATE TAX REFORM: ISSUES FOR CONGRESS

Jane G. Gravelle and Thomas L. Hungerford

SUMMARY

H.R. 3970, introduced in the 110th Congress by then-Chairman Charles Rangel of the House Committee on Ways and Means, includes corporate tax revisions, trading a lower rate for a broader tax base as part of the revenue neutral reform package. S. 3018, introduced by Senators Ron Wyden and Judd Gregg in the 111th Congress, also provides for a lower corporate tax rate in exchange for a somewhat broader corporate tax base. Some discussions by economists in opinion pieces suggest there is an urgent need to lower the corporate tax rate, but not necessarily to broaden the tax base.

Arguments for lowering the corporate tax rate include the traditional concerns about economic distortions arising from the corporate tax and newer concerns arising from the increasingly global nature of the economy. Some claims have been made that lowering the corporate tax rate would raise revenue because of the behavioral responses, an effect that is linked to an open economy. Although the corporate tax has generally been viewed as contributing to a more progressive tax system because the burden falls on capital income and thus on higher income individuals, claims have also been made that the burden falls not on owners of capital, but on labor income—an effect also linked to an open economy.

The analysis in this report suggests that many of the concerns expressed about the corporate tax are not supported by empirical data. Claims that behavioral responses could cause revenues to rise if rates were cut do not hold up on either a theoretical basis or an empirical basis. Studies that purport to show a revenue maximizing corporate tax rate of 30% (a rate lower than the current statutory tax rate) contain econometric errors that lead to biased and inconsistent results; when those problems are corrected the results disappear. Cross-country studies to provide direct evidence showing that the burden of the corporate tax actually falls on labor yield unreasonable results and prove to suffer from econometric flaws that also lead to a disappearance of the results when corrected, in those cases where data were obtained and the results replicated. Similarly, claims that high U.S. tax rates will create problems for the United States in a global economy suffer from a misrepresentation of the

U.S. tax rate compared to other countries and are less important when capital is imperfectly mobile, as it appears to be.

Although these new arguments appear to rely on questionable methods, the traditional concerns about the corporate tax appear valid. While an argument may be made that the tax is still needed as a backstop to individual tax collections, it does result in some economic distortions. These economic distortions, however, have declined substantially over time as corporate rates and shares of output have fallen. Moreover, it is difficult to lower the corporate tax without creating a way of sheltering individual income given the low rates of tax on dividends and capital gains.

A number of revenue-neutral changes are available that could reduce these distortions, allow for a lower corporate statutory tax rate, and lead to a more efficient corporate tax system. These changes include base broadening, reducing the benefits of debt finance through inflation indexing, and reducing the tax at the firm level offset by an increase at the individual level.

INTRODUCTION

On October 25, 2007, then-Ways and Means Committee Chairman Charles B. Rangel introduced H.R. 3970, a tax reform plan that included revisions in the corporate tax to lower the rate and broaden the base. This proposal would cut the corporate tax rate and, in a roughly revenue-neutral sub-section of the proposal, broaden the tax base. In the 111th Congress, S. 3018, introduced by Senators Ron Wyden and Judd Gregg, also provides for a lower corporate tax rate in exchange for a somewhat broader corporate tax base.

Interest in corporate rate cuts and other corporate revisions has been developing for some time. In November 2005, President George W. Bush's Advisory Panel on Tax Reform reported on a variety of proposals for major reform of the tax system, including those for corporate and business income taxes.[1] Hearings were held on these proposals in 2006, but no further action occurred. On July 16, 2007, *The Wall Street Journal* published an opinion article by Treasury Secretary Henry M. Paulson addressing concerns that the U.S. corporate tax rate is high relative to other countries and announcing a conference to be held July 26 that would examine the U.S. business tax system and its effects on the economy.[2]

On July 23, 2007, the Treasury Department released a background paper (hereafter, the Treasury Study) that addressed several issues associated with the corporate tax: (1) special tax provisions that narrow the corporate tax base; (2) the efficiency effects of the tax (distortions in the size and allocation of investment); (3) the size of the unincorporated sector; and (4) a comparison of corporate taxes in the United States with other countries.[3] The paper, however, did not discuss important justifications for a corporate tax, such as its role in the progressivity of federal taxes assuming the burden of the tax falls on capital, and the need for a corporate tax to avoid the use of the corporate form as a tax shelter by high income individuals.

While the Treasury Study focused largely on efficiency issues and international comparisons, on the day of the conference, R. Glenn Hubbard, President Bush's first chairman of the Council of Economic Advisors, also published an opinion article in *The Wall Street Journal* referring to the conference.[4] His article echoed some arguments that have been made in recent months that are based partly, or largely, on empirical studies of differences across countries. He addressed the distributional issue, but referred to some evidence that the burden of the corporate tax falls on labor. In addition to theoretical arguments, he cited an empirical paper by Kevin Hassett and Aparna Mathur of the American Enterprise Institute.[5] His article also discussed empirical evidence suggesting that the U.S. might raise revenue by cutting corporate tax rates because of large behavioral responses.[6] Hubbard concludes by suggesting that cutting the corporate tax rate would reduce a tax that is largely, or even fully, borne by labor and that behavioral responses would offset much of the static revenue cost.

During the conference, discussions included whether business representatives would trade tax preferences for lower rates, whether reform should take the form of lower rates or write-offs of investments, and methods of avoiding the corporate tax by income shifting in a global economy. Some participants complained that the corporate tax is outdated, too complex, distorts decisions, and undermines the ability of firms to complete in a global economy. Echoing some issues raised in Hubbard's article, Kevin Hassett indicated that the corporate tax was not an effective way to raise revenues and suggested that lowering the rate would raise revenues.[7]

Prior to the 2007 conference, Congress held hearings in 2006 on the Advisory Panel's proposals, with a general hearing followed by one concentrating on business tax issues. In the 110th Congress, attention to capital income taxes has been targeted to narrower issues such as the tax gap and offshore tax havens.[8] At the time of the Treasury conference, Chairman Charles B. Rangel of the House Ways and Means Committee released a statement inviting the Bush Administration to discuss such issues as tax reform, especially the Alternative Minimum Tax (AMT), addressing tax havens, and increasing equity and fairness in the tax structure.[9]

H.R. 3970 includes some of the base broadeners included in the Treasury Study and others that were not. The rate reduction, from 35% to 30.5% was not as large as that discussed in the Treasury Study, 27%. Base broadeners in H.R. 3970 have already been criticized by some business groups.[10]

The corporate tax debate continues to be in the news. In May 2008, N. Gregory Mankiw published an article suggesting that most of the burden of the tax falls on labor, and cites research suggesting the corporate tax is borne by labor and that revenue losses may be fully or largely offset by behavioral responses.[11]

This report provides an overview of corporate tax issues and discusses potential reforms in the context of these issues, with particular attention to some of the recent research concerning large behavioral responses and their implications for revenue and distribution. The first section reviews the size and history of the corporate income tax, and discusses an important issue that has been given little attention by those who propose deep cuts in the corporate tax: its role in preventing the use of the corporate form as a tax shelter by wealthy business owners. This section also discusses the potential effect of behavioral responses on corporate tax revenues. The second section examines the role of the corporate tax in contributing to a progressive tax system and discusses claims that the burden falls on workers. The third section reviews arguments relating to efficiency and revenue yield, and traditional criticisms of the corporate tax as one that causes important behavioral distortions. One aspect of this discussion is the question of how the tax might be viewed differently in a more global economy. The final section examines options for reform.

The Corporate Tax as a Revenue Source

The corporate tax is the third largest source of federal revenue, but its importance as a revenue source has diminished considerably over time.

Magnitude and Historical Pattern

Despite concerns expressed about the size of the corporate tax rate, current corporate taxes are extremely low by historical standards, whether measured as a share of output or a based on the effective tax rate on income. [12] In 1953, the corporate tax accounted for 5.6% of GDP and 30% of federal tax revenues. In recent years the tax has fluctuated round 2% of GDP and 10% of revenues, reaching a low of 1.2% of GDP in 2003, and standing at 2.7% in 2006. The tax is projected to continue to raise revenues of around 2% of GDP. Today, it is the third largest federal revenue source, lagging behind the individual income tax, which is about 8% of GDP and the payroll tax, which is about 6.5%. It is much more significant, however, than excise taxes, which are slightly over 0.5%, and estate and gift taxes at 0.2%. (Note that the income tax share is expected to grow and will exceed 10% if the 2001-2003 tax cuts are not made permanent; estate and gift tax revenues will also rise slightly.)

Much of the historical decline arises from legislated reductions in the corporate effective tax rate on the return to new investment, which has fallen from 63% of corporate profits in 2003 to about 30% today. These changes include a reduction in the top statutory rate from 52% to 35% and much more liberal depreciation rules. The total tax burden on corporate source income has declined even more due to lower rates on dividends and capital gains at the shareholder level and the increased fraction of stocks held in tax exempt form.

While a large fraction of the decline in corporate tax revenues is associated with these changes in rates and depreciation, other causes may be more liberal rules that allow firms to obtain benefits of corporate status (such as limited liability) while still being taxed as unincorporated businesses and tax evasion, particularly through international tax shelters. The Treasury Report documents the significant rise in the share of total business net income received by unincorporated businesses since 1980, from 21% of total net income to 50%. While the share of proprietorships (which have no limited liability) has declined slightly, from 17% to 14%, the share of Subchapter S firms (firms that are incorporated but are allowed to elect taxation as an unincorporated business) rose from 1% to 15%. These changes followed a dramatic increase in the number of shareholders allowed for the election (the limit of 10 was raised to 35 in 1982, to 75 in 1996, and to 100 in 2004). Partnerships (including limited liability corporations and limited liability partnerships) increased from 3% to 21%, with most of the increase occurring after 1990. This growth reflects in part the growth of limited liability corporations established under state law (the first state adopted such a provision in 1982), which qualify as unincorporated business for corporate tax purposes. While Subchapter S firms are constrained by the shareholder limit, partnerships are not.

Although it has declined considerably in importance, the corporate tax remains a major source of federal revenue, and a significant change in individual income taxes would be required to offset a substantial reduction in corporate taxes. Current pressures to find revenue sources to pay for relief from the AMT make an overall corporate tax cut difficult to envision.

For that reason, the Bush Administration has proposed trading off rate reductions, or possibly broad investment subsidies that reduce the effective burden on new investment, for base broadening, through reduction of corporate tax preferences.

The Role of the Corporate Tax in Backstopping the Individual Tax

Measuring corporate tax revenue falls short of describing the full role of the corporate tax in contributing to federal revenues because the corporate tax protects the collection of individual income taxes. As long as taxes on individual income are imposed, a significant corporate income tax is likely to be necessary to forestall the use of the corporation as a tax shelter. Without a corporate tax, high income individuals could channel funds into corporations, and, with a large part of earnings retained, obtain lower tax rates than if they operated in partnership or proprietorship form or in a way that allowed them to be taxed as such. As suggested by the growth in unincorporated business forms above, wealthy business owners may be quick to take advantage of tax rate differentials, which currently tend to favor unincorporated businesses. (Since 1986, when individual tax rates were lowered dramatically, the corporate tax rate has been high relative to the individual tax rate). The Treasury Study indicated that 61% of the income of unincorporated businesses was associated with taxpayers in the top income tax bracket.

Although the top tax rate on corporations is equal to the top individual rate (3 5%), the corporate tax is graduated. Consequently, for high income taxpayers, there is an advantage to shifting part of one's income into a corporation because corporate tax rates are graduated (15% on the first $50,000 and 25% on the next $25,000) and are lower than the top marginal tax. This opportunity, however, is restricted by (1) limiting to one the number of corporations income can be shifted to; (2) the amount on which rates are graduated; and (3) disallowing graduated rates for personal service corporations. There are over 600,000 corporations with earnings less than $50,000, according to Internal Revenue Service statistics, suggesting some shifting occurs. In recognition of the potential use of the corporation as a shelter, tax law has in the past contained a tax on accumulated earnings. As long as dividends were taxed as ordinary income and the accumulated earnings tax was strict enough, it was difficult to use the corporate form to shelter a great deal of income.

This tax shelter constraint on lowering the corporate rate is arguably more binding today because of the lower rates on dividends and capital gains enacted as part of the Administration's corporate relief package in 2003. Table 1 calculates the effective tax rate for operating through a corporation, versus an unincorporated business, for an individual in the 35% tax bracket. If dividends are taxed at 15% and the corporate rate is lowered to 27% as suggested in the Treasury conference, the tax rate in the corporate form would be less than the tax rate on unincorporated businesses. In fact, with a 15% rate on dividends, corporations that distributed less than 73% of their income would present a tax shelter opportunity with a 27% tax rate. This outcome would occur even without the benefit of graduated rates and could potentially benefit labor income as well as individual capital income. Moreover, although there are rules restricting accumulated earnings, it is common for corporations to reinvest a significant fraction of their earnings. This unlimited sheltering option would not exist as long as the corporate tax were as high as the individual tax, and its scope would be limited if dividends and capital gains were taxed at higher rates.

Table 1. Tax Rates For Alternative Forms of Organization Under Alternative Rate Structures, Individual at 35% Rate

	100% of Income Distributed	50% of Income Distributed	No Income Distributed
Corporate Business			
Dividends Taxed at 15% Rate			
Corporate Tax Rate of 35%	45	40	35
Corporate Tax Rate of 27%	38	32	27
Dividends Taxed at Ordinary Rates			
Corporate Tax Rate of 35%	58	46	35
Corporate Tax Rate of 27%	46	36	27
Unincorporated Business	35	35	35

Source: CRS analysis.

Some reforms might address these shelter issues directly, including raising tax rates on dividends and capital gains at the individual level while lowering the rate at the firm level, eliminating the graduated rate structure, and more formal methods of integrating the individual and corporate income taxes.

Behavioral Responses and Revenue Maximizing Tax Rate

Although it has long been recognized that there are behavioral responses to the corporate tax (even aside from the tax sheltering issues indicated above), and that these responses have important implications for the efficiency of the economy and the burden of the tax, the issue of a revenue maximizing tax rate, popularly associated with the "Laffer" curve, has rarely entered into the discussion. A Laffer curve graphs revenue against the tax rate, and is based on the notion that revenue is zero at a zero tax rate and zero at a 100% tax rate (at least with respect to some taxes).[13] In a Laffer curve, the revenue first rises with the tax rate and then falls, and at the point it reverses direction is the revenue-maximizing tax rate.

A Laffer curve for the corporate tax has been proposed or alluded to recently in several articles in the popular press. One is the article by Glenn Hubbard, cited above. In *National Review*, Kevin Hassett discusses the Laffer curve and presents a chart that he indicates is an illustration that appears to show a negative relationship between corporate revenues as a share of GDP and the tax rate. [14] Only 13 countries are shown on this graph, however, and the negative relationship is clearly strongly affected by an outlier, Ireland, which is a well known tax haven; most economists would not find this illustration persuasive proof. Another discussion of this issue appeared in an editorial in *The Wall Street Journal*, which also presented a chart with a number of OECD countries on it.[15] In this chart, the editors simply drew a curve, which passed through a couple of points. There was no statistical fitting to the data and no informative value to such an analysis; moreover the two points through which the freehand curve was drawn were questionable: one was the United Arab Emirates with no tax, which is neither a typical country nor in the OECD, and the other was Norway, whose corporate tax revenue tends to be high because of oil. The bulk of the data showed no obvious trend.[16]

The Hubbard and Hassett articles do, however, cite some more sophisticated research. Hassett referred to a paper by Kimberly Clausing,[17] and Hubbard referred to a paper by Michael Devereux.[18] In addition, Alex Brill and Kevin Hassett also prepared a statistical analysis examining the change in the relationship over time. [19] A cross country study was also prepared by Mintz.[20]. Clausing, who is referred to in the Hassett article, is quoted as claiming that the United States is likely to the right of the revenue maximizing point on the Laffer curve, but this statement, presumably from an earlier draft, is not found in her published article. That article finds a revenue maximizing tax rate of 33%, in her simple specification, but as she added variables and accounted for other features the revenue maximizing tax rate seemed to rise, as indicated in Table 2. Large countries and countries that are less open, such as the United States, have a revenue maximizing tax rate of 57%—much larger than the combined federal and state rate for U.S. firms of 39%.[21]

Michael Devereux's paper indicates that, while he finds a revenue maximizing rate of 33% under the same specification as Clausing, he finds only weak evidence of a relationship between tax rates and corporate tax revenues as a percentage of GDP. Many of his specifications do not yield statistically significant effects. Brill and Hassett find a rate of around 30%, which has been falling over time. Mintz finds a rate of 28%, but his data span only a few years (2001-2005).[22]

In the remainder of this section, we first discuss theoretical expectations of this relationship and then examine these empirical studies. Both the theoretical and empirical assessments suggest that the results of these analyses are questionable.

Theoretical Issues

The issue of a Laffer curve has not been a part of the debate because the notion of a revenue maximizing tax rate other than at very high tax rates is inconsistent with most of the models of the corporate tax. Traditionally, the main behavioral response associated with the corporate tax was the substitution of noncorporate capital for corporate capital within an economy where the amount of capital was fixed. Imposing a corporate tax (in excess of the noncorporate tax) caused capital to earn a lower return in the corporate sector and to flow out of that sector and into the noncorporate sector, thereby lowering the return in the noncorporate sector and raising the return, before taxes, in the corporate sector. The higher pre-tax return on capital also caused prices to go up in the corporate sector and fall in the noncorporate sector, causing a shift towards non- corporate sector total production. The corporate profits tax base, therefore, had two opposing forces: the amount of capital was falling but the profit rate was rising. The taxable base could, therefore, either increase as tax rates increased, or it could decrease. The direction depended on the substitutability of capital and labor in the corporate sector. The central tendency of most models (with unitary elasticities) suggested, however, that the tax base was relatively invariant to tax rates, and revenues would always rise with the tax rate. Consequently, under any reasonable set of assumptions there would either be no revenue maximizing tax rate or an extremely high one.[23]

Table 2. Revenue Maximizing Tax Rates and Share of Variance Explained in the Clausing Study

Specification	Tax Rate	R-Squared
(1) Basic	33%	0.13
(2) Additional Variables	39	0.43
(3) Additional Variables	42	0.46
(4) Additional Variables	41	0.23
(5) Additional Variables	37	0.21
(6) Openness	43	0.27
(7) Size	45	0.23
(8) Openness and size	57	0.28

Source: Kimberly Clausing (2007).

Note: The R-Squared is a statistical term that measures the share of the variance in the dependent variable explained by the independent variables.

If behavioral responses caused the total capital in the U.S. economy to contract, the outcome could be different. One such model, the open economy model, appears to be a motivation for the belief in a relatively low revenue maximizing tax rate. Brill and Hassett discuss elasticity estimates of foreign capital flows to after tax returns in the range of 1.5 to 3 (they also cite a recent study with an elasticity of 3.3) in their paper that finds a revenue maximizing tax rate of around 30%. They conclude that "[t]hese high elasticities are consistent with the view that reductions in corporate rates could lure a significant enough amount of economic activity to a locality to create a Laffer curve in the corporate tax space."[24]

As shown in the Appendix A, however, one cannot achieve this tax rate even with infinite elasticities. In the most extreme case, where (1) the country is too small to affect worldwide prices and rates of return; (2) capital is perfectly mobile; and (3) products in international trade are perfectly substitutable, the revenue maximizing tax rate would be the ratio of the labor share of income to the factor substitution elasticity. Assuming fairly common values for a model without depreciation of 75% for labor's share of income and a factor substitution elasticity of 1, the tax rate would be 75%—far above the rates of around 30% reported by Brill and Hassett. This rate could rise as these conditions are relaxed. If the U.S. is assumed to have 30% of world resources, the rate rises to 81%; if imperfect substitutability between investments across countries and between foreign and domestic products is allowed, it would rise further.

Although it is possible to have a revenue maximizing tax rate that does not asymptotically approach 100% it is probably not possible to find a rate that maximizes revenues as a percentage of GDP, because GDP falls as well as tax revenues. In this case, we are back to the same circumstances as in the reallocation of capital in the closed economy: with unitary elasticities, the corporate share of income is constant relative to GDP, and with other elasticities it can rise or fall.

A related circumstance where capital can contract would be in a model where savings responds so powerfully that the savings supply is infinitely elastic, that is, when a tax is imposed, the capital stock must contract so much, and the pre-tax rate of return rises so much that the after-tax return comes back to its original value. This extreme savings response model yields the same revenue maximizing tax rate as the extreme open economy, 75%, and probably no revenue maximizing tax rate for revenues as a percent of GDP. Moreover, the slowness with which the capital stock adjusts (most models allow 150 years for full adjustments) means that the revenue would be affected by tax rates in the past.

The result of this discussion makes it clear that revenue maximizing tax rates cannot arise from physical reallocations or contractions of capital. Nor are they likely to arise from a substitution between debt and equity, since the debt share has changed very little despite significant changes in the relative tax burden, and estimates of elasticities that do exist are small.

A remaining source of a different outcome is profit shifting. This could involve firms maintaining the same activity and shifting the form of operation to unincorporated businesses. This could be a possibility (although the point of revenue maximization would be much too low because much of the tax has not disappeared, but rather has shifted). But, at least in the United States, this shift is probably less the result of high corporate tax rates and more the result of increasingly loose restrictions on operating with limited liability outside the corporate form, actions that have not been taken by other countries.[25] The other profit shifting issue is the shifting of profits (rather than activity) to foreign countries. Such effects are possible, but it would seem unlikely that tax avoidance could be of this magnitude, given that only 5% of the U.S. capital stock is invested abroad. While a small low income country, as is characteristic of most tax havens, might have little enough domestic capital that they could afford the loss from lowering the rate in order to attract more capital, such an outcome is much less likely for the United States.

Empirical Analysis

As noted above, several recent studies have examined the relationship between corporate tax rates and corporate tax revenues as a percentage of gross domestic product (GDP). We obtained the data used for two of these studies to replicate and extend the analyses. Both studies and our analysis estimate the effect of the top corporate tax rate (and its square) on corporate tax revenues as a percentage of GDP. Panel data for 29 OECD countries is used for the analysis.

Brill and Hassett Study

In their study, Brill and Hassett use panel data for the OECD countries from 1981 to 2003.[26] They use regression analysis (OLS) to estimate the effects. Brill and Hassett find that the corporate tax rate has at first a positive effect on corporate tax revenues as a percentage of GDP and then a decreasing effect—the effect looks like an inverted U, the shape of the classic Laffer curve. All of their coefficient estimates are statistically significant. However, they do not account for problems often encountered with the use of panel data, and their coefficient estimates would appear to be biased and inconsistent.[27]

Table 3. Coefficient Estimates: Dependent Variable is Corporate Revenues as a Percentage of GDP (Brill and Hassett Model)

	1980-1986	1987-1992	1993-1997	1998-2003	1980-2003
A. Central government corporate tax revenues; federal corporate tax rate					
Tax rate	-0.037 (0.090)	-0.110 (0.081)	0.048 (0.087)	0.049 (0.117)	-0.040 (0.040)
Tax rate squared	0.087 (0.109)	0.122 (0.100)	-0.082 (0.129)	-0.060 (0.178)	0.052 (0.053)
F (joint)	5.15	1.21	0.33	0.21	0.51
Prob>F	0.008	0.303	0.719	0.809	0.603
B. Total government corporate tax revenues; total corporate tax rate					
Tax rate	0.204 (0.195)	-0.042 (0.077)	0.069 (0.076)	0.037 (0.094)	-0.016 (0.038)
Tax rate squared	-0.193 (0.214)	0.044 (0.091)	-0.106 (0.109)	-0.008 (0.123)	0.028 (0.047)
F (joint)	2.25	0.21	0.51	0.74	0.44
Prob>F	0.112	0.811	0.602	0.481	0.612

Source: Authors' analysis.

Notes: Standard errors in parenthesis. Fixed effects linear model with AR(1) disturbance. Other variables include time dummy variables.

The estimation results from our re-analysis of the Brill and Hassett study are reported in **Table 3**. The regression includes a tax rate and a tax rate squared to allow for a curve. Panel A of the table displays the results for central government corporate tax data (in the case of the U.S., this is federal government tax data). The coefficient estimates for the full time period (1980 to 2003) and the four subperiods defined by Brill and Hassett are reported. In all cases, the coefficient estimates are fairly small and none are statistically significant at conventional confidence levels.

Panel B of the table displays the results for total government (that is, governments at all levels) corporate tax data. Again, the coefficient estimates are fairly small and none are statistically significant. Once appropriate estimation methods are used to correct problems arising with panel data, there appears to be no statistically significant relation between corporate tax rates and corporate tax revenues as a percentage of GDP.

Clausing Study

Clausing uses panel data for the OECD countries from 1979 to 2002 to study the effect of corporate tax rates on corporate tax revenue as a percentage of GDP.[28] She includes more explanatory variables than did Brill and Hassett, but her overall research findings and conclusions are essentially the same as theirs—there is a Laffer curve relationship between corporate tax rates and corporate tax revenue as a percentage of GDP. However, her estimation methods would lead to biased and inconsistent coefficient estimates.[29]

The estimation results for five different specifications are reported in Table 4. The five specifications differ by what explanatory variables are included in the analysis. In all five specifications, the coefficient estimates of the corporate tax rate (and its square) are smaller than those estimated by Clausing and have the opposite signs. Most of the coefficient estimates are not statistically significant at conventional confidence levels, but two are statistically significant at the 10% level only. (In these cases where the coefficients are significant on the tax squared term they still do not produce the Laffer curve shape but rather suggest rising revenue with a rising tax rate). Overall, these results suggest that the corporate tax rate has little effect on corporate tax revenues as a percentage of GDP. Consequently, there is little evidence to support the existence of a corporate tax Laffer curve.

CROSS COUNTRY INVESTMENT ESTIMATES: THE DJANKOV STUDY

Cross country empirical studies, as noted above, have recently been employed to address the Laffer curve issue and, as will be discussed subsequently, the incidence of the corporate tax on wages. In addition to these direct estimates, there are numerous empirical studies that examine underlying relationships, such as the effect of the user cost of capital (which incorporates the tax rate along with other variables) on investment. Most of these studies have found modest effects on domestic investment and have employed times series estimates within the United States.[30]

One recent study on investment, Djankov et al.,[31] is similar to the other studies in that it employs a cross country data base and an independent variable reflecting the tax rate to directly estimate the effect of the corporate tax rate on investment, entrepreneurship and other variables. The study found no effect on investment for statutory tax rates, but very large effects for constructed first year and five year cash flow tax rates. This study, unlike the others discussed in this paper, is a single cross section, so there is no way to introduce fixed country effects.

Theoretical Issues

Several difficulties arise in the Djankov analysis. First, the cash flow tax rate variable they construct is hypothetical one (for a hypothetical firm) which is not representative of the capital stock or the firm size in a country (or in all countries). The denominator is income measured before labor income taxes paid by the firm (such as social security taxes in the United states) and economic depreciation. The first is very problematic because the capital income tax rate increases as the labor income tax rate falls, which is a relationship that seems to have no obvious economic justification. It also measures taxes on a cash flow basis for the first year (or the first five years in an alternative scenario), rather than over the life of the investment.

An examination of scatter-plots of their data suggest that the results are highly affected by outliers, particularly Bolivia (which has a very high tax rate and a very low investment rate) and Mongolia, a low tax country where investment has been flowing in recently due to mining.

Table 4. Coefficient Estimates: Dependent Variable is Corporate Revenues as a Percentage of GDP (Clausing Model)

	Specification				
	(1)	**(2)**	**(3)**	**(4)**	**(5)**
Tax rate	-0.055 (0.035)	-0.073 (0.111)	-0.075 (0.046)	-0.048 (0.036)	-0.067 (0.047)
Tax rate squared	0.078* (0.047)	0.118 (0.147)	0.102* (0.061)	0.069 (0.048)	0.093 (0.061)
Profit rate		X			
Corporate share		X			
Unemployment rate			X		X
Per capita GDP growth rate			X		X
Per capita GDP			X		X
Openness				X	X
F (joint)	1.39	0.75	1.45	1.04	1.21
Prob>F	0.251	0.473	0.236	0.354	0.298

Source: Authors' analysis.

Notes: Standard errors in parenthesis. Fixed effects linear model with AR(1) disturbance. Other variables include the indicated variables and time dummy variables. *significant at 10% level.

The tax rate for Bolivia is about twice the typical tax rate and is inconsistent with the corporate rate in Bolivia. According to the authors, the tax rate reflects an alternative transactions tax. However, a transactions tax is not a tax on corporate income but falls on all income in the economy. Assuming that about a quarter of income is capital incomes, the tax should be reduced by 75%.

As with the Laffer-curve estimates, the results of this study, at least for the United States, are not plausible. According to their estimates, a 10 percentage point drop in corporate tax increased investment by 2.2 percentage points. According to an open economy model developed by Gravelle and Smetters,[32] however, U.S. capital would increase a maximum of 0.7 percentage points with the elimination of corporate tax; with more reasonable elasticities, it would increase by 0.3 percentage points. (This study was directed at the question of tax incidence and will be discussed in more detail in the section below which addresses distributional issues and the burden on labor). Moreover, these effects may understate the investment effects because they do not take into account debt. Thus, their results suggest an investment increase that is at least 11 times too large and that could be 25 or more times too large.

Empirical Analysis

While the issue of fixed effects would cause this study to remain problematic in any case, this section explores the effects of the tax rate changes and of specifications that include multiple control variables.

Table 5. Coefficient Estimates: Key Independent Variable is Constructed Effective Tax Rate (Djankov, Ganser, McLiesh, Ramalho, and Shleifer Model)

Dependent Variable				
	Investment	**Foreign Direct Investment**	**Business Density per 100 People**	**Average Business Entry Rate**
Original Basic Estimate	-0.218*** (0.074)	-0.226*** (0.045)	-0.194*** (0.063)	-0.138*** (0.057)
Range of Estimate	-0.165 to -0.236	-0.189 to -0.233	-0.090 to -0.196	-0.110 to -0.141
Coefficient Estimates of Tax Rate Variable with Corrected Data				
Basic Estimate	-0.108 (0.073)	0.194*** (0.044)	-0.150** (0.060)	-0.116** (0.055)
PLUS				
Region Indicators	-0.046 (0.071)	-0.191*** (0.045)	-0.115* (0.058)	-0.126** (0.056)
PLUS				
Per Capital GDP	-0.031 (0.070)	-0.190*** (0.045)	-0.148*** (0.050)	-0.146** (0.055)
PLUS				
Number of Tax Payments				
Employment Rigidity Index	-0.025 (0.076)	-0.179*** (0.048)	-0.154*** (0.055)	-0.097* (0.057)
Procedures to Start a Business				

Source: Author's analysis.
Notes: Standard errors in parenthesis.
* significant at 10% level.
** significant at 5% level;
*** significant at 1% level

The Djankov et al. sample consists of 2004 tax and economic data for 85 countries. They examine the effect of the corporate tax rate on (1) aggregate investment, (2) foreign direct investment, and (3) two measures of entrepreneurial activity. The main results of their study and our reanalysis are reported in Table 5. The first row of the table displays the coefficient estimate of the effective corporate tax rate variable taken from the Djankov et al. study. Their basic specification includes only the tax rate as an independent variable. The second row of the table reports the range of estimates when a single additional independent variable is added—the authors add 10 variables, one at a time. In all but one instance, the estimates are statistically significant at the 1% or 5% confidence level, and at the 10% level in the remaining case.

We reanalyzed their data after correcting an error in their tax rate for Bolivia, and cumulatively added selected independent variables that Djankov et al. included in their analysis; we also included a region-of-the-world variable for each country. The first row of the bottom panel in Table 5 presents the coefficient estimates for the basic model with only a single independent variable: the effective corporate tax rate. For each dependent variable, the coefficient estimate of the tax rate variable is smaller than Djankov et al. 's estimate, which illustrates the importance of Bolivia to their results. Furthermore, the estimated effect of the tax rate on aggregate investment is not statistically significant. The final row of Table 5 reports the coefficient estimate of the tax rate when the full set of independent variables is included in the analysis. The estimated effect of the tax rate on aggregate investment is much smaller than Djankov et al. 's estimate and not statistically significant. The estimated effect of the corporate tax rate on foreign direct investment and entrepreneurial activity is somewhat smaller than the effects estimated by Djankov et al., but the estimates are statistically significant.

DISTRIBUTIONAL EFFECTS

A second issue that was a focus of the Hubbard article, but was not in the Treasury Report was the distributional effects of the corporate income tax. If the corporate tax falls on owners of the corporation, or on capital in general, it contributes to a progressive tax system, since higher income individuals have more income from capital than from labor. Based on tax data, for taxpayers with incomes up to $100,000, over 90% of income is labor income, while for those over $1,000,000, less than a third is labor income. [33] The traditional analysis of the corporate income tax indicates that the burden generally spread to all capital, but does not fall on labor income. Most government and private agencies that routinely do distributional analysis allocate the corporate tax to capital income.[34]

Hubbard refers to three studies in his article: one a working paper by economist Arnold Harberger,[35] one a working paper by William Randolph of the Congressional Budget Office,[36] and one a recent empirical cross-country study using data similar to the studies discussed above, by Hassett and Mathur.[37] Three other empirical studies that use cross country data have also been released recently, by Felix,[38] by Desai, Hines and Foley,[39] and by Arulampalam, Devereux, and Maffiini.[40] Mankiw refers to the Randolph and Arulampalam, Devereux, and Maffinni studies.

The Harberger and Randolph Studies

The first two studies explicitly focus on the effects of an open economy. It is a standard finding that for a small open single-good economy with perfect capital mobility and perfect product substitution, the burden of any source based capital income tax falls on labor (whereas for residence based taxes, that is taxes that apply to domestic owners of capital regardless of where they are domiciled, the burden would fall on capital). The corporate tax has some aspects of a source based tax and some of a residence based tax.

Both the Harberger and the Randolph studies are based on this simple model of perfect substitution, altered to account for the United States as a large county (which lowers the elasticities) and to account for multiple sectors. Randolph's study does not so much predict the burden of the tax as explore incidence in certain types of models; he acknowledges that less capital mobility causes the burden to shift from labor to capital. Harberger 's model has four sectors, corporate and non-corporate tradeable sectors and corporate and non-corporate nontradeable sectors. He assumes that the corporate tradeable sector is more capital intensive that the average industry, which leads to a burden of greater than 100% of the tax falling on capital. Despite the vision of the manufacturing sector as highly capital intensive, it actually is not: housing services, which are 100% capital, account for over a third of the capital stock in the country, and many other industries, such as utilities and agriculture are also more capital intensive than manufacturing. Using the same assumptions about mobility, but with a less capital intensive manufacturing sector, Randolph finds 70% of the corporate tax burden falls on labor.

To permit other than perfect substitutability, a much more complex computable general equilibrium model would be required, which neither Harberger nor Randolph has provided. Such a model has been developed by Gravelle and Smetters[41] who find, with reasonable elasticities, that capital still bears most of the burden, about 80%. A recent CBO working paper by Jennifer Gravelle provides an extensive review of the existing general equilibrium models and the factors that drive the results.[42] She finds that five factors tend to move the burden toward falling on capital: a smaller willingness of consumers to substitute between foreign and domestic products, a higher substitutability of labor and capital in the production process, a smaller willingness of investors to substitute investments in different countries, a less capital intensive corporate tradeable sector, and a larger country. Her review of the evidence on these factors suggests that, based on these models, the majority of the tax (about 60%) is born by capital, with results differing from the Gravelle and Smetters findings due to a lower substitution elasticity between capital and labor in production. She subsequently considers, however, other factors that could increase the burden on capital (and even benefit labor), including the use of debt (discussed below).

While the general equilibrium models can be very complex, they still abstract from some important features of the corporate tax. There are two other factors that would further push the corporate tax burden towards capital. First, the current corporate tax has elements of a residence based tax, and the burden of a residence based tax falls on capital. Second, the current corporate tax actually subsidizes debt finance at the firm level, and if debt is much more substitutable than equity, total capital would be less likely to be exported: indeed, raising the corporate tax could cause capital to flow in. A study by Grubert and Mutti[43] found that in a general equilibrium model that included debt, such a capital inflow occurred when capital income taxes were raised, an outcome that would lead to labor benefitting from the corporate tax.

Finally, note that as long as countries tend to choose tax rates similar to each other, which appears to be the case, the world becomes like the original closed economy, a model stressed by Harberger, with the burden falling on capital. According to the Treasury Study, the U.S. combined state and federal corporate statutory rate is 39%, the G-7 average is 36% and the OECD average is 31%. Effective tax rates, which should govern the movement of capital, are even closer together, and in some cases are lower for the U.S. than for other countries. Jennifer Gravelle uses OECD tax rates to estimate the share of the U.S. tax falling on labor using a global approach and finds that over 90% falls on capital.[44]

An argument is often made that the burden of any capital income tax tends to fall on labor because it reduces savings, an effect that would also occur in a closed economy. While one model predicts that the entire burden of a capital income tax eventually falls on labor, this model requires some extreme assumptions about human behavior such as perfect information, an infinite planning horizon, perfect liquidity, and asexual reproduction. Models allowing for finite lives (such as the life-cycle models) find results that vary, but if the revenue loss is made up by higher taxes on labor, there is little or no effect. Some economists believe that these models are inappropriate, as they assume too much information and skill on the part of individuals; they suggest that individuals use rules of thumb, such as fixed savings rates or targets, instead. These rules of thumb suggest that a cut in capital income taxes either has no effect on saving or reduces savings. These economists also point out that most empirical evidence does not point to an increase in savings; historically, savings rates do not appear to respond to reduced tax rates.[45]

The Hassett and Mathur Study

While the theoretical models do not provide much support for the corporate tax burden falling on labor, Hubbard also refers to an empirical study by Hassett and Mathur that uses the corporate tax rate to explain differences in manufacturing wages. They find a statistically significant result that indicates a 1% increase in the corporate tax causes manufacturing wages to fall by 0.8% to 1%.

These results are impossible, however, to reconcile with the magnitudes in the economy. Through competition, wage changes in manufacturing should be reflected in wages throughout the economy, implying that a 1% rise in corporate revenues would cause an 0.8% to 1% fall in wage income. However, corporate taxes are only about 2.5% of GDP, while labor income is about two thirds. These results imply that a dollar increase in the corporate tax would decrease wages by \$22 to \$26 dollars, an effect that no model could ever come close to predicting.[46]

The lack of theoretical reasonableness of the results may be explained by statistical issues. The Hassett and Mathur study used data from 72 developed and developing countries for the 1981 to 2003 period.[47] For their analysis, their dependent variable is the logarithm of the five-year average of the average manufacturing wage. They justify their use of the five-year average wage by (1) noting that due to capital adjustment costs, the economic effects of corporate tax rate changes show up over longer time periods, and (2) arguing that this may control for possible measurement error induced by the business cycle.[48] The wage rates for all countries were converted to U.S. dollars using annual exchange rates. Hassett and Mathur include the price level of consumption as an explanatory variable to capture cost of living differences across countries. The main explanatory variable of interest is the logarithm of the top corporate tax rate. Hassett and Mathur also use the average effective and marginal effective corporate tax rates (in logarithms) as explanatory variables in some specifications.

We repeated the Hassett and Mathur basic estimation exercise; the results are reported in the first row of Table 6.[49] The coefficient estimate reported in the first column (-0.759) suggests that a 10% increase in the top corporate tax rate will lead to an 7.6% decrease in the average manufacturing wage rate. This estimate is statistically significant at the 5% level.[50] The results are not as strong (the estimates are closer to zero) when using alternative measures of the corporate tax rate (see the next two columns of Table 6).

The exchange rate between two currencies reflects the relative supply and demand for those two currencies, and is affected by financial markets and government policies. Exchange rates may not be good indicators of the relative buying power of wage rates in two countries. Purchasing Power Parities (PPPs), however, are specifically designed to equalize the internal purchasing power of the currencies. Workers in Australia, for example, are concerned with what their wages will purchase in Australia, and not how many dollars their wages will buy. Using PPPs is a more appropriate way to convert national currencies to a common currency (U.S. dollars).

The second row of Table 6 reports the coefficient estimates when the wage rates are converted to U.S. dollars using the consumption PPPs. Consumption PPPs are more appropriate for converting wages than using general PPPs (over GDP) because they omit national expenditures for government and investment goods. Again, nominal wages are the dependent variable. The coefficient estimates are closer to zero than the estimates reported in the first row, but the coefficient estimate reported in the first column (-0.728) is statistically significant at the 5% level. The estimates for the alternative measures of the corporate tax rate are not statistically significant at the conventional confidence levels.

The most appropriate measure of wages is the inflation-adjusted consumption PPP-adjusted wage rate. Wages in each country were converted to U.S. dollars using the consumption PPP and then converted to constant (inflation-adjusted) dollars using the CPI-U before calculating the 5-year average. The final row of Table 6 displays the coefficient estimates for the model using this measure as the dependent variable. The estimates are closer to zero than in the other two cases. The coefficient estimate in the first column (-0.488) is statistically significant at the 10% level but not at the 5% level. The other two estimates in columns two and three are not statistically significant at the conventional confidence levels. While there is still some evidence of corporate tax rates having a negative influence on wage rates in manufacturing, the effect is smaller and less robust than reported in the Hassett and Mathur study.

Table 6. Coefficient Estimates: Dependent Variable is the Logarithm of the 5-Year Average of Wage Rates.

How Wage Variable Converted to U.S. Dollars	Corporate Tax Rate Variable		
	Top Tax Rate	Effective Average	Effective Marginal
Exchange Rate	-0.759** (0.297)	-0.630* (0.334)	-0.384* (0.226)
Purchasing Power Parity Exchange Rate (PPP)	-0.728** (0.303)	-0.528 (0.340)	-0.334 (0.230)
PPP—Constant Dollars	-0.488* (0.298)	-0.294 (0.318)	-0.218 (0.215)
Observations with 5-year Averages based on 5 Years of Data			
Exchange Rate	0.089 (0.353)	-0.229 (0.363)	-0.184 (0.240)
Purchasing Power Parity Exchange Rate (PPP)	-0.037 (0.354)	-0.187 (0.373)	-0.156 (0.246)
PPP—Constant Dollars	-0.064 (0.350)	-0.230 (0.351)	-0.180 (0.231)

Source: Authors' analysis.

Notes: Standard errors in parenthesis. Fixed effects linear model. Other variables include time dummies, log personal tax rate, log real value-added, log consumer price variable (except for real PPP). ** significant at 5% level; *significant at 10% level.

Table 7. Coefficient Estimates: Dependent Variable is Annual Logarithm of Real PPP-Adjusted Wage Rates

Tax Rate Lag	(1)	(2)	(3)	(4)	(5)	(6)	(7)
t	-0.031 (0.208)						0.010 (0.140)
t-1	-0.217 (0.188)					-0.219 (0.143)	
t-2	-0.076 (0.166)				-0.074 (0.144)		
t-3	-0.040 (0.159)			0.021 (0.145)			
t-4	-0.113 (0.156)		-0.070 (0.146)				
t-5	-0.154 (0.155)	-0.165 (0.147)					
F (joint)	0.49						
Prob>F	0.819						

Source: Authors' analysis.

Notes: Standard errors in parenthesis. Fixed effects linear model with AR(1) disturbance. Other variables include time dummies, log personal tax rate, log real value-added. ***significant at 1% level; ** significant at 5% level; *significant at 10% level.

Hassett and Mathur averaged wages over 5-year periods. They justify using 5-year averages by arguing that it helps to control for possible measurement error induced by the business cycle. But, because of missing values in the wage data, 66 observations have the average wage based on less than 5 years of data (60 observations use only 2 consecutive years of data for the calculation of the average, which would likely not affect any measurement error). The bottom panel of Table 6 reports the estimation results when these 66 observations are excluded from the analysis (leaving 153 observations). In all cases, the coefficient estimates for all measures of the corporate tax rate are not statistically significant.

Averaging the wage data over five years and using the beginning of period value for the explanatory variables, however, eliminates much of the variation in wages and tax rates, thus throwing away much of the information needed to estimate the economic effects. The statistical analysis is repeated using annual data and including various lagged values of the corporate tax rate as explanatory variables.[51] The results are reported in Table 7. The first column of the table displays the coefficient estimates for the current value of the corporate tax rate (labeled t in the first column) and the values for the previous five years (t-1 to t-5), which allows for longer term effects of tax rates on wages. In each case, the coefficient estimates are negative but very close to zero; none are statistically significant at the conventional confidence levels. Furthermore, all the tax rate variables in column (1) are not jointly statistically significant. The next six columns report the results when the corporate tax rate values (current and lagged) are entered individually. In every case, the coefficient estimates are close to zero and are not statistically significant at conventional confidence levels. In using annual data, we can find no evidence that changes in the top corporate tax rate affects wage rates in manufacturing.[52]

Other Cross Country Wage Studies

Three other recent studies using cross country data have examined the incidence of the tax on labor income. Felix,[53] in a study that controls for education, finds much smaller effects than Hassett and Mathur, but ones that are still too large to be predicted by a theoretical model (about $4 dollars for each dollar of corporate tax revenue). This study has problems similar to those that for Hassett and Mathur and, in addition, does not control for country fixed effects, and thus reflect cross country variation. The sample is unusual as well, with 19 countries covered for varying years. Out of the total of 65 observations (countries and years), about a quarter of the sample is drawn from Italy and Mexico and seven of the 19 countries had only one or two years of data.

A second study, by Desai, Foley and Hines[54] uses observations on foreign owned affiliates of U.S. firms across countries and in different time periods. This study uses data on multinational subsidiaries of U.S. firms to estimate the allocation of the tax burden between labor and capital using a seeming unrelated regression for capital income (which they measure by the interest rate) and labor income. In their model, labor and capital burdens are restricted to the total of taxes, and they impose a cross-equation restriction on the estimated burdens. They find the share of the burden falling on labor income to fall between about 45% and 75% of the total, a number that is not inconsistent with theoretical expectations.

This approach, however, has the fundamental theoretical problem that wages at an individual firm should not reflect tax burdens at an individual firm. In deriving a model that assumes it does, they assume that the price level of their goods is fixed and base their results only on their sample of firms (which is comprised solely of multinational corporate sector firms). This approach creates both econometric problems in their analysis and also means that their results cannot be construed as reflecting actual burdens in any of their economies, as discussed in more detail in Appendix C.

They have also represented equity returns through the interest rate, under the assumptions that investors equate (net of risk) debt and equity returns. If these assets are generally substitutable, the increase in corporate tax should cause portfolios to shift toward debt and drive the interest rate up (while driving the equity return down). Moreover, the tax burdens on debt and equity differ at the individual level and those differences depend, among other things, on any special tax rates for dividends and capital gains, the deferral advantage of capital gains and the inflation rate.

Aside from these theoretical problems, an important issue with their study is that it appears that their results are forced by the cross equation restriction. Bill Randolph, a discussant at a recent conference, found that if the restriction is eliminated there are no statistically significant results from their study.[55] In an example he presented, the estimates of the wage effect was 48% of the burden, with a standard error of 18% in the original study; in a regression without the restriction the share was 19% with a standard error of 100%.[56] Randolph considered a number of other specifications, including excluding the largest countries, but found no statistically significant results. He also suggested that only manufacturing subsidiaries be considered since other subsidiaries may be involved in tax sheltering operations. In the case where he considered only manufacturing subsidiaries, the sign reversed (indicating labor benefitted from the tax) but it was not statistically significant.

A third study, by Arulampalam, Devereux, and Maffini, uses firm level data (for about 55,000 firms) from several European countries (primarily France, Italy, Spain and Germany) over a relatively short time frame of 1996-2003.[57] It controls for firm-specific effects. About a quarter of the observations are for only 4 years and about 45% only 5 years so that the panel, like that of Felix, shows changes over the short run. The same authors had a earlier version of their study with a smaller sample.[58] Although the authors control for firm level fixed effects, they do not control for country-specific effects.

The premise of this study is quite different from the premise of the other empirical studies or the theoretical literature on the incidence of the corporate income tax. The authors present a bargaining model, where capital and labor split the excess profit (profit over a normal required return). Thus, the theoretical motivation is not driven by shifts in capital in response to changes in return, but by other factors that do not have implications for capital income distortions.

The study reports, for the preferred specification, that labor bears 96% of an increase in tax in the short run, and 92% in the long run. (These numbers were considerably different in an earlier version of the study, which found that labor bore 54% in the short run and 176% in the long run, at least for the specification that the authors reported.)

There are several reservations about this study, with the estimation results, the plausibility of the findings, and the underlying theory and execution. Perhaps the most serious of these reservations is in translating from the motivating theory to the actual estimation process. The theory addresses a bargaining division of excess profits (including the taxes on those excess profits) between labor and capital as a steady state long-run relationship. But the actual empirical implementation examines the change in wages as a function of the change in output and taxes. It does not allow for normal profit or taxes on normal profit, or for possible changes in options. It is thus an estimate of the short run incidence of a tax change that could fall on both normal return and excess profits, not the long-run sharing of the tax on rents. Traditionally, economists have assumed that the burden of the corporate tax falls on owners of the firm in the short run since capital cannot be easily shifted.

Even though it is technically possible to derive a long-run elasticity if the regression includes lagged dependent variables,[59] these short-term data are unlikely to be useful. As a long-run specification, the estimating relationship is deeply flawed because the factors that determine the incidence of the tax on normal returns, which are held fixed in the model, can also change. For this part of the tax, the burden on labor arises from general equilibrium effects in the economy and the effects on wages in a particular firm bears no relationship to the tax burden of that firm.

To the extent that the study is measuring the short-run effects, the results, as reported, are not plausible. To expect that labor would bear all of the short-run burden of a corporate tax in a bargaining model would seem unreasonable. There are implicit or explicit multi-year contracts that likely make short-run adjustments of this nature difficult. In the more intermediate term, if all firms are considered, labor is free to move from the firms with high taxes per worker to those with lower taxes.

At the same time, it is not clear that the results do imply such a large share is born by labor. The regression is estimated in logarithms, for reasons that are not apparent—such as specification is not consistent with the model presented and implies a burden that rises as the wage rises relative to taxes. A change in wages due to a change in taxes equals the estimated coefficient, multiplied by the rate of wages per worker to taxes per worker times the change in taxes. The authors report the value calculated at the median. If one took such a formula literally, it would imply that burdens for more labor-intensive firms would be more than 100% of the change, an implausible outcome for bargaining. The normal way to report results of this nature is to measure them at the mean. In this case, the short run incidence would fall from 96% to around 52%, based on data reported in the study.

There are also some important reservations about the econometric methods. Panel data with short time periods (where persistence effects can be serious) and the need to control for firm specific effects face some significant econometric problems. The authors use a number of different specifications, with widely varying results, which suggest that the results are not robust.[60] There are several other aspects of the econometrics that are not transparent.[61]

Overall, it is not clear what relationship or phenomenon the study is measuring. We are interested ideally in how an exogenous tax change affects incomes. Yet for some of the countries that constitute a large share of the data, there were no changes in tax rates. In others tax rate changes were virtually all declines, with most of those declines occurring during the growth period of the late 1 990s, when productivity and output was rising. It is possible that the results are capturing that phenomenon.

Economic Efficiency Issues

The traditional criticism of the corporate tax, as spelled out in the Treasury Study, is that the tax causes distortions, and that these distortions are exacerbated by corporate tax preferences that prevent, for a given level of tax revenue, a lower tax rate. The issues discussed in this section include allocation of capital within the domestic economy, savings effects, and international capital flows.

Allocation of Capital within the Domestic Economy

Traditionally, the efficiency concern about the corporate tax is related to the misallocation of resources between corporate and noncorporate production (including owner-occupied housing). Over time, efficiency issues have also encompassed differential taxation of the returns to assets of different physical types, and financial distortions, which affect the debt-equity ratio, payout choice, and decision to realize capital gains.

Some efficiency costs, including those that alter the mix of a firm's physical assets, arise not so much from the existence of a corporate tax but from its design. Table 8 captures the effects of the two most significant generally available provisions that affect tax burdens on different assets: depreciation rules and the recently enacted production activities deduction, which in effect allows a lower tax rate on certain domestic activities that are deemed production (manufacturing, construction, etc.). The tax rates in this table account only for the corporate tax (that is, they do not include the benefits of deducting interest or the tax at the individual level on interest, dividends, and capital gains). They are also forward looking and marginal: they estimate the share of the return on a prospective investment that is paid in tax.

If income were correctly measured and taxed that share would be the statutory rate; most assets face lower tax rates.

The variations within a column illustrate the distortions firms face in choosing the mix of capital within a firm. Overall the variations not only distort the mix of capital within a firm, but also the allocation of capital across different industries. In general, the most favored major industry is oil and gas extraction where a large fraction of investment is deducted when incurred. Other things equal, firms eligible for the production activities deduction and firms that have a larger share of their capital stock in equipment than average will be favored.

Table 8. Differential Tax Rates across Asset Types.

Asset	No Production Deduction	With Production Deduction
Autos	34	31
Office/Computing Equipment	31	28
Trucks/Buses/Trailers	29	26
Aircraft	29	26
Construction Machinery	23	21
Mining/Oilfield Equipment	28	25
Service Industry Equipment	28	25
Tractors	27	24
Instruments	28	25
Other Equipment	27	24
General Industrial Equipment	25	23
Metalworking Machinery	23	21
Electric Transmission Equipment	33	30
Communications Equipment	19	17
Other Electrical Equipment	24	21
Furniture and Fixtures	23	20
Special Industrial Equipment	21	19
Agricultural Equipment	21	19
Fabricated Metal	29	26
Engines and Turbines	36	33
Ships and Boats	17	15
Railroad Equipment	18	16
Mining Structures	7	6
Other Structures	40	37
Industrial Structures	37	34
Public Utility Structures	27	24
Commercial Structures	34	31
Farm Structures	26	23
Residential Structures	31	NA

Source: Congressional Research Service, from CRS Report RL33545, *The Advisory Panel's Tax Reform Proposals*, by Jane G. Gravelle.

Table 9. Effective Tax Rates by Sector and Type of Finance

Sector	Treasury Estimates	CRS Estimates, No Tax Exempt Investment	CRS Estimates, Half of Investment Tax Exempt
All Business	26	28	22
Corporate Business	30	32	25
Debt	-2	9	-11
Equity	40	37	33
Non-corporate business	20	20	14
Owner Occupied Housing	4	-3	-13
Economy wide	17	18	11

Source: Treasury Report; CRS Report RL33545, The Advisory Panel's Tax Reform Proposals, by Jane G. Gravelle.

In the aggregate, the tax rate on equipment is estimated at about 25%, a full 10 percentage points below the statutory tax rate, while structures (covering the last seven rows of **Table 8**) are subject to a 30% rate. Inventories are subject to a 37% rate and the overall rate on reproducible capital is 29%.[62]

The Treasury Study reports aggregated asset specific data, which provide a similar result, indicating that equipment is favored. Their measures include the total tax burden, including the benefit of deducting interest, and individual level taxes. They estimate a tax rate of 25% on equipment, 34% on structures, and 33% on land and inventories.

These estimates are somewhat overstated because they do not include intangible investments, such as research and advertising. Some research and experimentation expenditures are expensed (leading to a zero tax rate on those expenditures) and eligible for a credit as well (leading to a negative rate, but only intangible expenditures, however, are eligible). Spending on advertising is expensed and subject to a zero rate even though some advertising has future benefits.

Table 9 reports the types of distortions that are an artifact of the corporate tax as a separate tax. These estimates, unlike those in Table 8, take into account all levels of taxes. One of the complications of estimating these tax rates is whether the estimates should consider the significant (over 50%) fraction of individual passive income that is held in tax exempt form through pensions, IRAs, life insurance annuities and non-profits. In some ways, these sources can be viewed largely as not affecting marginal investment (for example, overall savings) because they are capped or not controlled directly by the investors and in other ways they affect choices (such as debt or equity of pension funds). For this reason, in addition to the estimates presented by Treasury, two sets of CRS estimates are provided which assume either no tax exempt investment or half is tax exempt.

Within the corporate sector, in addition to asset differences, there is a larger differential with respect to debt versus equity finance. The aggregate tax burden on debt is slightly negative, while equity is taxed at close to 40%. If economic income were measured correctly, interest would be subject to the individual income tax rate, which is typically slightly above 20%. Debt is subsidized at the firm level, however, because nominal interest is deducted (including the inflation premium) while corporate profits before this deduction are effectively taxed at a rate below the statutory rate on real income. The result is that at the firm level, equity is subject to a tax rate of around 30% while debt is subsidized at about the same level (a negative 32% tax rate). At the individual level, the tax on interest for taxable recipients is higher than the statutory rate because nominal interest is taxed, which pushes the overall tax rate towards a small but negative rate.

Evidence on the size of this distortion is limited, but since there appears to be limited substitution between debt and equity, it is probably less than 5% of corporate tax revenue.[63] Some simple measures, however, could significantly reduce this distortion (such as indexing interest payments for inflation). Lower corporate tax rates would also reduce this distortion.

The distortion that has probably received the most attention by those studying the corporate tax is the misallocation of capital between the corporate and noncorporate sectors. One source of the distortion arising from the corporate tax system is the taxation of corporate business at around 30%, while unincorporated business is taxed at only 20%. The higher corporate tax also contributes to a larger wedge between corporate production and owner-occupied housing, which is generally taxed at a negligible rate. The magnitude of the estimated distortion produced by having a separate corporate tax varies depending on the model used and ranges from less than 10% of corporate tax revenue to about a third.[64] Since the deadweight loss varies with the square of the tax rate, the recent decline in the differential due to lower tax rates on dividends and capital gains suggests the distortion relative to revenue would be smaller—probably no more than 4% to 7% of revenue.[65]

A distortion not captured in Table 9 is the one that affects corporate payouts. Given that appreciation in stock values is not taxed until realized, there is a benefit to retaining earnings. There is a dispute about what determines payout ratios, and what the consequences of the tax are, but, in general, the welfare cost is small. There is also some distortion due to the lock-in effect for capital gains realizations.[66]

Considering all of these distortions together, they are probably in the range of 10% to 15% of corporate tax revenues, a magnitude that could be considered as a significant component of the burden of the tax. However, given the revenue needs of the government, there would also be distortions, perhaps smaller, associated with alternative taxes. Ways to reduce these distortions may, however, be worth considering.

Savings Effects

Much of the Treasury Study's discussion emphasized effects on savings although this is not normally the focus of efficiency concerns about the corporate income tax. This distortion is not unique to corporate income taxes, but occurs with all capital income taxes. There are many difficulties with analyzing this issue. The first is that, as noted above in the discussion about the potential effect of savings on the wage rate, the economic distortion depends on the behavioral response of savings to tax changes, and what tax replaces them. Some economists have a strong view that taxes on the rate of return are always distorting, but these views are based on dynamic infinite-horizon models that may not be very realistic. With life-cycle models, the distortions depend on what revenue substitute is provided; substituting taxes on wages for taxes on capital, the most likely substitute in the U.S. tax system, could potentially increase distortions, depending on the responses in the models.[67] In models of bounded rationality, where savings are based on rules of thumb such as fixed shares of income or fixed targets, there is no response, or only an income effect, which would not produce a distorting effect.

International Capital Flows

Tax rules can affect the efficiency of allocation of capital around the world, and, if the U.S. rate is different from other countries, it can cause misallocations of capital. Despite claims that the U. S. tax rate is much higher than other countries, its rate of 39% (including state and local rates) is only slightly above the G-7 rate of 36% according to data in the Treasury Study. Since the production activities deduction acts in the same way as a statutory tax rate reduction, the actual U.S. rate is not 39%, but rather about 37%, virtually the same as the G-7 average.[68] The G-7 rate would be higher if weighted by GDP. The U.S. rate is below the 38% rate in Germany and 40% rate in Japan, the two largest of the G-7 other than the U.S. In addition, it is at the same rate as Italy, just above the 36% rate of Canada, and slightly above the 30% rate of Great Britain. The 19 OECD countries had an average of 31%, but this average would be higher if weighted by country size because larger countries have higher rates (if Ireland, with a 13% tax rate were eliminated, the average would be 33%). Although these rates put the United States rate close to those of other large developed countries, the report also indicates that several countries, in particular Germany, are planning to cut their corporate tax rates.

The Treasury Study also reports effective marginal tax rates on equipment investment (which accounts for tax preferences such as depreciation): the effective tax rate for the United States at 24%, was the same as the G-7 average, and just 4 percentage points above the 19 OECD country average. For debt finance, the U.S. had a higher negative rate, -46% (and thus more beneficial tax treatment) than the G-7 average at -39%, and the average for 19 OECD countries of -32%. If the measure is simply the average tax rate (corporate tax dividend by corporate surplus), which accounts for various corporate preferences, the U.S. average rate is 17%, which is below the OECD average of 22%.

These data do not indicate the U.S. is a high tax country with respect to investment, and would probably not become so even if some reductions occur in the future in other countries. The main source of international distortion, therefore, is probably the increased investment that occurs in low tax and tax haven countries because the United States and other developed countries do not tax that income at all or tax it on a deferred basis. This inefficiency is not due to the corporate effective tax rate, but rather is due to the provision of a tax benefit for investment abroad.[69]

Even when tax rates diverge, the efficiency costs may not be significant because the evidence suggests, as noted in previous sections, limited mobility of capital as a result of varying tax rates.

Potential Revisions in the Corporate Tax

There are a variety of potential revisions that could be made to the corporate tax to permit lowering the rate. The revisions discussed here include (1) broadening the corporate tax base and using the revenues to reduce the rate or to provide investment incentives, (2) correcting interest deductions and income for inflation, and (3) increasing the individual level tax to permit a lower tax at the firm level.

Eliminating Corporate Tax Preferences

One type of revision that would probably be supported by most economic analysts, is to eliminate corporate preferences in exchange for a lower statutory corporate tax rate. The Treasury Study estimates that eliminating corporate preferences would allow the tax rate to be lowered to 27%. Table 10 shows the preferences the Treasury Study lists and the FY2008-FY2017 revenue costs.

The largest preference in the list is expensing and accelerated depreciation ($410 billion) and the second largest is the production activities deduction ($210 billion); both provisions are captured in effective tax rates cited above. Other significant provisions (worth over $100 billion each in these years) include the exclusion of interest on state and local bonds, the research and experimentation tax credit, and the deferral of income from foreign sources, which is probably responsible for much of the international distortions.[70]

Interestingly, their list does not include graduated rates for small corporations, which costs slightly over $4 billion per year, and would, allowing for growth, raise over $50 billion in revenue over the period if were eliminated. Since owners of small corporations are typically as wealthy (or more wealthy) than owners of large ones, there appears to be little economic justification for not including these rates.

Table 10. Corporate Tax Preferences and Projected Revenue Costs, FY2008-FY2017

Preference	Revenue Cost ($ Billions)
Expensing and accelerated depreciation	410
Deduction for U.S. production activities	210
Exclusion of interest on state and local debt	135
Research and experimentation (R&E) credit	132
Deferral of income of controlled foreign corporations	120
Low income housing credit	55
Exclusion of interest on life insurance savings	30
Inventory property sales source rule	29
Deductibility of charitable contributions	28
Special Employee Stock Ownership Plan (ESOP) rules	23
Exemption of credit union income	19
New technology credit	8
Special Blue Cross/Blue Shield Deduction	8
Excess of percentage over cost depletion	7
Other corporate preferences.	27

Source: Treasury Study.

A full discussion of the economic merits of these provisions is beyond the scope of this paper, but are discussed in the Senate Budget Committee Print, *Tax Expenditure Compendium*;[71] most would be regarded as provisions that lead to economic distortions. One possible exception is the Research and Experimentation (R&E) credit, since social returns to research and development appear higher than private returns, but many economists believe that the credit is probably poorly targeted and possibly abused. Arguments could also be made that the tax exempt bond benefit is shifted to state and local governments (which can charge lower interest rates) and that these assets and revenue loss would be shifted to individuals. Arguments could also be made that the benefits of the charitable contribution deduction and the low income housing credit ultimately accrue to charities and lower income tenants, at least in part. Many other provisions have some support, and may, therefore, be difficult to repeal.

H.R. 3970 (110th Congress) would lower the tax rate to 30.5% (at a 10 year cost in FY2008- FY20 17 of $363.8 billion), as well as a permanent extension of provisions allowing expensing for small business (at a cost of $20.5 billion). As shown in Table 11, eliminating the production activities deduction is the proposal's largest base broadener. It also includes a provision that is somewhat more limited than eliminating deferral: disallowing expenses associated with foreign source income that is tax-deferred. The proposal also includes two other international provisions, one eliminating a provision adopted in 2004 that included worldwide (rather than domestic) interest in allocation rules for the foreign tax credit limit and one restricting the availability of lower withholding tax rates on income invested in the United States under treaty rules. Another major revenue raiser is a restriction in inventory accounting rules. The only depreciation base broadener in the proposal is one to extend the depreciation period for acquired intangibles. As is often the case in tax legislative proposals, revenue raisers are not always in the tax expenditure list.

Table 11. Corporate Revenue Raisers in H.R. 3970

Provision	10-Year Revenue Gain ($billions)
Production Activities Deduction	114.932
Allocation of Expenses for Deferred Income	106.385
Repeal of Worldwide Allocation of Interest	26.204
Limitation Eligibility for Reduced Treaty Withholding	6.397
Repeal Last-In First-Out Inventory Accounting	106.506
Repeal Lower of Cost or Market Inventory Method	7.146
Special Rule for Service Providers	0.225
20-Year Amortization of Intangibles	20.967
Economic Substance Doctrine	3.787
Reduction in Dividends Received Deduction	4.596
Ordinary Tax on S Corporation Stock Options in an ESOP	0.606
Terminate Domestic International Sales Corporation Benefit	0.881
Tax Debt Securities as a Tax Free Spin Off	0.235

Source: Joint Committee on Taxation.

S. 3018, introduced by Senators Wyden and Gregg in the current Congress, would also eliminate a range of corporate tax preferences and lower the rate to 24%. This legislation would eliminate several of the provisions in Table 10 (accelerated depreciation, the production activities deduction, deferral, the inventory property sales source rule, and some smaller provisions), as well as index corporate debt for inflation (discussed below).

The Treasury Study also discussed the possibility of using this base broadening to provide an investment incentive, such as a partial expensing. Such a provision would have a larger effect on lowering the tax rate on new investment than is the case for a rate reduction. It is difficult, however, to design investment subsidies in a fashion that is both neutral across types of assets and generates an even revenue loss pattern over time. Historically, investment subsidies have been restricted to equipment. The provision used most frequently in the past is the investment tax credit which, if allowed at a flat rate, favors short-lived assets. Partial expensing is neutral across investments if allowed for all types but its revenue loss is very large in the short run. Accelerated depreciation can be designed to be neutral, but it also has an uneven revenue loss pattern and cannot be applied to non-depreciable assets, such as inventories. A benefit of lowering the statutory rate is that it reduces the incentive to shift profits abroad to tax havens, although that incentive would probably be considerably lessened in any case if deferral of taxation of foreign source income were ended, as proposed in H.R. 3018.

The ending of deferral might be a controversial provision, and indeed some pressure has been exerted to move in the other direction, toward a territorial tax.[72] There are, however, some more limited approaches. For example, the President's advisory panel proposed to exempt dividends of active businesses but disallow costs such as interest to the extent income is exempt. And, as proposed in H.R. 3970, one could also defer interest deductions associated with deferred income without making any other changes, or direct restrictive rules to tax havens.

Interest Deduction Inflation Correction

If the inflation premium were disallowed for interest deductions, assuming that about half of interest is inflation, the savings would eventually be $30 billion per year at the corporate level, which would be offset by about a $10 billion loss at the individual level. This could allow a 2.5 percentage point reduction in the corporate tax rate. The important aspect of this change is that it would virtually eliminate the distortion between debt and equity, which is responsible for a significant portion of the overall distortion in the corporate tax, while maintaining the overall corporate tax burden. S. 3018 makes this revision at the corporate level.

Reducing Tax at the Firm Level and Increasing Individual Level Taxes

Given the value of lowering the corporate tax rate to reduce the shifting of income into tax havens and concerns over the U.S. position among other countries, one change that would allow this reduction is to raise the tax at the individual level and use the revenues to lower the corporate tax rate. Since individual taxes tend to be collected regardless of where income is earned, these taxes are neutral with respect to international allocation. This approach also allows more scope for lowering corporate tax rates without creating sheltering opportunities for high income individuals. If the 2003 tax changes that lowered rates on dividends and capital gains to 15% were rolled back, the federal corporate tax rate could be reduced to 31%.[73] Taxing capital gains at full rates, as was enacted in 1986 and remained largely in place until 1997 would allow two or three more percentage points in reduction. One could go even further, by taxing corporate capital gains on an accrual basis, which would yield dramatically more revenue. This type of change would also eliminate distortions arising from payout policies and realizations response. Even lower corporate rates could be achieved by taxing non-profits enough to offset their savings from the lower corporate rates—a change that would leave them unaffected, but would simply shift the source of tax collection. These latter proposals would arguably be broad enough to move much of the way towards an integration of the corporate and individual income taxes.

CONCLUSION

Is there an urgent need to lower the corporate tax rate, as some recent discussions and analyses have suggested? On the whole, many of the new concerns expressed about the tax appear not to stand up under empirical examination. The claims that behavioral responses could cause revenues to rise if rates were cut does not hold up on both a theoretical basis and an empirical basis.

Studies that purport to show a revenue maximizing tax rate of 30% contain econometric errors that produce biased and inconsistent results; when those problems are corrected the results disappear. Cross-country studies to provide direct evidence showing that the burden of the corporate tax actually falls on labor yield unreasonable results and prove to suffer from econometric flaws that also lead to a disappearance of the results when corrected. Similarly, claims that high U.S. tax rates will create problems for the United States in a global economy suffer from a misrepresentation of the U.S. tax rate compared to other countries and are less important when capital is imperfectly mobile, as it appears to be.

While these new arguments appear to rely on questionable data, the traditional concerns about the corporate tax appear valid. While many economists believe that the tax is still needed as a backstop to individual tax collections, it does result in some economic distortions. These economic distortions, however, have declined substantially over time as corporate rates and shares of output have fallen. There are a number of revenue-neutral changes that could reduce these distortions, allow for a lower corporate statutory tax rate, and lead to a more efficient corporate tax system.

APPENDIX A. REVENUE MAXIMIZING TAX RATES IN AN OPEN ECONOMY

For an exploration of corporate tax revenue, consider a very simplified example where there is a U.S. corporate sector and the rest of the world with no tax. The lowest revenue maximizing rate would apply in a case where there is a small country which is a price-taker (that is, worldwide price and rate of return after tax are fixed because there is perfect capital mobility and perfect product substitutability). To determine the revenue maximizing tax rate, begin with the equation for corporate tax revenues:

$$REV = \frac{tRK}{1-t} \tag{A1}$$

where K , the corporate capital stock, and R , the after-tax rate of return, are potentially functions of the tax rate, t . Revenue is maximized when the total differential of equation (A1) with respect to taxes is equal to zero, which is:

$$(1-t)\left(tR\frac{dK}{dt} + tK\frac{dR}{dt}\right) + RK = 0 \tag{A2}$$

Assuming the rest of the world can be treated as a aggregate and has a zero capital income tax rate, Gravelle and Smetters[74] show that, in a case of a small country with perfect substitutability, R does not change and

$$\frac{dK}{K} = -\frac{\mu}{\sigma}\frac{dt}{(1-t)} \tag{A3}$$

where μ is the labor share of income and a is the factor substitution elasticity.

Substituting equation (A3) into equation (A2) we obtain the revenue maximizing rate of μ/σ . To use some common values, if μ is 0.75 and σ is 1, the revenue maximizing rate is 75%.

Since the United States is a large country, the rates would be even higher, because the tax can affect the world wide interest rate. The Gravelle and Smetters paper provide effects for R and K for a given country share, which can also be substituted into equation (A2). As a result, the revenue-maximizing tax rate is $\mu/(\mu\gamma + \mu(1-\gamma))$ where γ is the output share. For example, if the United States has approximately 30% of the total output, the tax rate would be 81%. The rates would rise further if capital were not perfectly mobile or products not perfectly substitutable, since these factors would allow R to fall further. At the extreme, it would return to a closed economy solution. Gravelle and Smetters present evidence to suggest that the outcome is more similar to a closed economy than a small open economy solution.

This same outcome, a 75% rate, would also apply for the most extreme case of growth models, the Ramsey model, where the supply of savings is perfectly elastic.

Note that in both of these extreme cases, the after tax return is fixed and the total burden falls on wage income, so that labor income would fall. One could also calculate a corporate tax rate than maximizes revenue while taking into account the effect on wages and keeping the wage rate constant. Again, relying on the model in Gravelle and Smetters and maximizing,

$$REV = \frac{tRK}{(1-t)} + t_l WL \tag{A4}$$

Where t_l is the tax rate wages, we obtain a revenue maximizing corporate tax rate of $t = (\mu(1-t_l))/(\sigma - t_l\mu)$. With an approximate 20% tax rate on labor income, the revenue maximizing corporate tax rate is 70%. Note however, that this is not the rate that would be found in the cross-section analysis.

APPENDIX B. DATA AND ESTIMATION METHODS

We obtained the data used in the Hassett and Mathur study and the Clausing study.[75] The data used to replicate the Brill and Hassett study were obtained from the original sources cited in the study.[76] We were able to replicate the results reported for all studies.

The data we use are for several countries for a period of several years, and are known as panel data. The model of the relationship between the corporate tax rate (the independent variable) and the various dependent variables takes a linear form:

$$t = (\mu(1-t_l))/(\sigma - t_l\mu) \tag{B1}$$

where Y_{it} is the dependent variable, X_{it} is the independent variable (the corporate tax rate in our case), α and β are the regression parameters to be estimated, and ε_{it} is a random error term.[77] The subscripts, i and t, indicate that information for a particular observation comes from country I for year t (for example, information for Australia for 1992). The random error term, ε_{it} , is a random variable and captures omitted and unobservable factors or variables that affect the dependent variable. The error term will be discussed in further detail below.

If the following conditions are met:

- the expected value (mean) of the random error term, ε_{it} , is zero;
- the variance of the random error term is constant for all observations;
- the random error term for one observation is uncorrelated with the error term for another observation; and
- the random error terms are uncorrelated with the explanatory variables...

then the ordinary least squares (OLS) estimators will yield the best linear unbiased estimators of the parameters (α and β). The β parameter shows the true relationship between the dependent variable and the independent variable, and is the parameter of interest to us. Denote the estimate of β as $\hat{\beta}$. Since is an estimate, it is a random variable drawn from a probability or sampling distribution with an expected value (mean) and variance. This estimator will have the following desirable properties:

- unbiased: the expected value of $\hat{\beta}$ is β;
- efficient: the variance of $\hat{\beta}$ is smaller than the variance of all other unbiased estimators; and
- consistent: the probability distribution of $\hat{\beta}$ collapses on β as the number of observations gets arbitrarily large.

Estimation problems often arise with panel data because one or more of the conditions listed above are not met. The result is the OLS estimator will be biased and inconsistent. Problems arise with panel data, as is demonstrated when equation (B1) is rewritten as:

$$Y_{it} = \alpha + \beta X_{it} + v_i + \phi_t + \eta_{it}. \qquad \text{(B2)}$$

The term v_i is an effect (unobserved heterogeneity) specific to a particular country capturing differences among countries in (1) the measurement of economic data, (2) economic institutions, (3) laws and regulations applying to business, and (4) attitudes toward business, among other things. The term ϕ_t is a time specific effect capturing such things as the international business cycle. Since the corporate tax rate is a reflection of the attitudes toward business in a country, X_{it} and v_i will be correlated. Ignoring the country-specific unobserved heterogeneity means that the OLS estimate of β is biased and inconsistent because the error term in equation (B 1) is correlated with the explanatory variable—one of the conditions listed above is violated. Another problem often encountered with data that has a time dimension is the error terms are correlated from one year to the next year (called autocorrelation). Statistical tests indicate that these problems exist with the data we obtained. Consequently, we estimate the parameters of the model using the fixed effect estimation procedure allowing for an AR(1) error structure.[78]

Table B-1. Standard Deviation of Corporate Tax Rate Variables in the Three Data Sets

	Brill and Hassett Data	Clausing Data	Hassett and Mathur Data
Variable	Corporate tax rate	Corporate tax rate	Logarithm of corporate tax rate
Mean	0.362	0.354	-1.106
Overall Standard Deviation	0.092	0.101	0.396
Between Component	0.065	0.078	0.307
Within Component	0.064	0.063	0.248

Source: Authors' analysis of data.

Identification

Neither Brill and Hassett nor Clausing offer any justification in their studies for using OLS rather than the fixed effects method to estimate the parameters of their model. A well-known drawback of the fixed effects method is variables that vary across countries, but not across time within a country, cannot be included in the estimation (that is, the parameters associated with these variables are not identified). Devereux (2006) claims "changes in the statutory [corporate tax] rate within a country are comparatively rare. In practice, as found by Clausing (2006), there is not enough variation within country to identify an effect of the statutory rate, conditional on country fixed effects."[79]

To check the correctness of this statement and the justification for using OLS, we directly examine the variation of the corporate tax rate across countries and over time. Table B-1 displays the results for the data from the three studies we reanalyzed. The first row displays the relevant explanatory corporate tax rate variable used in the study. The second row reports of mean of the variable. The third row reports the standard deviation (a measure of variation of a variable) of the corporate tax rate variable. The last two rows decompose the standard deviation into the between country component and the within country component. If there is no variation in the variable over time within countries, then the within component of the standard deviation will be zero. Consequently, the effect of that variable on the dependent variable is not identified conditional on fixed effects (that is, it cannot be estimated using the fixed effects procedure). As can be seen from the table, there is almost as much variation within countries (the within component) as there is between countries (the between component).

In addition, we find that all OECD countries changed their corporate tax rate at least once between 1979 and 2002. Four countries (Ireland, Norway, Spain, and Switzerland) changed their corporate tax rate only once during this period. In contrast, Luxembourg changed their corporate rate 12 times over this period. On average, OECD countries changed their corporate tax rates once every five years. Therefore, we can find no evidence to support the argument that the effect of the corporate tax rate on corporate tax revenues is not identified conditional on fixed effects.

Appendix C. Modeling Problems of the Desai, Foley, and Hines Study

This appendix explains in further detail the modeling problems associated with the Desai, Foley, and Hines study (hereafter DFH) study, which include the failure to recognize price variability. This means that their cross-equation restriction is not justified (and that restriction is what gives rise to their results). The DFH study also fails to correctly interpret their results given that other sectors exist in the economy.

The DFH model effectively begins with an equation that forms a basic part of any general equilibrium model, namely that a percentage change in price is a weighted average of the percentage in costs for small changes. In the case of an imposition of a tax, that is:

$$\hat{p} = \alpha(\hat{r} + \hat{\tau}) + (1 - \alpha)\hat{w} \tag{1}$$

where p is price, r is rate of return, w is the wage rate, τ is the tax rate and α is the share of capital income. The hat notation refers to a percentage change except in the case of the tax variable, where the hat means the change in tax rate divided by one minus the tax rate. Beginning with a no tax world, that variable is simply $d\tau$. This relationship can be derived from a profit maximization problem. DFH derive such an equation to motivate their seemingly unrelated regression model. They then assume that p, the price of the good, does not change, which produces an equation of the form:

$$0 = \alpha(\hat{r} + \hat{\tau}) + (1 - \alpha)\hat{w} \tag{2}$$

Since τ is an exogenous variable this equation indicates that the change in the tax would be shared by interest rates and wages, and this is the basis for the two seemingly unrelated regressions where the dependent variables are r and w, and the coefficients are constrained so that the burden will add up to one.

The argument for keeping the price fixed is that such a good would have its price fixed due to trade (e.g., all commodities have to sell at the same price). There are two difficulties with this assumption. First, if consumers in different countries have different preferences for goods based, in part, on country of origin (i.e., they do not consider French wine and German wine to be perfect substitutes) these prices will not be fixed. Indeed, this phenomenon is widely recognized, and the price responses are referred to as Armington elasticities—and they have been estimated empirically. Second, their observations are the weighted average of firms in each country but the firms themselves produce heterogeneous products, and all of these product prices cannot stay fixed because they have different capital intensities and because the products will vary from one country to another. Indeed, the trading of heterogeneous products means that fixed prices cannot be assumed because, in such a model, countries could not produce, consume and trade numerous products with differential taxation because such a world economy would be characterized by corner solutions (i.e., no internal equilibrium).

This problem means that there is another variable, price, that is affecting the results and presumably is correlated with the error term (that is, the price would tend to be higher when the tax rate is higher, making the regression suspect and that the coefficient restriction is not appropriate.

Even if these problems did not exist, there is an additional problem with the interpretation of their findings, namely that they did not adjust for other sectors in the economy, including non-traded sectors and sectors not subject to the corporate tax. Incidence results must be adjusted for the fact that the tax is only a partial one.

To illustrate in the simplest fashion, suppose the remaining sector of the economy is a non- corporate non-traded sector of the economy whose price is denoted by a capital P:

$$\hat{P} = \beta(\hat{r}) + (1 - \beta)\hat{w} \tag{3}$$

This commodity has no taxes and if we estimate the effects on r and w, those can be used to determine the change in P.

What we ultimately want to determine is the fraction of the tax, $rK_c\, d\tau$(where K_c is the capital in the corporate traded sector) that falls on labor, that is what share of Ldw, where L is total labor in the economy, is of $rK_c\, d\tau$.

To derive the real change in wages, we want the change in nominal wage divided by the change in total price level in the economy, or, if the corporate sector is responsible for $(1- \theta)$ of output in the economy the percentage change in real wage (which we denote with a capital W) can be expressed as follows:

$$\hat{W} = \hat{w} - (1-\theta)\hat{p} - \theta\hat{P} \tag{4}$$

If s is the share of the burden falling on labor income, from equation (1), and

$$\hat{r} = -(1-s)d\tau \quad \hat{w} = -\frac{-s\alpha d\tau}{(1-\alpha)}$$

And, by substitution of these values into (3) and in turn into (4), and allowing the initial price level to be normalized at 1, we obtain the equation for incidence in the economy, noting that $\alpha/(1-\alpha)$ equals rK_c/wL_c:

$$Ldw = -(L/L_c)(s - \theta s(1-\beta) - \theta(1-s)(1-\alpha)\beta/\alpha)rK_c d\tau \tag{5}$$

The first term, total labor divided by labor in the tax sector reflects the increased burden from the spread of the nominal fall in wages to the other sector, while the negative terms inside the next parenthesis reflects the rise in real wages due to the fall in the price of the untaxed sector. Whether the burden rises or falls depends on a variety of factors. As the capital intensity of the untaxed sector rises the burden falls; at the extreme when β becomes 1, the first term collapses to 1 and the second term is less than s, so the total burden on labor is less in the economy than it is in the estimation. This possibility is more important than it might initially appear, because one of the most important uses of capital not subject to the corporate income tax is in housing in the United States.

End Notes

1 *Simple, Fair, and Pro-Growth: Proposals to Fix America's Tax System*, November 2005, which can be found at http://www.taxreformpanel.gov/.

2 Henry M. Paulson, Jr., "Our Broken Corporate Tax Code," *The Wall Street Journal*, July 19, 2007.

3 United States Department of the Treasury, "Treasury Tax Conference on Business Taxation and Global Competitiveness: Background Paper," July 30, 2007, at http://www.ustreas.gov/press/releases/hp500.htm.

4 R. Glenn Hubbard, "The Corporate Tax Myth," *The Wall Street Journal*, July 26, 2007.

5 Kevin A. Hassett and Aparna Mathur, *Taxes and Wages*, American Enterprise Institute, working paper, March 6, 2006, presented at a conference of the American Enterprise Institute on May 2, 2006.

6 Hubbard's article cites Michael Devereux, and apparently refers to a paper also presented at the American Enterprise Institute Symposium.

7 This summary and other references to the issues discussed at the conference are based on two detailed media accounts of the conference; although the conference was televised, there is no transcript at this time. The articles are Heidi Glenn, "Business Leaders would Give Up Tax Breaks for Lower Rates," *Tax Notes,* July 30, 2007, pp. 324-327, and Joanne M. Weiner, "U.S. Corporate Tax Reform: All Talk, No Action," *Tax Notes*, August 27, 2007, pp. 7 16-728.

[8] Hearings were held by the Senate Finance Committee on August 3, 2006, with a follow-up focused on business tax issues on September 20, 2006. The committee also held hearings on May 3, 2007 on tax havens.

[9] Statement released by the Honorable Charles B. Rangel, Chairman, Ways and Means Committee, July 26, 2007.

[10] See Jeffrey H. Birnbaum, "Democrat Overhall of Taxes: Rangel Would Annul AMT, Shift Burden," *Washington Post*, October 26, 2007, p. D1.

[11] N. Gregory Mankiw, "The Problem with the Corporate Tax," *New York Times*, June 2, 2008. For empirical evidence on incidence he cites an empirical study by Wiji Aralampalam, Michael P. Devereux, and Giorgia Maffini, *The Direct Incidence of Corporate Income Tax on Wages*, Oxford University Center for Business Taxation, May, 2008. For empirical evidence on the feedback effects on revenue, he cites Alex Brill and Kevin Hassett, *Revenue Maximizing Corporate Income Taxes*, AEI working paper # 137, American Enterprise Institute, July 31, 2007.

[12] The data discussed in this paragraph are taken from Jane G. Gravelle, "The Corporate Tax: Where Has it Been and Where is it Going?," *National Tax Journal,* vol. 57 (December 2004), pp. 903-923; U.S. Congressional Budget Office, Historical Data, http://cbo.gov/budget/historical.shtml and The Budget and Economic Outlook, Fiscal Years 2008- 2017, http://www.cbo.gov/ftpdoc.cfm?index=7731&type=0.

[13] Excise taxes can be set at more than 100% and still yield revenue. Taxes on real capital income in excess of 100% can also yield revenues because inflation is an implicit tax on the holding of cash.

[14] Kevin A. Hassett, "Art Laffer, Righter Than Ever," *National Review*, February 13, 2006.

[15] "We're Number One, Alas," *The Wall Street Journal*, July 13, 2007, p. A12.

[16] For insight into how this graph was viewed by economists, see Brad DeLong, an economist at Stanford and author of a website, *Brad DeL ong 's Daily Journal*, who titled his entry "Most Dishonest Wall Street Journal Editorial Ever." There was some perception, which was incorrect, that this graph was prepared by Kevin Hassett because he was mentioned as a source, but that was not the case; he provided some of the data (personal communication with Kevin Hassett). Based on data provided by one of the correspondents in that debate, a simple regression of corporate share on tax and tax squared showed no significant coefficients for tax variables, indicating no relationship: http://delong.typepad.com/sdj/2007/07/most-dishonest-.html.

[17] Kimberly A. Clausing, "Corporate Tax Revenues in OECD Countries," *International Tax and Public Finance*, vol. 14 (April 2007), pp. 115-133.

[18] Michael P. Devereux, *Developments in the Taxation of Corporate Profit in the OECD Since 1965: Rates, Bases and Revenues*, May 2006 presented at a conference of the Alliance for Competitive Taxation and the American Enterprise Institute, June 2, 2006.

[19] Alex Brill and Kevin Hassett, *Revenue Maximizing Corporate Income Taxes*, AEI working paper # 137, American Enterprise Institute, July 31, 2007.

[20] Jack M. Mintz, *2007 Tax Competitiveness Report: A Call for comprehensive Tax Reform*, C.D. Howe Institute, No. 254, September 2007.

[21] The 33% tax rate is from the simplest regression; the other regressions, which include other variables, or control for country size and/or openness, lead to higher revenue maximizing rates.

[22] Hence, most of the variation is across countries, which, as discussed below, is a potentially serious problem.

[23] An invariant tax base would occur when both production and utility were of the Cobb Douglas form, that is unitary factor substitution elasticities and unitary product substitution elasticities. At 100% tax rate a corner solution would be presumably be reached where the corporate sector would entirely disappear, but only at that extreme rate would such an effect occur.

[24] Brill and Hassett, *Revenue Maximizing Corporate Income Taxes*, p. 6.

[25] The Treasury Study provides data on the growth over time in unincorporated business forms and suggests that the large share of this income in the United States relative to other countries is due to the ability to avoid the corporate tax and still retain limited liability in the United States. The growth in Subchapter S income (partnerships that can elect to be taxed as corporations) corresponds to increasing limits on the number of permissible shareholders, and the growth in partnership income to the growth in the number of states allowing limited liability companies that do not fall under the corporate tax. Proprietorship income shares have changed very little. In any case, this growth occurred during a period when the corporate tax was constant or falling.

[26] See Alex Brill and Kevin A. Hassett, *Revenue-Maximizing Corporate Income Taxes: The Laffer Curve in OECD Countries*. We obtained our data from the same sources as Brill and Hassett.

[27] The terms "biased" and "inconsistent" are technical statistical terms. See Appendix B for a description and the consequences of these problems, and the statistical definitions for biased and inconsistent.

[28] See Kimberly A. Clausing, "Corporate Tax Revenues in OECD Countries." The authors thank Kimberly Clausing for providing her data.

[29] Clausing included two variables in her analysis indicating the type of corporate tax system that do not vary over time for a country. The coefficients of these variables are not identified when using the fixed effect estimation method, which is probably why she estimated the coefficients using OLS. While she obtained coefficient estimates for these two variables, the estimates are biased and inconsistent.

[30] For reviews see Robert Chirinko, "Investment Tax Credits," in *The Encyclopedia of Taxation and Tax Policy*, ed. by Joseph J. Cordes, Robert D. Ebel and Jane G. Gravelle, Washington, D.C., the Urban Institute. 2005, pp.

226-229 and Kevin A. Hassett and R. Glenn Hubbard, "Tax Policy and Business Investment", *Handbook of Public Economics*, New York, Elsiever, 2002, pp. 1293-1343.

[31] Simeon Djankov, Tim Ganser, Caralee McLiesh, Rita Ramalho, and Andrei Shleifer, "The Effect of Corporate Taxes on Investment and Entreprenuership," National Bureau of Economic Research, Canbridge, MA, Working Paper 13756, January 2008.

[32] Jane G. Gravelle and Kent A. Smetters, "Does the Open Economy Assumption Really Mean That Labor Bears the Burden of a Capital Income Tax?" *Advances in Economic Policy and Analysis*, vol. 6, No. 1, 2006.

[33] See CRS Report RL33285, *Tax Reform and Distributional Issues*, by Jane G. Gravelle.

[34] This is the allocation used by the Congressional Budget Office, the Treasury Department, and the Urban-Brookings Tax Policy Center.

[35] It is not clear which of Harberger's papers is being referred to, but it is presumably the more recent one: Arnold C. Harberger, *Corporate Tax Incidence: What is Known, Unknown, and Unknowable*, University of California, 2006. This paper was presented at a conference at Rice University in 2006, and will be published with other papers.

[36] The paper in question is not an official CBO paper but rather a working paper by William Randolph. William C. Randolph, *International Burdens of the Corporate Tax*, CBO working paper 2006-09, August 2006.

[37] Kevin A. Hassett and Aparna Mathur, *Taxes and Wages*, American Enterprise Institute, working paper, April 2008.

[38] Rachel Alison Felix, *Passing the Burden: Corporate Tax Incidence in Open Economies*, November 2006. This paper was a dissertation essay, University of Michigan.

[39] Mihir A. Desai, C. Fritz Foley, and James R. Hines, Jr., *Labor and Capital shares of the corporate Tax Burden: International Evidence*. Prepared for the International Tax forum and Urban-Brookings Tax Policy Center conference on Who Pays the Corporate Tax in an Open Economy, December 18, 2007.

[40] Wiji Aralampalam, Michael P. Devereux, and Giorgia Maffini, *The Direct Incidence of Corporate Income Tax on Wages*, Oxford University Center for Business Taxation, May, 2008.

[41] Jane G. Gravelle and Kent A. Smetters, "Does the Open Economy Assumption Really Mean That Labor Bears the Burden of a Capital Income Tax?" *Advances in Economic Policy and Analysis*, vol. 6, No. 1, 2006.

[42] Jennifer Gravelle, *Corporate Tax Incidence: Review of General Equilibrium Estimates and Analysis*, Congressional Budget Office Working Paper 2010-03, May 2010, http://www.cbo.gov/ftpdocs/115xx/doc11519/05-2010-Working_Paper-Corp_Tax_Incidence-Review_of_Gen_Eq_Estimates.pdf.

[43] Harry Grubert and John Mutti, International Aspects of Corporate Tax Itegration: The Role of Debt and Equity Flows, National Tax Journal, vol. 47, March, 1994, pp. 111-133.

[44] Jennifer Gravelle, *Corporate Tax Incidence: Review of General Equilibrium Estimates and Analysis, op cit.*

[45] These issues surrounding savings are discussed in greater detail in CRS Report RL325 17, *Distributional Effects of Taxes on Corporate Profits, Investment Income, and Estates*, by Jane G. Gravelle; CRS Report RL33545, *The Advisory Panel's Tax Reform Proposals*, by Jane G. Gravelle; and CRS Report RL33482, *Saving Incentives: What May Work, What May Not*, by Thomas L. Hungerford. The recognition that replacement of capital income taxes by wage taxes in a life cycle model could have little effect on savings or contract them can be found in numerous simulation studies, for example, Alan Auerbach and Laurence Kotlikoff, *Dynamic Fiscal Policy* (Cambridge, MA: Cambridge University Press, 1987).

[46] Two other studies using cross country data have examined the incidence of the tax on labor income. Passing the Burden: Corporate Tax Incidence in Open Economies, by Rachel Alison Felix, November 2006, finds smaller effects than Hassett and Mathur, but ones that are still too large to be predicted by a theoretical model. This study has problems similar to those that are discussed subsequently and, in addition, do not control for country fixed effects.

[47] Hassett and Mathur, *Taxes and Wages*. We are grateful to Kevin Hassett and Aparna Mathur for providing their data. Several of the countries only have data for shorter periods.

[48] Their independent or explanatory variables take their value from the beginning of the five-year period over which wages are averaged. It should also be noted that Hassett and Mathur calculate the five-year average with nominal wages (that is, they are not corrected for inflation).

[49] See Appendix B for a description of the estimation method. Visual inspection of the Hassett and Mathur data uncovered some errors with their 5-year averages of wage rates—some averages were based on 6 years of data and others were based on less than 5 years of data. We corrected the errors so that each 5-year period for each country contains 5 years of data. Some of the averages are based on less than 5 years of data because of missing values in the wage series; most of the missing valued are in the 2001 to 2005 period.

[50] The specific test of statistical significance of the coefficient estimates is the t-test. This is a test of whether or not the estimate is equal to zero (the null hypothesis is the estimate is equal to zero). The significance level indicates the risk of rejecting the null hypothesis when it is, in fact, true. A significance level of 5% indicates that the null hypothesis will be inadvertently rejected only 5% of the time. Significance levels commonly used in empirical social science work are the 1%, 5%, and 10% levels.

[51] Including the lagged values of the corporate tax rate allows the tax rates for the previous five years to individually have an impact on wages. All tax rates are entered into the model in logarithms.

[52] We obtain the same estimation results when the exchange rate is used to convert wage rates to U.S. dollars—the method used by Hassett and Mathur.

[53] Rachael Alison Felix, Paaing the Burden: Corporate Tax Incidence in Open Economies, November 2006. This paper was a dissertation essay at the University of Michigan.

[54] Mehir A. Desai, C. Fritz Foley, and James R. Hines, Jr., "Labor and Capital Shares of the Corporate Tax Burden: International Evidence," Prepared for the International Tax Policy Forum and Urban-Brookings Tax Policy Center conference on Who Pays the Corporate Tax in an Open Economy?, December 18, 2007.

[55] His remarks were made at a seminar at the American Enterprise Institute, March 17, 2008.

[56] The coefficient must be close to twice the standard error to be statistically significant; thus the result from the unrestricted regression showed no relationship between taxes and wages.

[57] Arulampalam, Wiji, Michael P. Devereux, and Georgia Maffinin, The Direct Incidence of Corporate Income Tax on Wages, Oxford University Centre for Business Taxation, May 2008.

[58] Arulampalam, Wiji, Michael P. Devereux, and Georgia Maffinin, The Incidence of Corporate Income Tax on Wages, Oxford University Centre for Business Taxation, April 2007.

[59] One can trace an infinite series of tax changes through a lagged dependent variable. For example, if there is an effect of the tax rate in this year and an effect of the wage rate last year, then the wage rate last year is a function of the tax rate last year and the wage rate two years before, which is in turn a function of tax and wage rates. By continuous substitution the taxes can be traced back infinitely long and converge on a long run effect.

[60] The tests used by the authors to determine their preferred specification are not without problems. See David Roodman, "How to Do xtabond2: An Introduction to "Difference" and "System" GMM in Stata," Center for Global Development, Working Paper 103, December 2006.

[61] For example, no reason is presented for using a dynamic specification or the specific number of lagged variables, and the number of instruments was not reported.

[62] These estimates are reported in CRS Report RL33545, *The Advisory Panel's Tax Reform Proposals*, by Jane G. Gravelle.

[63] See Jane G. Gravelle, *The Economic Effects of Taxing Capital Income* (Cambridge: MIT Press, 1994), pp. 82-83, suggesting a distortion of about 0.17% of total consumption. With consumption (including government spending) about 83% of output, and the corporate tax 2.7%, this amounts to about 5% of corporate revenue. This amount has fallen slightly due to lower rates on capital gains and dividends.

[64] See the review in Gravelle, The Economic Effects of Taxing Capital Income, pp. 77-82.

[65] The distortion is proportional to the square of the wedge between pretax returns, which is $tc(1-tc)-t(1-t)$, where tc is the corporate tax rate and t the unincorporated. The corporate tax fell from about 44% in the mid-1980s to 32% today, while the noncorporate tax fell from 22% to 20% and the rate on owner occupied housing remained about the same (roughly zero). Holding the after-tax return constant, the wedge between corporate and noncorporate capital fell by over a half, and the square of the wedge by 80%. A calculation for owner-occupied housing suggests that the wedge fell by 40% and the deadweight loss by two thirds. For the largest deadweight loss estimates, virtually all of the distortion was due to the corporate non-corporate differential, so that the current deadweight loss would be only 20% as large, while for the others, both assets played an important role.

[66] Estimates of 0.04% to 0.11% of consumption translate into 1% to 4% of corporate revenues, see Gravelle, *The Economic Effects of Taxing Capital Income*, p. 89. With the reduction in tax rates of almost 50%, and the welfare cost proportional to the square of the tax wedge, the welfare cost would be about 30% of its former value or less than 1%. There is also a welfare cost from the realizations response of about 1%, but recent evidence has shown this response to be small, about the same size as the pay-out distortion.

[67] See Jane G. Gravelle, "Income Consumption and Wage Taxation in a Life Cycle Model: Separating Efficiency from Redistribution," *American Economic Review*, vol. 81, no. 4 (September 1991), pp. 985-995.

[68] This reduction of two percentage points was based on the estimates for the production activities deduction relative to corporate revenues presented in the paper.

[69] The issues of efficiency in international taxation are discussed in much more detail in CRS Report RL341 15, *Reform of U.S. International Taxation: Alternatives*, by Jane G. Gravelle.

[70] The purpose of most of the provisions is self explanatory; note, however, the property sales source rule (also known as the title passage rule) is effectively an export subsidy. Percentage depletion benefits independent oil and gas producers and mineral and coal producers and allows a deduction of costs based on a percentage of receipts rather than the actual costs.

[71] See U.S. Congress, Senate Committee on the Budget, *Tax Expenditures*, committee print, 109th Cong., 2nd sess., December 2006, S. Prt. 109-072 (Washington: GPO, 2006). The document is posted at http://frwebgate.access.gpo.gov/cgi-bin/useftp.cgi?IPaddress=162.140.64.88&filename=31188.pdf&directory=/diskb/wais/data/109_cong_senate_committeejrints.

[72] A territorial tax system is one where the tax is imposed only in the country where business activity occurs and not in the country of ownership. While the present international tax system results in distortions, it is not clear how moving to a territorial tax would reduce these distortions, and even less clear how it would improve tax

compliance and profit shifting. For a more detailed discussion, see CRS Report RL341 15, *Reform of U.S. International Taxation: Alternatives*, by Jane G. Gravelle.

[73] Details of these proposals are provided in CRS Report RL341 15, *Reform of U.S. International Taxation: Alternatives*, by Jane G. Gravelle.

[74] Jane G. Gravelle and Kent A. Smetters, "Does the Open Economy Assumption Really Mean That Labor Bears the Burden of a Capital Income Tax?" *Advances in Economic Policy and Analysis*, vol. 6, No. 1, 2006.

[75] We thank the authors for providing their data to us. The studies are Kevin A. Hassett and Aparna Mathur, *Taxes and Wages*, American Enterprise Institute, working paper, 2006; and Kimberly A. Clausing, "Corporate Tax Revenues in OECD Countries," *International Tax and Public Finance*, vol. 14 (2007), pp. 115-133.

[76] Alex Brill and Kevin A. Hassett, *Revenue-Maximizing Corporate Income Taxes: The Laffer Curve in OECD Countries*, AEI working paper #137, American Enterprise Institute, July 31, 2007.

[77] For ease of exposition only one independent variable is written in the equation. Generally, several independent variables are included in the linear model. This simplification does not change the following discussion of our model and estimation techniques.

[78] See Christopher F. Baum, *An Introduction to Modern Econometrics Using Stata* (College Station, TX: Stata Press, 2006) for a description of this technique. Our overall results and conclusions are not changed when using the random effects estimation procedure allowing for an AR(1) error structure.

[79] Michael P. Devereux, *Developments in the Taxation of Corporate Profit in the OECD Since 1965: Rates, Bases and Revenues*, University of Warwick, working paper, May 2006, p. 20.

In: Corporate and International Taxation
Editor: Allison S. Garner and Daniel C. Murphy

ISBN: 978-1-61324-616-0

Chapter 4

FIRMS THAT INCORPORATE ABROAD FOR TAX PURPOSES: CORPORATE "INVERSIONS" AND "EXPATRIATION"

Donald J. Marples

SUMMARY

In the early 2000s, reports indicated that an increasing number of U.S. firms have altered their structure by substituting a foreign parent corporation for a domestic one. Such "inversions" typically involved the creation of a new foreign corporation in a country with low tax rates (a "tax haven") that becomes the parent of the firm's foreign and U.S. component corporations. A chief motive for inversions was apparently savings by firms on their U.S. corporate income tax. One source of savings was tax on a firm's foreign income: the United States taxes corporations chartered in the United States on both U.S. and foreign income but taxes foreign-chartered corporations only on their U.S.-source income. An inversion can thus potentially reduce a firm's U.S. taxes on foreign income. Other tax savings apparently result from "earnings stripping," or the shifting of U.S.-source income from taxable U.S. components of the firm to the tax-exempt foreign parts.

In the long run, inversions may be accompanied by some increased level of U.S. investment abroad; a firm that inverts reduces its tax burden on foreign investment. However, any such shift may be small, and the recent corporate inversions do not appear to be accompanied by substantive shifts of economic activity from the United States. This leaves the impact of inversions on tax revenues as probably the leading near-term economic effect. As a consequence, one policy issue inversions present is that of tax equity: unless offset by spending cuts or larger budget deficits, the lost revenue is made up with higher taxes on other U.S. taxpayers. Several bills introduced in the 108th Congress appear to have had the revenue losses and tax equity as their primary concern, and tax legislation aimed at restricting inversions was included in the American Jobs Creation Act of 2004 (P.L. 108-357), an omnibus tax bill addressing business and international tax issues. In 2006, additional tax restrictions were proposed in the Senate-passed version of the Tax Increase Prevention and

Reconciliation Act (TIPRA; P.L. 109-222) but were not contained in the final act. In March 2007, the Senate passed a tax package that included inversion provisions as part of H.R. 1591, a supplemental appropriations bill. However, the measure was not included in the conference agreement on the bill. There are indications that the 111th Congress may again look to the corporate income tax as an area where revenue-raising measures might be found to offset tax cuts provided elsewhere.

Some have viewed inversions as symptomatic of a burden they believe the U.S. tax system places on the international competitiveness of U.S. firms. A May 2002 U.S. Treasury report saw inversions as just one result of competitive problems posed by U.S. taxes and called for a more general reexamination of the U.S. international tax system. The report's near-term recommendations for more stringent tax rules are confined to changes aimed at protecting the domestic tax base rather than U.S. tax revenue from foreign income. Recent policy discussions of the U.S. international tax system have included calls by some for adoption of a "territorial" tax system, under which U.S. taxes would no longer apply to foreign-source income. Inversions can be viewed in this larger context; they have been described as "do-it-yourself" territoriality and present many of the same policy issues.

INTRODUCTION

News reports and articles in professional tax journals in the early 2000s drew the attention of policymakers and the public to a phenomenon sometimes called corporate "inversions" or "expatriations": instances where firms that consist of multiple corporations reorganize their structure so that the "parent" element of the group is a foreign corporation rather than a corporation chartered in the United States. A May 2002 study by the U.S. Treasury Department concluded that while inversions are not new—the statutory framework making them possible has long been in existence—there has been a "marked increase" in their frequency, size, and visibility.[1] A comprehensive list of firms that have inverted has not been compiled. Some of the more high-profile inversions, however, include Ingersoll-Rand, Tyco, the PXRE Group, Foster Wheeler, Nabors Industries, Coopers Industries, and Stanley Works. (Stanley Works, however, subsequently announced that it would not undertake its planned reorganization.) According to the U.S. Treasury Department, the transactions are increasing in size, scope, and frequency.[2]

Firms engaged in the inversions cite a number of reasons for undertaking them, including creating greater "operational flexibility," improved cash management, and an enhanced ability to access international capital markets.[3] Prominent, if not primary, however, is the role of taxes: each of the firms in the above list expects significant tax savings from its reorganization.

The tax structure that permits tax savings through inversions has long been a part of the U.S. tax system. The question then arises: why now? One plausible explanation is the decline in the stock market that followed the bull market of the 1 990s. As described in more detail below, an inversion is accompanied by a required payment of tax by individual shareholders on capital gains. The capital gains tax may thus serve as a brake on inversions. Lower stock prices, however, may mean that capital gains are smaller and capital gains taxes less onerous. Another suggestion has been that increased globalization of markets has exposed U.S. firms to more competitive pressures, leading them to more avidly pursue tax-saving strategies. And yet another reason is simply momentum: firms may have been reluctant to incorporate abroad for fear of public relations damage. Once several firms undertook reorganizations, the damage potential may have been perceived to have fallen, and other firms followed.[4]

The corporate inversions apparently involve little, if any, shifts in actual economic activity from the United States abroad, at least in the near term. (See, however, the section below on "Policy Issues" for a discussion of possible long-run effects.) Bermuda and the Cayman Islands are the location of many of the newly created parent corporations—jurisdictions that have no corporate income tax but that do have highly developed legal, institutional, and communications infrastructures. But the actual headquarters of inverted firms typically remain in the United States, and an inversion does not apparently involve the outflow of capital from the United States abroad or the shifting of corporate jobs to foreign locations.

Instead, the chief near-term economic impact of inversions is on U.S. federal tax revenues, which are reduced by the reorganizations, and concern has been expressed about the potential erosion of the U.S. corporate tax base.[5] This has also led some to draw conclusions about their impact on tax equity: unless federal spending is cut or the deficit is increased, the reduction in tax revenue must be made up by tax increases on other taxpayers.[6] Some policymakers have sought a remedy within the existing U.S. system for taxing international transactions. As discussed below in the section on "Alternative Policy Responses and Proposals," the 107th and 108th Congresses have considered a variety of proposals aimed at stemming the growth of inversions. The proposals range from re-imposing U.S. taxes in a manner that would undo the effect of the inversion to more incremental approaches, such as denying the applicability of foreign tax credits and net operating losses to one-time U.S. "toll" taxes that may be triggered by an inversion. The latter, more incremental approach was taken by the enacted version of the American Jobs Creation Act of 2004 (P.L. 108-357).

Others view inversions as symptomatic of more general problems with the U.S. tax system that have become evident as the world economy has become more integrated. Rather than disallowing inversions, they recommend a more general reevaluation of the tax code "that drives them to do such a thing."[7] The U.S. Treasury Department views inversions as evidence of competitive problems with the U.S. tax system. The Administration initiated a study of inversions in February, 2002 and issued a preliminary report in May 2002. The report stated that a near-term response to inversions should ensure that inversions "cannot be used to reduce inappropriately the U.S. tax on income from U.S. operations," and thus makes several proposals designed to protect U.S. tax revenues generated by U.S. income.[8] In keeping with its concern for competitiveness, however, the report does not propose more stringent rules for foreign-source income and calls for a reexamination of the U.S. international tax system.

Inversions have thus been discussed in terms of tax equity and competitiveness. A more detailed look at their implications for the U.S. tax system in general is presented below in the section entitled "Policy Issues." First, however, it is useful to look at the mechanics of inversions and how they generate tax savings.

How Inversions Generate Tax Savings

Anatomy of an Inversion

Although each corporate inversion has unique features, a common reorganization is apparently a "triangular" stock transaction merger, where a new foreign corporation is created that is chartered in a foreign country with low tax rates. The new foreign entity creates a U.S.-chartered "merger subsidiary," owned by the new foreign corporation. The U.S. parent corporation is then merged into the domestic merger subsidiary and becomes a subsidiary of the new foreign parent. For stockholders of the U.S. corporation—for example, individuals, institutional investors, and other firms—shares of the old U.S. parent automatically becomes shares of the new foreign parent.[9] Other forms of inversions are "asset transfers," where the domestic parent transfers its assets to a newly created foreign corporation, and "drop-down" transactions, where the domestic parent transfers its assets to a foreign corporation, but the foreign corporation transfers some of those assets to a domestic subsidiary.[10]

The Basic Structure of U.S. International Taxation

To see how inversions such as these generate tax savings, it is useful first to look at the general structure of the U.S. international tax system. In the international context, the United States bases its tax jurisdiction on residence: it taxes corporations chartered in the 50 states or the District of Columbia on their worldwide income, foreign as well as domestic. At the same time, the United States generally exempts corporations chartered in foreign countries from U.S. tax on their foreign-source income.[11]

Under the residence system, a firm's U.S. tax on foreign income depends on how the firm's foreign operations are organized, and a result of the system is a feature known as the "deferral principle," or simply "deferral." Under deferral, income that a U.S.-chartered corporation earns directly through a branch that is not separately incorporated is generally taxed by the United States on a current basis since the income is earned by a U.S. "resident." In contrast, foreign income earned through a separate foreign subsidiary corporation is generally not subject to U.S. tax until it is remitted to the U.S. parent corporation as dividends or other income: it is tax- deferred. Because of discounting,[12] this deferral confers a tax benefit on income earned in foreign countries with relatively low tax rates.

The system has several additional complicating features. One is the U.S. foreign tax credit, which is designed to alleviate double-taxation where foreign countries tax U.S. firms' foreign income. Under its provisions, the United States permits its taxpayers to credit foreign taxes they or their foreign subsidiaries pay against U.S. taxes they would otherwise owe. The foreign tax credit is generally limited to offsetting U.S. tax on foreign and not domestic income, but if a firm pays sufficient foreign taxes, it may use the credit to eliminate its entire U.S. tax liability on foreign- source income, whether U.S. pre-credit taxes are deferred or apply on a current basis.

Another important feature is a set of "anti-deferral" regimes that limit the availability of deferral in some cases. The broadest and most important of these is the tax code's Subpart F provisions that were enacted in 1962 as a means to limit the concentration of passive-investment income by firms in tax havens. Under Subpart F, U.S. parent firms can in some cases be taxed on particular types of subsidiary income, even if it is not repatriated to the U.S. parent firm. Subpart F, however, only applies where a foreign subsidiary is controlled (more than 50%-owned) by those U.S. stockholders who own large blocs (at least 10%) of the subsidiary's stock. The type of income subject to Subpart F is generally income from passive investment and certain types of income whose source is thought to be easily manipulated.

A second anti-deferral regime is the passive foreign investment company, or PFIC rules. In contrast to Subpart F, the PFIC provisions apply to foreign corporations that invest intensively in passive-type assets, regardless of the degree or concentration of U.S. ownership and even to income that is not itself from passive investment. Although the PFIC rules permit a deferral of U.S. tax in some cases, the rules apply an interest charge to the delayed tax payment, thus negating the benefit of deferral.

Before explaining how an inversion within this U.S. tax structure generates tax savings, we first note that foreign taxes are not irrelevant. Foreign countries frequently tax corporations chartered within their borders—as does the United States. Thus, whatever U.S. tax savings an inversion generates could be offset if the country where the new parent corporation is chartered were not to have corporate tax rates lower than those of the United States. Indeed, Bermuda and the Cayman Islands have been a frequent destination for recent inversions, and neither imposes a corporate income tax.[13]

U.S. Tax Consequences of Inversions

Given the U.S. tax structure, inversions potentially provide tax savings in two general ways: by reducing U.S. tax on foreign source income; and by reducing U.S. tax on U.S. income that is shifted outside the United States in "earnings stripping" or similar transactions. Where they occur, these tax savings are ongoing but only save taxes at the corporate level under the corporate income tax. Inversions can potentially trigger a one-time tax on gain that is required to be recognized when an inversion occurs; the capital gains tax can apply to individual stockholders or at the corporate level. Further, inversions may be unable to generate tax savings to firms whose foreign tax credits have eliminated U.S. tax on foreign income.

To see how these results occur, we look at the straightforward example of a firm that is initially "uninverted"; the firm includes a U.S.-chartered parent corporation that is publicly owned and traded on U.S. stock exchanges. The parent corporation earns foreign income through foreign subsidiaries. Under current law, as long as a firm has a dearth of foreign tax credits, at least some U.S. tax burden applies to the firm's foreign income. Some of the income may be taxed on a current basis either through Subpart F or the PFIC provisions. And while other foreign income may be tax-deferred, it is nonetheless ultimately taxed when it is repatriated. At the stockholder level, shareholders who are private individuals generally pay individual income tax on dividends from the U.S. parent corporation and on capital gains when the stock is sold. However, some shareholders may hold their stock in tax free vehicles—for example, individual retirement accounts (IRAs)—while other shareholders—for example pension funds—may be tax exempt.

Now, suppose the firm inverts, so that the both the former U.S. parent corporation and the foreign subsidiaries become subsidiary to a new foreign parent corporation. First, since the conglomerate's foreign income is now earned by a foreign-chartered corporation, U.S. corporate- level tax on the foreign income that was either deferred or currently paid under the anti-deferral regimes is eliminated. Thus, one source of tax saving is U.S. tax on foreign income.

Inverted firms may also employ earnings stripping to reduce U.S. tax on domestic income. Earnings stripping shifts U.S.-source income from a U.S. corporation to a foreign parent by means of transactions between the related parts of the firm. While the transactions can take a variety of forms, a prototypical earnings stripping transaction involves a foreign parent lending funds to a domestic subsidiary; the subsidiary is able to deduct interest payments to its parent from its U.S. taxable income, thereby reducing its U.S. tax liability. According to the Treasury report on inversions, "a feature common to many inversions is the presence of substantial indebtedness from the former U.S. group to the new foreign parent or one of its foreign subsidiaries."[14] Foreign corporations are generally subject to a U.S. "withholding tax" on U.S.- source interest received from related U.S. corporations; the withholding tax rate is generally 30%. However, the withholding tax is in many cases reduced or eliminated by tax-treaty provisions. Thus, if an earnings-stripping transaction is structured so that interest payments are made to a related lender in a treaty country, the tax can be avoided.

Provisions designed to limit earnings stripping by foreign firms investing in the United States were enacted with the Omnibus Budget Reconciliation Act of 1989 (P.L. 10 1-239). The provisions deny deductions for interest payments to related corporations, but apply only after a certain threshold of interest payments and level of debt-finance is exceeded. [15]

As noted above, although inversions can generate ongoing tax savings at the corporate level under the corporate income tax, they may generate taxes at the shareholder level, under the individual income tax. One source of new taxes may be capital gains: Section 367 of the tax code and Treasury regulations issued under that section impose capital gains tax on transfers of stock by U.S. stockholders to foreign corporations. Thus, for a shareholder of an inverted firm's domestic parent, any appreciation that occurred from the time of purchase to the time of the inversion is generally subject to capital gains tax.[16] The purpose of the provision is to prevent capital gains from flowing out of U.S. tax jurisdiction without being subject to U.S. tax at some point.[17]

The triggering of capital gains tax suggests a divergence of interests among an inverting firm's stockholders, with those of taxable shareholders differing from those whose stock is not taxed (e.g., pension funds and those with holdings in IRAs). Indeed, lawsuits were filed by some Ingersoll-Rand shareholders that sought to block the firm's inversion, although stockholders subsequently voted overwhelmingly to approve the reorganization and the lawsuits were settled.[18] For its part, Stanley Works has pointed out that only 40% of its shares are in taxable accounts. [19]

The anti-deferral regimes may also be a factor at the shareholder level. Inversions commonly result in stockholders at large owning the new foreign parent corporation. Subpart F, with its thresholds requiring control and concentration of ownership, are not likely to be a factor. The PFIC rules, however, may be more likely to apply. If a foreign parent passes the PFIC passive- investment and income thresholds, individual stockholders may be subject to the PFIC regime where they previously were not.[20]

ECONOMIC EFFECTS OF INVERSIONS

Tax Equity

As noted above, the chief near-term economic effect of inversions is to reduce U.S. tax revenue.[21] If the U.S. government has a fixed revenue requirement, inversions' revenue loss has implications for fairness: the lost revenue is made up by higher taxes elsewhere, either on other corporations and businesses, or on individual taxpayers. Equity is one of the chief grounds on which inversions' critics have assailed them.

Economic theory, however, points out that equity is a difficult concept to apply in the case of the corporate income tax. To begin, corporations are not people but agglomerations of stockholders, employees, creditors, and managers, each of whom has his own particular income and wealth characteristics. It is therefore not very informative to compare the tax burden of a corporation with that of an individual, no matter how eye-catching the comparison may be. To make equity comparisons even more difficult, the ultimate repository of the tax's burden is difficult to determine with any certainty. In the short run, the burden of corporate income tax (or the benefit of its reduction, as with inversions) likely falls on the corporate stockholders. In the long run, however, economic analysis suggests that market adjustments and behavioral reactions to the tax result in its burden being spread beyond corporate stockholders to all owners of capital. Thus, inversions may reduce the tax burden on capital in general relative to the burden on labor income. And to the extent capital income is associated with individuals with higher incomes, inversions may reduce the progressivity of the tax system.

Investment and "Competitiveness"

In the short run, inversions probably have little impact on real economic activity. Firms undertaking inversions have indicated that they are only changes in legal structure and substantive headquarters functions will continue to be conducted in the United States. At the same time, however, inversions do reduce the corporate tax burden on foreign-source income relative to that on domestic income. An inverted firm may face a lower overall tax rate on investment in low-tax countries than it does on investment in the United States. As a consequence, a more long- run result may be for inverted firms to shift some amount of investment and business operations from the United States to locations where foreign income taxes are low.

What are the implications of this possible impact on investment flows? In assessing the impact of taxes on investment, economic analysis focuses on economic efficiency and, ultimately, on economic welfare. According to traditional economic theory, taxes best promote economic efficiency when they are least distorting of investment decisions; when taxes do not distort investment decisions, investment is generally employed in its most productive location. As a consequence, economic welfare is maximized. Economic theory also holds that taxes are least distorting of the location of investment when the tax burden on investment is the same in every location. In the international context, taxes do not distort investment location when the tax burden on foreign source income is the same as that on domestic income. (In tax parlance, a tax policy that promotes equal taxation of foreign and domestic investment is a policy of "capital export neutrality.") Since inversions reduce the tax burden on foreign income compared to domestic income, their availability likely nudges the U.S. tax system away from capital export neutrality with a corresponding loss in economic efficiency and economic welfare.

But any loss in economic efficiency that may result from inversions is not likely to be large, because features of the U.S. tax system that exist quite apart from inversions already reduce the tax burden on foreign investment. The ability of firms to defer U.S. tax on subsidiary earnings in low-tax countries reduces the tax burden on foreign investment as do certain U.S. foreign tax credit rules. While inversions likely do reduce the tax burden on foreign income by granting a permanent tax exemption rather than just a deferral of tax, it is likely their incremental change in the tax burden is not enormous.

While capital export neutrality is thought by economists to maximize world economic welfare, business leaders and others have emphasized the importance of taxes' impact on U.S. competitiveness and the ability of U.S. firms to compete in world markets. This analysis recommends a policy sometimes called "capital import neutrality" under which the United States would not tax income from foreign business operations, and would limit its tax jurisdiction to U.S.-source income. For example, several European countries operate "territorial" tax systems that do not apply home-country taxes to foreign income; it is argued that the United States should likewise adopt a territorial system to place its firms on the same tax footing as firms from territorial countries.

The availability of corporate inversions introduces an element of capital import neutrality into the U.S. system. Supporters of capital import neutrality are likely to view inversions in a more positive light than supporters of capital export neutrality; capital import neutrality recommends an exemption for foreign income and inversions accomplish that for inverted firms. And as noted above, some policymakers have suggested that inversions may signal a need for tax changes that would make the U.S. tax system more "competitive."

Alternative Policy Responses and Proposals

Proposed policy responses to inversions vary widely, depending on what is viewed as their chief threat. For example, those that are chiefly concerned about the revenue and tax equity results of inversions make little distinction between inversions' loss of tax revenue from U.S. source- income, on the one hand, and foreign-source income, on the other. Their proposals seek to reimpose U.S. taxes on firms when inversions occur. In contrast, others view inversions as symptomatic of a competitive burden imposed by the U.S. tax system, and have suggested more general reforms of the U.S. method of taxing foreign-source income may be in order. The 2002 Treasury Department report, for example, recommended more stringent treatment of U.S.-, but not foreign-source income—for example, more effective measures of limiting earningsstripping—and called for a general reexamination of the U.S. system of taxing foreign income.

Congressional Proposals

The House and Senate ETI Bills

A number of bills were introduced in the 108th Congress that addressed inversions. Prominent among these were two broad business tax bills passed in 2004 by the Senate and House—S. 1637 and H.R. 4520, respectively—that had as a primary focus the controversy over the U.S. extraterritorial income exclusion (ETI) tax benefit for exporting. Both bills proposed to repeal the ETI benefit and proposed a variety of tax cuts both for domestic and overseas investment. The bills contained many overlapping provisions but also contained differences, including some in the area of inversions. The differences between the bills were resolved in October by a conference committee, and the conference committee version of H.R. 4520 was enacted as the American Jobs Creation Act of 2004 (P.L. 108-357).

S. 1637 (Senator Grassley) was approved by the Senate Finance Committee on October 1, 2003, and included several inversion-related provisions among a variety of revenue-raising proposals designed to offset the cost of the bill's investment tax benefits.[22] S. 1637 proposed to impose two new tax regimes on inversions, depending on ownership thresholds and on when the inversions occurred. Under the first regime, S. 1637 would have taxed a foreign parent corporation like a domestic corporation if it passed a continuity-of-ownership threshold, thus nullifying much of the tax benefit an inversion can generate. The test would be met if at least 80% of the foreign corporation is owned by the former shareholders of a domestic corporation or partnership that had transferred substantially all of its property to the foreign parent. The threshold also required the foreign parent and its affiliates not have "substantial business activities" in the country of incorporation, and applied only to inversions that occur after March 20, 2002.

S. 1637' s second regime was based on a 50% ownership test and would potentially have applied whether the inversion occured before or after March 20, 2002. (The second set of rules would not apply, however, to post-March 20 inversions subject to the bill's first regime.) The second regime would act as a type of toll tax on the shifting of the firm's foreign subsidiaries from the former U.S. parent to the new foreign parent. The tax would apply the highest corporate tax rate (or the highest individual tax rate, in the case of partnerships) to stock received by the former domestic parent from the new foreign parent in exchange for ownership of the firm's foreign subsidiary corporations. Neither foreign tax credits nor net operating losses would be permitted to offset the tax.

An additional provision of S. 1637 proposed to impose an excise tax on stock options related to inversions, thus addressing an area in which the interests of corporate officers with respect to inversions might diverge from those of stockholders. (See the discussion of capital gains taxes at the shareholder level, above on page 5.) Under the provision, officers, directors, and 10% owners of inverted firms would be subject to a 20% excise tax on compensation that is directly linked to the value of an inverting corporation's stock. Such compensation would include stock, certain stock options (generally nonqualified stock options), and other stock-based compensation. For stock options, the tax would apply to the value of the option at the time of the inversion, determined by an option-pricing model specified by the Treasury Department. The excise tax would apply, however, only when the inversion in question triggers recognition of shareholder- level capital gains. The bill also contained provisions that would extend current law's earnings- stripping restrictions on the deductibility of interest paid to related corporations (see page 4, above) to partnerships and S corporations. The restrictions currently apply only to corporations.

According to estimates by the Joint Committee on Taxation, S. 1637's inversion provisions would have increased tax revenue by $2.6 billion over 10 years.

The House passed H.R. 4520 (Representative Thomas) on June 17, 2004. Like S. 1637, H.R. 4520 included more stringent treatment of inversions in conjunction with a broad set of unrelated provisions that would repeal ETI while enacting other investment tax benefits. The House bill's inversion provisions, however, were generally narrower than those of the Senate bill. (Note however, that a temporary inversion provision comparable in scope to that of S. 1637 was included in H.R. 6, the House-passed energy bill, as described below.) Under current law, the transfer of foreign subsidiaries or other assets from a U.S. parent corporation to a new foreign parent corporation may give rise to corporate-level tax (sometimes referred to as "toll charges") under several different tax code provisions. However, "tax attributes" such as foreign tax credits or net operating losses (if available) may offset the tax. H.R. 4520 proposed to deny the applicability of tax attributes in the case of inversions.

Like the Senate bill, the House bill contained a provision that applied an excise tax on stock options related to inverted corporations. The applicable rate of the tax, however, would be 15% rather the 20% rate imposed by S. 1637.

Unlike S. 1637, the House-passed bill did not contain restrictions on interest deductions aimed at limiting earnings stripping. In this respect, it is distinct from the 2003 Ways and Means Committee bill (H.R. 2896), which did contain earnings stripping provisions.

According to Joint Committee on Taxation estimates, the House bill's inversion and earnings stripping provisions would together increase tax revenue by an estimated $488 million over fiscal years (FY) 2004-2014.

The American Jobs Creation Act (AJCA; P.L. 108-357)

Like the Senate bill, the conference agreement on H.R. 4520 adopted two alternative tax regimes applicable to inversions; which one applies depends on continuity-of-ownership thresholds. The new rules applied to inversions occurring after March 4, 2003. The new law provides that when a new foreign parent is at least 80% owned by the former parent's stockholders, the new law treats the foreign parent as a domestic corporation, thus generally denying to the firm the tax benefits of the inversion. The second regime applies when there is at least 60% continuity of ownership but less than 80%. In the latter case, the new foreign parent is not taxed like a domestic corporation, but (in a manner similar to the House bill) any toll taxes that apply to transfers of assets to the new entity are not permitted to be offset by foreign tax credits or net operating losses.

The conference agreement provides an excise tax on stock options, as did both the House and Senate bills. The rate of the tax, however, will be the maximum capital gains tax rate for an individual: 15% through 2008 and 20% thereafter.

According to JCT estimates, the conference agreement's inversion provisions will increase tax revenue by $937 million over 10 years.

Contracting Restrictions

Several bills not directly pertaining to taxes have contained anti-inversion provisions. In the 107th Congress, Section 835 of the Homeland Security Act (P.L. 107-296) contained restrictions on the agency's contracting with inverted corporations. The measure that was approved contained broader waiver conditions than those in the earlier House or Senate bills and provided that the prohibition can be waived in the interests of homeland security, to prevent the loss of jobs, or to prevent the government from incurring higher costs.

In the 108th Congress, the Senate returned to the procurement restrictions issue. On January 23, 2003, the Senate approved an omnibus appropriations bill (H.J.Res. 2) that would tighten the enacted waiver conditions by making a waiver of the contracting restrictions possible only if the Secretary of Homeland Security certifies that it is essential to national security. The provision was included in section 101 of division L of the conference committee version of the bill that became P.L. 108-7.

2006 Budget Reconciliation Legislation (H.R. 4297)

Additional tax legislation aimed at restricting inversions was included as one of several revenue- raising "offsets" in the version of budget reconciliation legislation passed by the Senate in November, 2005. The proposal would have applied restrictions to inversions occurring after March 20, 2002, rather than those occurring after March 20, 2003, as under the AJCA. In addition, the plan would have reduced the 60% threshold that applies to AJCA's second inversion regime to a 50% continuity-of-ownership threshold, thus expanding the scope of AJCA's restrictions. The proposal would also have tightened the tax code's earnings-stripping restrictions (see above) in the case of inverting firms. The Senate proposal was not contained in the final version of reconciliation legislation enacted in May 2006 (Tax Increase Prevention and Reconciliation Act; P.L. 109-222).

2007 Senate Small Business Tax Bill

On January 17, 2007, the Senate Finance Committee approved S. 349, containing a package of tax benefits for small business along with a set of revenue-raising measures designed to offset part of the tax benefits' revenue loss. The bill included expanded restrictions on inversions, a scaled-back version of the 2005 proposals described above, as one of the revenue-raisers. The provisions were subsequently included in H.R. 2, the minimum wage bill passed by the full Senate in February, and in H.R. 1591, the supplemental appropriations bill approved by the Senate in March. The inversion measure was not, however, included in the conference agreement reached on H.R. 1591, nor was it in the small business tax package that Congress ultimately passed as H.R. 2206 (P.L. 110-28).

The Senate inversion provision generally applied a part of AJCA's anti-inversion regime, which are the provisions applicable to firms meeting the 80%-or-greater test, to inversions occurring up to (approximately) a year earlier than the effective date specified by AJCA. As described above, AJCA's provisions apply to inversions occurring after March 4, 2003. With some modifications, the Senate measure also applied the AJCA provisions to inversions occurring after March 20, 2002. The modifications were apparently designed to limit the retroactivity of the expanded date. Under their terms, the tax regime that AJCA applied to 80% inversions—treatment of the new offshore parent as a domestic corporation—do not apply until the first year after tax years beginning in 2006.

Other Approaches

An approach to inversions that is similar to those contained in the legislative proposals would modify the "anti-deferral" regimes contained in subpart F or the PFIC provisions. These proposals have not, however, been introduced as legislation. As with the legislative proposals, these suggestions would identify reorganizations that qualify as inversions and apply their tax rules in such situations. The subpart F or PFIC rules would be modified so that the stockholders of foreign-chartered inverted parent corporations would be subject to U.S. tax on at least some of its foreign income.[23]

In contrast to the proposals that would apply only when inversions occur, another suggested approach would modify the tax code's concept of residence. Such an approach would be more fundamental, and might be viewed as treating the cause rather than the symptoms. One analyst has pointed out that the residence test applied by the British tax system looks beyond the place of incorporation and generally establishes a firm's residence as the country from which the firm is centrally managed and controlled. Such a system would appear to avoid some potential administrative problems inherent in attempting to identify inversions by means of thresholds, as do the legislative proposals. On the other hand, the British system has apparently encountered difficulties in identifying the substantive location of management and control: control can in some cases be established in tax havens simply by conducting *pro forma* board meetings there.[24]

The May 2002 Treasury Report

The Treasury Department's May 2002 report voiced three principal concerns: that the earnings- stripping opportunities from inversion may erode the part of the U.S. tax base consisting of U.S.- source income; that the current tax system may give foreign-controlled firms a competitive advantage; and that inversions "reduce confidence in the fairness of the tax system."[25]

The Treasury Department report noted that earnings stripping is not confined to inversions, but can occur within foreign-controlled groups in general. The report's concern with the practice was reflected in a number of proposals aimed at restraining the practice. As described above, the tax code already places limitations on interest deductions when certain thresholds are exceeded; the Treasury concluded that "the prevalent use of foreign related-party debt in inversion transactions is evidence that these rules should be revisited." The report listed a number of specific ways the rules could be tightened.[26] The report also suggested that "further work is needed" in income- shifting areas apart from related-party debt, specifically, the tax system's transfer pricing rules in the area of intangible assets.[27]

As with earnings stripping, the Treasury report's concern for competitiveness was broader than just inversions. The report viewed inversions as being one aspect of a more general result of the U.S. tax system. The report's analysis concluded that the U.S. system places U.S.-controlled and headquartered firms in general at a disadvantage relative to foreign-controlled firms, a disadvantage that is believed to occur because the United States taxes the worldwide income of its corporations while some foreign countries use "territorial" systems that exempt foreign income.[28] The report viewed not only inversions, but a growing number of acquisitions of U.S. firms by foreign companies as possible symptoms of the disadvantage.[29]

As a result of its concern for competitiveness, the Treasury report stopped short of proposals that would negate the tax savings on foreign-source as well as domestic-source income, a contrast with bills listed above. Instead, the report stated:

> the policy response to the recent corporate inversion activity should be broad enough to address the underlying differences in the tax treatment of U.S.-based companies and foreign-based-companies, without regard to how foreign-based status is achieved. Measures designed simply to halt inversion activity may address these transactions in the short run, but there is a serious risk that measures targeted too narrowly would have the unintended effect of encouraging a shift to other forms of transactions to the detriment of the U.S. economy in the long run.[30]

As a more general response, the report recommended evaluating the merits of exempting foreign-source business income and re-evaluating the usefulness of the anti-deferral regimes and limitations on the foreign tax credit.[31]

The report was generally confined to describing the current legal framework and presenting policy options; it does not present a rigorous economic analysis of inversions or the broader impact of U.S. taxes in the international context. With its focus, however, on protecting the domestic rather than foreign U.S. tax base and its concern with competitiveness, the report's perspective appeared more closely akin to the capital import neutrality perspective described above.

Conclusion

The apparent recent increase in corporate inversions has aroused concern in its own right. The spectacle of U.S. corporations engaging in "expatriation" in a tax-saving technique not available to most individual taxpayers may, in the words of the Treasury Department, "reduce confidence in the fairness of the tax system." But inversions can be viewed in a broader context. Recent tax policy debate has tended to focus on the international economy, sparked in part by the European Union's successful challenge of the U.S. Foreign Sales Corporation export tax benefit, and in part by the perceived new challenges posed by an increasingly integrated world economy. Some observers and policymakers have suggested that the time is right to consider fundamental reform of the U.S. tax system; one approach might be to adopt a territorial tax system under which the United States would exempt foreign business income from tax.

Inversions present many of the same policy issues as would be presented by adoption of a territorial system. The end result of an inversion, after all, is the exemption from U.S. tax of a firm's foreign income. [32] Accordingly, the debate over the respective merits of capital import neutrality and capital export neutrality occur in much the same manner over inversions as they occur in a debate over territoriality. And the administrative problems inversions present in protecting the U.S. domestic tax base—the problems presented by earnings stripping and income shifting transactions—would be presented by a territorial tax system. Thus, if the question of adopting a territorial tax system moves to the fore of the tax policy debate, the debate over inversions may have provided a preview.

ACKNOWLEDGMENTS

This report was originally written by David L Brumbaugh, Specialist in Public Finance.

End Notes

[1] U.S. Department of the Treasury, Office of Tax Policy, *Corporate Inversion Transactions: Tax Policy Implications* (Washington: May, 2002), p. 1.

[2] BNA *Daily Tax Report*, May 13, 2002, p. G-10.

[3] These reasons are cited by Stanley Works in a February 8, 2002, press release. See also the November 2, 2001 proxy statement by Ingersoll-Rand, which cites "a variety of potential business, financial and strategic benefits." The statement is available on the IR website at http://www.shareholder.com/ir/edgar.cfm?Page=2.

[4] For an analysis of the reasons firms undertake inversions, see Mihir A. Desai and James R. Hines, Jr., "Expectations and Expatriations: Tracing the Causes and Consequences of Corporate Inversions," *National Tax Journal*, vol. 55, September 2002, pp. 409-439.

[5] One commentator maintains that they may result in a "significant" erosion in the corporate income tax base, and terms them "the most significant policy question the Congress and the U.S. Treasury Department face regarding the federal corporate income tax." Samuel C. Thompson, Jr., "Section 367: A 'Wimp' for Inversions and a 'Bully' for Real Cross- Border Acquisitions," *Tax Notes*, vol. 94, March 18, 2002, p. 1506. Another analyst, however, maintains that "corporate inversions are not a threat to the U.S. tax system." Willard B. Taylor, "Corporate Expatriation—Why Not?," *Taxes*, vol. 78, March 2002, pp. 146-152. The U.S. Treasury Department has expressed concern over tax-base erosion, but only in connection with the ability of inverted firms to shift U.S.-source income to the foreign parent corporation. U.S. Department of the Treasury, Office of Tax Policy, *Corporate Inversion Transactions: Tax Policy Implications*, May 2002, p. 2. Available online at http://www.treas.gov/press/releases/docs/ inversion.pdf?IMAGE.X=33\&IMAGE.Y=12.

[6] For example, columnist Robert Trigaux of the St. Petersburg Times compares the tax savings by inverting firms with liabilities of individual taxpayers, and asks: "If more companies head offshore, guess who's going to be stuck with the bills?" Robert Trigaux, "Maybe Evading Taxes Isn't Such a Great Idea," *St. Petersburg Times*, March 10, 2002, p. 1H.

[7] House Ways and Means Committee Chairman William Thomas, as quoted in BNA *Daily Tax Report*, April 16, 2002, p. G-7.

[8] U.S. Department of the Treasury, Office of Tax Policy, *Corporate Inversion Transactions: Tax Policy Implications*, May, 2002, p. 30.

[9] This is the form taken by the recent Ingersoll-Rand inversion. See Lee A. Sheppard, "Ingersoll-Rand's Permanent Holiday," *Tax Notes International*, January 14, 2002, pp. 107-111.

[10] For a more detailed description of these categories and specific examples of each, see Willard B. Taylor, "Corporate Expatriation—Why Not?" *Taxes*, vol. 78, March 2002, pp. 146-152.

[11] U.S. taxes generally do apply, however, to a foreign corporation's income from the conduct of a U.S. trade or business and on certain investment income earned in the United States.

[12] Discounting is the fundamental economic principle that a given increment of funds—say, a dollar—is more valuable the sooner an economic actor has control of it. For a firm, this is because the sooner a dollar is received, the sooner it can be invested and earn a return.

[13] As an illustration, Ingersoll-Rand reported to its shareholders that the firm's payments to Bermuda will be limited to a fixed annual fee whose current amount is $27,825. In addition, Bermuda's Minister of Finance has assured Ingersoll- Rand that even if Bermuda enacts an income tax, it will not apply such a tax to Ingersoll-Rand until 2016. See the proxy statement posted at http://www.shareholder.com/ir/edgar.cfm?Page=2.

[14] U.S. Department of the Treasury, Office of Tax Policy, *Corporate Inversion Transactions: Tax Policy Implications*, p. 22.

[15] For further information on the earnings stripping provisions, see Aaron A. Rubenstein and Todd Tuckner, "Financing U.S. Investments After the Revenue Reconciliation Act of 1993," *Tax Adviser*, vol. 25, February 1994, pp. 111-117.

[16] For a detailed description of Section 367, see Vikram A. Gosain, "Working With the New Section 367 Rules After the Final Regs. And TRA '97," *Journal of Taxation*, vol. 87, November 1997, pp. 310-314.

[17] U.S. Congress, Joint Committee on Taxation, *General Explanation of the Revenue Provisions of the Deficit Reduction Act of 1984*, joint committee print, 98th Cong., 2nd sess. (Washington: GPO, 1984), p. 427.

[18] Pamela Sebastian Ridge, "Economy Hinders Progress of Ingersoll-Rand Revamping," *The Wall Street Journal,* December 26, 2001, p. B3.

[19] John M. Moran, "Stanley Tax Plan Could be Double-Edged Sword," *Hartford Courant*, February 9, 2002, p. E1.

[20] In the Ingersoll-Rand (IR) reorganization, its domestic corporations received "class B" non-voting stock amounting to 45% of the value of all the new Bermuda parent's shares. IR's proxy statement states that IR does not expect its new Bermuda corporation to be classified as a CFC. However, the statement mentions the possibility that the Internal Revenue Service may classify the class B stock as voting stock, which could trigger the application of Subpart F. The statement also states that IR does not expect the Bermuda parent to be classified as a PFIC. The statement is available on the IR website at http://www.shareholder.com/ir/edgar.cfm?Page=14.

[21] The Joint Committee on Taxation has estimated that H.R. 3884, a bill aimed at limiting inversions, would increase federal tax revenues by $4 billion over 10 years. BNA *Daily Tax Report*, June 3, 2002, p. G-1.

[22] The inversion proposals were similar to those contained in the Senate-passed version of the May, 2003 tax-cut bill (JGTRRA, the Jobs and Growth Tax Relief and Reconciliation Act; P.L. 108-27), but which were not included in the conference committee bill.

[23] Samuel C. Thompson, Jr., "Section 367: A 'Wimp' for Inversions and a 'Bully' for Real Cross-Border Acquisitions," *Tax Notes*, vol. 94, March 18, 2002, p. 1506; and Jim Ditkoff, "Closing the Bermuda Loophole: An Easier Approach Than the REPO Bill," BNA *Daily Tax Report*, April 26, 2002, p. J-1.

[24] For a discussion of the British system and how it compares to U.S. legislative proposals, see Lee A. Sheppard, "Preventing Corporate Inversions," pp. 10-11.

[25] U.S. Department of the Treasury, Office of Tax Policy, *Corporate Inversion Transactions: Tax Policy Implications*, May 2002, p. 21.

[26] Ibid., pp. 21-25.

[27] Ibid., p. 26.

[28] Two examples of countries with "territorial" systems are France and the Netherlands.

[29] Ibid., p. 19.

[30] Ibid., p. 2.

[31] Ibid., p. 29.

[32] However, an inversion exempts all foreign income from U.S. tax, including income from passive investment. Some territorial tax proposals would only exempt income from active business operations.

In: Corporate and International Taxation
Editor: Allison S. Garner and Daniel C. Murphy

ISBN: 978-1-61324-616-0

Chapter 5

TAX HAVENS: INTERNATIONAL TAX AVOIDANCE AND EVASION

Jane G. Gravelle

SUMMARY

The federal government loses both individual and corporate income tax revenue from the shifting of profits and income into low-tax countries, often referred to as tax havens. The revenue losses from this tax avoidance and evasion are difficult to estimate, but some have suggested that the annual cost of offshore tax abuses may be around $100 billion per year. International tax avoidance can arise from large multinational corporations who shift profits into low-tax foreign subsidiaries or wealthy individual investors who set up secret bank accounts in tax haven countries.

Recent actions by the Organization for Economic Cooperation and Development (OECD) and the G-20 industrialized nations have targeted tax haven countries, focusing primarily on evasion issues. The recently adopted HIRE Act (P.L. 111-147) included a number of anti-evasion provisions, and P.L. 111-226 included foreign tax credit provisions. Some of these proposals, and some not adopted, are in the American Jobs and Closing Loopholes Act (H.R. 4213); the Stop Tax Haven Abuse Act (S. 506, H.R. 1265); draft proposals by the Senate Finance Committee; two other related bills, S. 386 and S. 569; the Bipartisan Tax Fairness and Simplification Act (S. 3018); and proposals by President Obama.

Multinational firms can artificially shift profits from high-tax to low-tax jurisdictions using a variety of techniques, such as shifting debt to high-tax jurisdictions. Since tax on the income of foreign subsidiaries (except for certain passive income) is deferred until repatriated, this income can avoid current U.S. taxes and perhaps do so indefinitely. The taxation of passive income (called Subpart F income) has been reduced, perhaps significantly, through the use of "hybrid entities" that are treated differently in different jurisdictions. The use of hybrid entities was greatly expanded by a new regulation (termed "check-the-box") introduced in the late 1 990s that had unintended consequences for foreign firms. In addition, earnings from income that is taxed can often be shielded by foreign tax credits on other income. On average very little tax is paid on the foreign source income of U.S. firms. Ample evidence of a significant amount of profit shifting exists, but the revenue cost estimates vary from about $10 billion to $60 billion per year.

Individuals can evade taxes on passive income, such as interest, dividends, and capital gains, by not reporting income earned abroad. In addition, since interest paid to foreign recipients is not taxed, individuals can also evade taxes on U.S. source income by setting up shell corporations and trusts in foreign haven countries to channel funds. There is no general third party reporting of income as is the case for ordinary passive income earned domestically; the IRS relies on qualified intermediaries (QIs) who certify nationality without revealing the beneficial owners. Estimates of the cost of individual evasion have ranged from $40 billion to $70 billion.

Most provisions to address profit shifting by multinational firms would involve changing the tax law: repealing or limiting deferral, limiting the ability of the foreign tax credit to offset income, addressing check-the-box, or even formula apportionment. President Obama's proposals include a proposal to disallow overall deductions and foreign tax credits for deferred income and restrictions on the use of hybrid entities. Provisions to address individual evasion include increased information reporting and provisions to increase enforcement, such as shifting the burden of proof to the taxpayer, increased penalties, and increased resources. Individual tax evasion is the main target of the HIRE Act, the proposed Stop Tax Haven Abuse Act, and the Senate Finance Committee proposals; some revisions are also included in President Obama's plan.

INTRODUCTION

The federal government loses both individual and corporate income tax revenue from the shifting of profits and income into low-tax countries. The revenue losses from this tax avoidance and evasion are difficult to estimate, but some have suggested that the annual cost of offshore tax abuses may be around $100 billion per year.[1] International tax avoidance can arise from wealthy individual investors and from large multinational corporations; it can reflect both legal and illegal actions.

Tax avoidance is sometimes used to refer to a legal reduction in taxes, whereas evasion refers to tax reductions that are illegal. Both types are discussed in this report, although the dividing line is not entirely clear. A multinational firm that constructs a factory in a low-tax jurisdiction rather than in the United States to take advantage of low foreign corporate tax rates is engaged in avoidance, whereas a U.S. citizen who sets up a secret bank account in the Caribbean and does not report the interest income is engaged in evasion. There are, however, many activities, particularly by corporations, that are often referred to as avoidance but could be classified as evasion. One example is transfer pricing, where firms charge low prices for sales to low-tax affiliates but pay high prices for purchases from them. If these prices, which are supposed to be at arms-length, are set at an artificial level, then this activity might be viewed by some as evasion, even if such pricing is not overturned in court because evidence to establish pricing is not available.

Most of the international tax reduction of individuals reflects evasion, and this amount has been estimated to range from about $40 billion to about $70 billion a year.[2] This evasion occurs in part because the United States does not withhold tax on many types of passive income (such as interest) paid to foreign entities; if U.S. individuals can channel their investments through a foreign entity and do not report the holdings of these assets on their tax returns, they evade a tax that they are legally required to pay. In addition, individuals investing in foreign assets may not report income from them.

Corporate tax reductions arising from profit shifting have also been estimated. As discussed below, estimates of the revenue losses from corporate profit shifting vary substantially, ranging from about $10 billion to about $60 billion.

In addition to differentiating between individual and corporate activities, and evasion and avoidance, there are also variations in the features used to characterize tax havens. Some restrictive definitions would limit tax havens to those countries that, in addition to having low or non-existent tax rates on some types of income, also have such other characteristics as the lack of transparency, bank secrecy and the lack of information sharing, and requiring little or no economic activity for an entity to obtain legal status. A definition incorporating compounding factors such as these was used by the Organization for Economic Development and Cooperation (OECD) in their tax shelter initiative. Others, particularly economists, might characterize as a tax haven any low-tax country with a goal of attracting capital, or simply any country that has low or non-existent taxes. This report addresses tax havens in their broader sense as well as in their narrower sense.

Although international tax avoidance can be differentiated by whether it is associated with individuals or corporations, whether it is illegal evasion or legal avoidance, and whether it arises in a tax haven narrowly defined or broadly defined, it can also be characterized by what measures might be taken to reduce this loss. In general, revenue losses from individual taxes are more likely to be associated with evasion and more likely to be associated with narrowly defined tax havens, while corporate tax avoidance occurs in both narrowly and broadly defined tax havens and can arise from either legal avoidance or illegal evasion. Evasion is often a problem of lack of information, and remedies may include resources for enforcement, along with incentives and sanctions designed to increase information sharing, and possibly a move towards greater withholding. Avoidance may be more likely to be remedied with changes in the tax code.

Several legislative proposals have been advanced that address international tax issues. President Obama has proposed several international corporate tax revisions which relate to multinational corporations, including profit shifting, as well as individual tax evasion. Some of the provisions relating to multinationals had earlier been included in a bill introduced in the 110th Congress by Chairman Rangel of the Ways and Means Committee (H.R. 3970). Major revisions to corporate international tax rules are also included in S. 3018, a general tax reform act introduced by Senators Wyden and Gregg, and provisions that address techniques used by corporations to reduce taxes are included in pending legislation, the American Jobs and Closing Loopholes Act (H.R. 4213) passed by the House on May 28, 2010.

The Senate Permanent Subcommittee on Investigations has been engaged in international tax investigations since 2001, holding hearings proposing legislation.[3] In the 111th Congress, the Stop Tax Haven Abuse Act, S. 506, was introduced by the chairman of that committee, Senator Levin, with a companion bill, H.R. 1265, introduced by Representative Doggett. The Senate Finance Committee also has circulated draft proposals addressing individual tax evasion issues. A number of these anti-evasion provisions (including provisions in President Obama's budget outline) have been adopted in the Hiring Incentives to Restore Employment (HIRE) Act, P.L. 111-147. S. 386, introduced by Chairman Leahy of the Senate Judiciary

Committee, would expand the money- laundering provisions to include tax evasion and provide additional funding for the tax division of the Justice Department. S. 569, also introduced by Chairman Levin, would impose requirements on the states for determination of beneficial owners of corporations formed under their laws. This proposal has implications for the potential use of incorporation in certain states as a part of an international tax haven plan.

Table 1. Countries Listed on Various Tax Haven Lists

Caribbean/West Indies	Anguilla, Antigua and Barbuda, Aruba, Bahamas, Barbados,[d,e] British Virgin Islands, Cayman Islands, Dominica, Grenada, Montserrat,[a] Netherlands Antilles, St. Kitts and Nevis, St. Lucia, St. Vincent and Grenadines, Turks and Caicos, U.S. Virgin Islands[a,e]
Central America	Belize, Costa Rica,[b,c] Panama
Coast of East Asia	Hong Kong,[b,e] Macau,[a,b,e] Singapore[b]
Europe/Mediterranean	Andorra,[a] Channel Islands (Guernsey and Jersey),[e] Cyprus,[e] Gibralter, Isle of Man,[e] Ireland,[a,b,e] Liechtenstein, Luxembourg,[a,b,e] Malta,[e] Monaco,[a] San Marino,[a,e] Switzerland[a,b]
Indian Ocean	Maldives,[a,d] Mauritius,[a,c,e] Seychelles[a,e]
Middle East	Bahrain, Jordan,[a,b] Lebanona[,b]
North Atlantic	Bermuda[e]
Pacific, South Pacific	Cook Islands, Marshall Islands,[a] Samoa, Nauru,[c] Niue,[a,c] Tonga,[a,c,d] Vanuatu
West Africa	Liberia

Sources: Organization for Economic Development and Cooperation (OECD), *Towards Global Tax Competition*, 2000; Dhammika Dharmapala and James R. Hines, "Which Countries Become Tax Havens?" Journal of Public Economics, Vol. 93, 0ctober 2009, pp. 1058-1068; Tax Justice Network, "Identifying Tax Havens and Offshore Finance Centers: http://www.taxjustice.net/cms/upload/pdf/Identifying_Tax_Havens_Jul_07.pdf. The OECD's "gray" list is posted at http://www.oecd.org/dataoecd/38/14/42497950.pdf. The countries in Table 1 are the same as the countries, with the exception of Tonga, in a recent GAO Report, *International Taxation: Large U.S. Corporations and Federal Contractors with Subsidiaries in Jurisdictions Listed as Tax Havens or Financial Privacy Jurisdictions*, GAO-09- 157, December 2008.

Notes: The Dharmapala and HInes paper cited above reproduces the Hines and Rice list. That list was more oriented to business issues; four countries—Ireland, Jordan, Luxembourg, and Switzerland—appear only on that list. The Hines and Rice list is older and is itself based on earlier lists; some countries on those earlier lists were eliminated because they had higher tax rates.

St. Kitts may also be referred to as St. Christopher. The Channel Islands are sometimes listed as a group and sometimes Jersey and Guernsey are listed separately. S. 506 and H.R. 1245 specifically mention Jersey, and also refer to Gurensey/Sark/Alderney, the latter two are islands associated with Guernsey.

a. Not included in S. 506, H.R. 1245.

b. Not included in original OECD tax haven list.

c. Not included in Hines and Rice (1994).

d. Removed from OECD's List; Subsequently determined they should not be included.

e. Not included in OECD's "gray" list as of August 17, 2009; currently on the OECD "white" list. Note that the "gray" list is divided into countries that are tax havens and countries that are other financial centers. The latter classification includes three countries listed in Table 1 (Luxembourg, Singapore, and Switzerland) and five that are not (Austria, Belgium, Brunei, Chile, and Guatemala). Of the four countries moved from the "black" to the "gray" list, one, Costa Rica, is in Table 1 and three, Malaysia, Uruguay and the Philippines are not.

The first section of this report reviews what countries might be considered tax havens, including a discussion of the Organization for Economic Development and Cooperation (OECD) initiatives and lists. The next two sections discuss, in turn, the corporate profit-shifting mechanisms and evidence on the existence and magnitude of profit shifting activity. The following two sections provide the same analysis for individual tax evasion. The report concludes with overviews of alternative policy options and a summary of specific legislative proposals.

WHERE ARE THE TAX HAVENS?

There is no precise definition of a tax haven. The OECD initially defined the following features of tax havens: no or low taxes, lack of effective exchange of information, lack of transparency, and no requirement of substantial activity.[4] Other lists have been developed in legislative proposals and by researchers. Also, a number of other jurisdictions have been identified as having tax haven characteristics.

Formal Lists of Tax Havens

The OECD created an initial list of tax havens in 2000. A similar list was used in S. 396, introduced in the 110th Congress, which would treat firms incorporated in certain tax havens as domestic companies; the only difference between this list and the OECD list was the exclusion of the U.S. Virgin Islands from the list in S. 396. Legislation introduced in the 111th Congress to address tax haven abuse (S. 506, H.R. 1265) uses a different list taken from IRS court filings, but has many countries in common. The definition by the OECD excluded low-tax jurisdictions, some of which are OECD members, that were thought by many to be tax havens, such as Ireland and Switzerland. These countries were included in an important study of tax havens by Hines and Rice.[5] GAO also provided a list.[6]

Table 1 lists the countries that appear on various lists, arranged by geographic location. These tax havens tend to be concentrated in certain areas, including the Caribbean and West Indies and Europe, locations close to large developed countries. There are 50 altogether.

Developments in the OECD Tax Haven List

The OECD list, the most prominent list, has changed over time. Nine of the countries in Table 1 did not appear on the earliest OECD list. These countries not appearing on the original list tend to be more developed larger countries and include some that are members of the OECD (e.g., Switzerland and Luxembourg).

It is also important to distinguish between OECD 's original list and its blacklist. OECD subsequently focused on information exchange and removed countries from a "blacklist if they agree to cooperate." OECD initially examined 47 jurisdictions and identified a number as not meeting the criteria for a tax haven; it also initially excluded six countries with advance agreements to share information (Bermuda, the Cayman Islands, Cyprus, Malta, Mauritius, and San Marino). The 2000 OECD blacklist included 35 countries; this list did not include the six countries eliminated due to advance agreement. The OECD had also subsequently determined that three countries should not be included in the list of tax havens (Barbados, the Maldives, and Tonga). Over time, as more tax havens made agreements to share information, the blacklist dwindled until it included only three countries: Andorra, Liechtenstein, and Monaco.

A study of the OECD initiative on global tax coordination by Sharman, also discussed in a book review by Sullivan, argues that the reduction in the OECD list was not because of actual progress towards cooperation so much as due to the withdrawal of U.S. support in 2001, which resulted in the OECD focusing on information on request and not requiring reforms until all parties had signed on.[7] This analysis suggests that the large countries were not successful in this initiative to rein in on tax havens. A similar analysis by Spencer and Sharman suggests little real progress has been made in reducing tax haven practices.[8]

Interest in tax haven actions has increased recently. The scandals surrounding the Swiss bank UBS AG (UBS) and the Liechtenstein Global Trust Group (LGT), which led to legal actions by the United States and other countries, focused greater attention on international tax issues, primarily information reporting and individual evasion.[9] The credit crunch and provision of public funds to banks has also heightened public interest. The tax haven issue was revived recently with a meeting of the G20 industrialized and developing countries that proposed sanctions, and a number of countries began to indicate commitments to information sharing agreements. [10]

The OECD currently has three lists: a "white list" of countries implementing an agreed-upon standard, a "gray" list of countries that have committed to such a standard, and a "black" list of countries that have not committed. On April 7, 2009, the last four countries on the "black" list, which were countries not included on the original OECD list—Costa Rica, Malaysia, the Philippines, and Uruguay—were moved to the "gray" list.[11] The gray list includes countries not identified as tax havens but as "other financial centers." According to news reports, Hong Kong and Macau were omitted from the OECD's list because of objections from China, but are mentioned in a footnote as having committed to the standards; they also noted that a "recent flurry of commitments brought 11 jurisdictions, including Austria, Liechtenstein, Luxembourg, Singapore, and Switzerland into the committed category."[12] As of September 3, 2010, only nine countries appeared on the gray list for tax havens and four appeared as financial centers.[13]

Many countries that were listed on the OECD's original blacklist protested because of the negative publicity and many now point to having signed agreements to negotiate tax information exchange agreements (TIEA) and some have negotiated agreements. The identification of tax havens can have legal ramifications if laws and sanctions are contingent on that identification, as is the case of some current proposals in the United States and of potential sanctions by international bodies.

Other Jurisdictions with Tax Haven Characteristics

Criticisms have been made by a range of commentators that many countries are tax havens or have aspects of tax havens and have been overlooked. These jurisdictions include major countries such as the United States, the UK, the Netherlands, Denmark, Hungary,

Iceland, Israel, Portugal, and Canada. Attention has also been directed at three states in the United States: Delaware, Nevada, and Wyoming. Finally there are a number of smaller countries or areas in countries, such as Campione d'Italia, an Italian town located within Switzerland, that have been characterized as tax havens.

A country not on the list in Table 1, but which is often considered a tax haven, especially for corporations, is the Netherlands, which allows firms to reduce taxes on dividends and capital gains from subsidiaries and has a wide range of treaties that reduce taxes.[14] In 2006, for example, Bono and other members of the U2 band moved their music publishing company from Ireland to the Netherlands after Ireland changed its tax treatment of music royalties. [15]

Some have identified the United States and the United Kingdom as having tax haven characteristics. Luxembourg Prime Minister Jean-Claude Junker urged other EU member states to challenge the United States for tax havens in Delaware, Nevada, and Wyoming. [16] One website offering offshore services mentions, in their view, several overlooked tax havens which include the United States, United Kingdom, Denmark, Iceland, Israel, and Portugal's Madeira Island.[17] (Others on their list and not listed in Table 1 were Hungary, Brunei, Uruguay, and Labuan [Malaysia]).[18] In the case of the United States the article mentions the lack of reporting requirements and the failure to tax interest and other exempt passive income paid to foreign entities, the limited liability corporation which allows a flexible corporate vehicle not subject to taxation, and the ease of incorporating in certain states (Delaware, Nevada, and Wyoming).

Another website includes in its list of tax havens Delaware, Wyoming, and Puerto Rico, along with other jurisdictions not listed in Table 1: the Netherlands, Campione d'Italia, a separate listing for Sark (identified as the only remaining "fiscal paradise"), the United Kingdom, and a coming discussion for Canada.[19] Sark is an island country associated with Guernsey, part of the Channel Islands, and Campione d'Italia is an Italian town located within Switzerland.

The Economist reported a study by a political scientist experimenting with setting up sham corporations; the author succeeded in incorporating in Wyoming and Nevada, as well as the United Kingdom and several other places.[20] Michael McIntyre discusses three U.S. practices that aid international evasion: the failure to collect information on tax exempt interest income paid to foreign entities, the system of foreign institutions that act as qualified intermediaries (see discussion below) but do not reveal their clients, and the practices of states such as Delaware and Wyoming that allow people to keep secret their identities as stockholder or depositor.[21]

In a meeting in late April 2009, Eduardo Silva, of the Cayman Islands Financial Services Association, claimed that Delaware, Nevada, Wyoming, and the United Kingdom were the greatest offenders with respect to, among other issues, tax fraud. He suggested that Nevada and Wyoming were worse than Delaware because they permit companies to have bearer shares, which allows anonymous ownership. A U.S. participant at the conference noted that legislation in the United States, S. 569, would require disclosure of beneficial owners in the United States.[22]

In addition, any country with a low tax rate could be considered as a potential location for shifting income to. In addition to Ireland, three other countries in the OECD not included in **Table 1** have tax rates below 20%: Iceland, Poland, and the Slovak Republic.[23] Most of the eastern European countries not included in the OECD have tax rates below 20%.[24]

The Tax Justice Network probably has the largest list of tax havens, and includes some specific cities and areas.[25] In addition to the countries listed in Table 1, they include in the Americas and Caribbean, New York and Uruguay; in Africa, Mellila, Sao Tome e Principe, Somalia, and South Africa; in the Middle East and Asia, Dubai, Labuan (Malaysia), Tel Aviv, and Taipei; in Europe, Alderney, Belgium, Campione d'Italia, City of London, Dublin, Ingushetia, Madeira, Sark, Trieste, Turkish Republic of Northern Cyprus, and Frankfurt; and in the Indian and Pacific oceans, the Marianas. The only county listed in Table 1 and not included in their list was Jordan.

METHODS OF CORPORATE TAX AVOIDANCE

U.S. multinationals are not taxed on income earned by foreign subsidiaries until it is repatriated to the U.S. parent as dividends, although some passive and related company income that is easily shifted is taxed currently under anti-abuse rules referred to as Subpart F. (Foreign affiliates or subsidiaries that are majority owned U.S. owned are referred to as controlled foreign corporations, or CFCs, and many of these related firms are wholly owned.) Taxes on income that is repatriated (or, less commonly, earned by branches and taxed currently) are allowed a credit for foreign income taxes paid. (A part of a parent company treated as a branch is not a separate entity for tax purposes, and all income is part of the parent's income.)

Foreign tax credits are limited to the amount of tax imposed by the United States, so that they, in theory, cannot offset taxes on domestic income. This limit is imposed on an overall basis, allowing excess credits in high-tax countries to offset U.S. tax liability on income earned in low- tax countries, although separate limits apply to passive and active income. Other countries either employ this system of deferral and credit or, more commonly, exempt income earned in foreign jurisdictions. Most countries have some form of anti-abuse rules similar to Subpart F.

If a firm can shift profits to a low-tax jurisdiction from a high-tax one, its taxes will be reduced without affecting other aspects of the company. Tax differences also affect real economic activity, which in turn affects revenues, but it is this artificial shifting of profits that is the focus of this report.[26]

Because the United States taxes all income earned in its borders as well as imposing a residual tax on income earned abroad by U.S. persons, tax avoidance relates both to U.S. parent companies shifting profits abroad to low-tax jurisdictions and the shifting of profits out of the United States by foreign parents of U.S. subsidiaries. In the case of U.S. multinationals, one study suggested that about half the difference between profitability in low-tax and high-tax countries, which could arise from artificial income shifting, was due to transfers of intellectual property (or intangibles) and most of the rest through the allocation of debt.[27] However, a study examining import and export prices suggests a very large effect of transfer pricing in goods (as discussed below).[28] Some evidence of the importance of intellectual property can also be found from the types of firms that repatriated profits abroad following a temporary tax reduction enacted in 2004; one- third of the repatriations were in the pharmaceutical and medicine industry and almost 20% in the computer and electronic equipment industry.[29]

Allocation of Debt and Earnings Stripping

One method of shifting profits from a high-tax jurisdiction to a low-tax one is to borrow more in the high-tax jurisdiction and less in the low-tax one. This shifting of debt can be achieved without changing the overall debt exposure of the firm. A more specific practice is referred to as earnings stripping where either debt is associated with related firms or unrelated debt is not subject to tax by the recipient. As an example of the former earnings stripping method, a foreign parent may lend to its U.S. subsidiary. Alternatively, an unrelated foreign borrower not subject to tax on U.S. interest income might lend to a U.S. firm.

The U.S. tax code currently contains provisions to address interest deductions and earnings stripping. It applies an allocation of the U.S. parent's interest for purposes of the limit on the foreign tax credit. The amount of foreign source income is reduced when part of U.S. interest is allocated and the maximum amount of foreign tax credits taken is limited, a provision that affects firms with excess foreign tax credits.[30] There is no allocation rule, however, to address deferral, so that a U.S. parent could operate its subsidiary with all equity finance in a low-tax jurisdiction and take all of the interest on the overall firm's debt as a deduction. A bill introduced in 2007 (H.R. 3970) by Chairman Rangel of the Ways and Means Committee would introduce such an allocation rule, so that a portion of interest and other overhead costs would not be deducted until the income is repatriated.[31] This provision is also included in President Obama's proposals for international tax revision.

While allocation-of-interest approaches could be used to address allocation of interest to high-tax countries in the case of U.S. multinationals, they cannot be applied to U.S. subsidiaries of foreign corporations. To limit the scope of earnings stripping in either case, the United States has thin capitalization rules. (Most of the United States' major trading partners have similar rules.) A section of the Internal Revenue Code (163(j)) applies to a corporation with a debt-to-equity ratio above 1.5 to 1 and with net interest exceeding 50% of adjusted taxable income (generally taxable income plus interest plus depreciation). Interest in excess of the 50% limit paid to a related corporation is not deductible if the corporation is not subject to U.S. income tax. This interest restriction also applies to interest paid to unrelated parties that are not taxed to the recipient.

The possibility of earnings stripping received more attention after a number of U.S. firms inverted, that is, arranged to move their parent firm abroad so that U.S. operations became a subsidiary of that parent. The American Jobs Creation Act (AJCA) of 2004 addressed the general problem of inversion by treating firms that subsequently inverted as U.S. firms. During consideration of this legislation there were also proposals for broader earnings stripping restrictions as an approach to this problem that would have reduced the excess interest deductions. This general earnings stripping proposal was not adopted. However, the AJCA mandated a Treasury Department study on this and other issues; that study focused on U.S. subsidiaries of foreign parents and was not able to find clear evidence on the magnitude.[32]

An noted in the Treasury's mandated study, there is relatively straightforward evidence that U.S. multinationals allocate more interest to high-tax jurisdictions, but it is more difficult to assess earnings stripping by foreign parents of U.S. subsidiaries, because the entire firm's accounts are not available. The Treasury study focused on this issue and used an approach that had been used in the past of comparing these subsidiaries to U.S. firms. The study was not able to provide conclusive evidence about the shifting of profits out of the United States due to high leverage rates for U.S. subsidiaries of foreign firms but did find evidence of shifting for inverted firms.

Transfer Pricing

The second major way that firms can shift profits from high-tax to low-tax jurisdictions is through the pricing of goods and services sold between affiliates. To properly reflect income, prices of goods and services sold by related companies should be the same as the prices that would be paid by unrelated parties. By lowering the price of goods and services sold by parents and affiliates in high-tax jurisdictions and raising the price of purchases, income can be shifted.

An important and growing issue of transfer pricing is with the transfers to rights to intellectual property, or intangibles. If a patent developed in the U.S. is licensed to an affiliate in a low-tax country income will be shifted if the royalty or other payment is lower than the true value of the license. For many goods there are similar products sold or other methods (such as cost plus a markup) that can be used to determine whether prices are set appropriately. Intangibles, such as new inventions or new drugs, tend not to have comparables, and it is very difficult to know the royalty that would be paid in an arms-length price. Therefore, intangibles represent particular problems for policing transfer pricing.

Investment in intangibles is favorably treated in the United States because costs, other than capital equipment and buildings, are expensed for research and development, which is also eligible for a tax credit. In addition, advertising to establish brand names is also deductible. Overall these treatments tend to produce an effective low, zero, or negative tax rate for overall investment in intangibles. Thus, there are significant incentives to make these investments in the United States. On average, the benefit of tax deductions or credits when making the investment tend to offset the future taxes on the return to the investment. However, for those investments that tend to be successful, it is advantageous to shift profits to a low-tax jurisdiction, so that there are tax savings on investment and little or no tax on returns. As a result, these investments can be subject to negative tax rates, or subsidies, which can be significant.

Transfer pricing rules with respect to intellectual property are further complicated because of cost sharing agreements, where different affiliates contribute to the cost.[33] If an intangible is already partially developed by the parent firm, affiliates contribute a buy-in payment. It is very difficult to determine arms-length pricing in these cases where a technology is partially developed and there is risk associated with the expected outcome. One study found some evidence that firms with cost sharing arrangements were more likely to engage in profit shifting.[34]

Contract Manufacturing

When a subsidiary is set up in a low-tax country and profit shifting occurs, as in the acquisition of rights to an intangible, a further problem occurs: this low-tax country may not be a desirable place to actually manufacture and sell the product. For example, an Irish subsidiary's market may be in Germany and it would be desirable to manufacture in

Germany. But to earn profits in Germany with its higher tax rate does not minimize taxes. Instead the Irish firm may contract with a German firm as a contract manufacturer, who will produce the item for cost plus a fixed markup. Subpart F taxes on a current basis certain profits from sales income, so the arrangement must be structured to qualify as an exception from this rule. There are complex and changing regulations on this issue.[35]

Check-the-Box, Hybrid Entities, and Hybrid Instruments

Another technique for shifting profit to low-tax jurisdictions was greatly expanded with the "check-the-box" provisions. These provisions were originally intended to simplify questions of whether a firm was a corporation or partnership. Their application to foreign circumstances through the "disregarded entity" rules has led to the expansion of hybrid entities, where an entity can be recognized as a corporation by one jurisdiction but not by another. For example, a U.S. parent's subsidiary in a low-tax country can lend to its subsidiary in a high-tax country, with the interest deductible because the high-tax country recognizes the firm as a separate corporation. Normally, interest received by the subsidiary in the low-tax country would be considered passive or "tainted" income subject to current U.S. tax under Subpart F. However, under check-the-box rules, the high-tax corporation can elect to be disregarded as a separate entity, and thus from the perspective of the United States there is no interest income paid because the two are the same entity. Check-the-box and similar hybrid entity operations can also be used to avoid other types of Subpart F income, for example from contract manufacturing arrangements. According to Sicular, this provision, which began as a regulation, has been effectively codified, albeit temporarily.[36]

Hybrid entities relate to issues other than Subpart F. For example, a reverse hybrid entity can be used to allow U.S. corporations to benefit from the foreign tax credit without having to recognize the underlying income. As an example, a U.S. parent can set up a holding company in a county that is treated as a disregarded entity, and the holding company can own a corporation that is treated as a partnership in another foreign jurisdiction. Under flow through rules, the holding company is liable for the foreign tax and, because it is not a separate entity, the U.S. parent corporation is therefore liable, but the income can be retained in the foreign corporation that is viewed as a separate corporate entity from the U.S. point of view. In this case, the entity is structured so that it is a partnership for foreign purposes but a corporation for U.S. purposes.[37]

In addition to hybrid entities that achieve tax benefits by being treated differently in the United States and the foreign jurisdiction, there are also hybrid instruments that can avoid taxation by being treated as debt in one jurisdiction and equity in another.[38]

Cross Crediting and Sourcing Rules for Foreign Tax Credits

Income from a low-tax country that is received in the United States can escape taxes because of cross crediting: the use of excess foreign taxes paid in one jurisdiction or on one type of income to offset U.S. tax that would be due on other income. In some periods in the past the foreign tax credit limit was proposed on a country-by-country basis, although that rule proved to be difficult to enforce given the potential to use holding companies. Foreign tax credits have subsequently been separated into different baskets to limit cross crediting; these baskets were reduced from nine to two (active and passive) in the American Jobs Creation Act of 2004 (P.L. 108-357).

Because firms can choose when to repatriate income, they can arrange realizations to maximize the benefits of the overall limit on the foreign tax credit. That is, firms that have income from jurisdictions with taxes in excess of U.S. taxes can also elect to realize income from jurisdictions with low taxes and use the excess credits to offset U.S. tax due on that income. Studies suggest that between cross crediting and deferral, U.S. multinationals typically pay virtually no U.S. tax on foreign source income.[39]

This ability to reduce U.S. tax due to cross crediting is increased, it can be argued, because income that should be considered U.S. source income is treated as foreign source income, thereby raising the foreign tax credit limit. This includes income from U.S. exports which is U.S. source income, because a tax provision (referred to as the title passage rule) allows half of export income to be allocated to the country in which the title passes. Another important type of income that is considered foreign source and thus can be shielded with foreign tax credits is royalty income from active business, which has become an increasingly important source of foreign income. This benefit can occur in high-tax countries because royalties are generally deductible from income. (Note that the shifting of income due to transfer pricing of intangibles, advantageous in low-tax countries, is a different issue.) Interest income is another type of income that may benefit from this foreign tax credit rule.

Since all of this income arises from investment in the United States, one could argue that this income is appropriately U.S. source income, or that, failing that, it should be put in a different foreign tax credit basket so that excess credits generated by dividends cannot be used to offset such income. Two studies, by Grubert and by Grubert and Altshuler, have discussed this sourcing rule in the context of a proposal to eliminate the tax on active dividends.[40] In that proposal, the revenue loss from exempting active dividends from U.S. tax would be offset by gains from taxes on royalties.

In addition to these general policy issues, there are numerous other narrower techniques that might be used to enhance foreign tax credits; a number of these are the focus of pending legislation in H.R. 4213, the American Jobs and Loophole Closing Act.

THE MAGNITUDE OF CORPORATE PROFIT SHIFTING

This section examines the evidence on the existence and magnitude of profit shifting and the techniques that are most likely to contribute to it.

Evidence on the Scope of Profit Shifting

There is ample, and simple, evidence that profits appear in countries inconsistent with an economic motivation. This section first examines the profit share of income of controlled corporations compared to the share of gross domestic product.[41] The first set of countries, acting as a reference point, are the remaining G-7 countries that are also among the United States' major trading partners. They account for 32% of pre-tax profits and 38% of rest-of-world gross domestic product. The second group of countries are larger countries from **Table 1** (with GDP of at least $10 billion), plus the Netherlands, which is widely considered a tax conduit for U.S. multinationals because of their holding company rules. These countries account for about 30% of earnings and 5% of rest-of-world GDP. The third group of countries are smaller countries listed in Table 1, with GDP less than $10 billion. These countries account for 14% of earnings and less than 1% of rest-of-world GDP.

As indicated in Table 2, income to GDP ratios in the large G-7 countries range from 0.2% to 2.6%, the latter reflecting in part the United States' relationships with some of its closest trading partners. Overall, this income as a share of GDP is 0.6%. Outside the United Kingdom and Canada, they are around 0.2% to 0.3% and do not vary with country size (Japan, for example, has over twice the GDP of Italy). Note also that Canada and the United Kingdom have also appeared on some tax haven lists and the larger income shares could partially reflect that.[42]

Table 2. U.S. Company Foreign Profits Relative to GDP, G-7

Country	Profits of U.S. Controlled Foreign Corporations as a Percentage of GDP
Canada	2.6
France	0.3
Germany	0.2
Italy	0.2
Japan	0.3
United Kingdom	1.3
Weighted Average	0.6

Source: CRS calculations, see text.

Table 3. U.S. Foreign Company Profits Relative to GDP, Larger Countries (GDP At Least $10 billion) on Tax Haven Lists and the Netherlands.

	Profits of U.S. Controlled Corporations Country as a Percentage of GDP
Costa Rica	1.2
Cyprus	9.8
Hong Kong	2.8
Ireland	7.6
Luxembourg	18.2
Netherlands	4.6
Panama	3.0
Singapore	3.4
Switzerland	3.5
Taiwan	0.7

Source: CRS calculations, see text.

Table 3 reports the share for the larger tax havens listed in Table 1 for which data are available, plus the Netherlands. In general, U.S. source profits as a percentage of GDP are considerably larger than those in Table 2. In the case of Luxembourg, these profits are 18% of output. Shares are also very large in Cyprus and Ireland. In all but two cases, the shares are well in excess of those in Table 2.

Table 4 examines the small tax havens listed in Table 1 for which data are available. In three of the islands off the U.S. coast (in the Caribbean and Atlantic) profits are multiples of total GDP. Profits are well in excess of GDP in four jurisdictions. In other jurisdictions they are a large share of output. These numbers clearly indicate that the profits in these countries do not appear to derive from economic motives related to productive inputs or markets, but rather reflect income easily transferred to low-tax jurisdictions.

Evidence of profit shifting has been presented in many other studies. Grubert and Altshuler report that profits of controlled foreign corporations in manufacturing relative to sales in Ireland are three times the group mean.[43] GAO reported higher shares of pretax profits of U.S. multinationals than of value added, tangible assets, sales, compensation or employees in low-tax countries such as Bermuda, Ireland, the UK Caribbean, Singapore, and Switzerland.[44] Martin Sullivan reports the return on assets for 1998 averaged 8.4% for U.S. manufacturing subsidiaries, but with returns of 23.8% in Ireland, 17.9% in Switzerland, and 16.6% in the Cayman Islands.[45] More recently, he noted that of the 10 countries that accounted for the most foreign multinational profits, the five countries with the highest manufacturing returns for 2004 (the Netherlands, Bermuda, Ireland, Switzerland, and China) all had effective tax rates below 12% while the five countries with lower returns (Canada, Japan, Mexico, Australia, and the United Kingdom) had effective tax rates in excess of 23%.[46] A number of econometric studies of this issue have been done.[47]

Table 4. U.S. Foreign Company Profits Relative to GDP, Small Countries on Tax Haven Lists

Country	Profits of U.S. Controlled Corporations as a Percentage of GDP
Bahamas	43.3
Barbados	13.2
Bermuda	645.7
British Virgin Islands	354.7
Cayman Islands	546.7
Guernsey	11.2
Jersey	35.3
Liberia	61.1
Malta	0.5
Marshall Islands	339.8
Mauritius	4.2
Netherland Antilles	8.9

Source: CRS calculations, see text.

Estimates of the Cost and Sources of Corporate Tax Avoidance

There are no official estimates of the cost of international corporate tax avoidance, although a number of researchers have made estimates, nor are there official estimates of the individual tax gap.[48] In general, the estimates are not reflected in the overall tax gap estimate. The magnitude of corporate tax avoidance has been estimated through a variety of techniques and not all are for total avoidance. Some address only avoidance by U.S. multinationals and not by foreign parents of U.S. subsidiaries. Some focus only on a particular source of avoidance.

Estimates of the potential revenue cost of income shifting by multinational corporations varies considerably, with estimates as high as $60 billion. The only study by the IRS in this area is an estimate of the international gross tax gap (not accounting for increased taxes collected on audit) related to transfer pricing based on audits of returns. They estimated a cost of about $3 billion, based on examinations of tax returns for 1996-1 998.[49] This estimate would reflect an estimate not of legal avoidance, but of non-compliance, and for reasons stressed in the study has a number of limitations. One of those is that an audit does not detect all non-compliance, and it would not detect avoidance mechanisms which are, or appear to be, legal.

Some idea of the potential magnitude of the revenue lost from profit shifting by U.S. multinationals might be found in the estimates of the revenue gain from eliminating deferral. If most of the profit in low-tax countries has been shifted there to avoid U.S. tax rates, the projected revenue gain from ending deferral would provide an idea of the general magnitude of the revenue cost of profit shifting by U.S. parent firms. The Joint Committee on Taxation projects the revenue gain from ending deferral to be about $11 billion in FY20 10.[50] This estimate could be either an overstatement or an understatement of the cost of tax avoidance. It could be an overstatement because some of the profits abroad accrue to real investments in countries that have lower tax rates than the United States and thus do not reflect artificial shifting. It could be an understatement because it does not reflect the tax that could be collected by the United States rather than foreign jurisdictions on profits shifted to low-tax countries. For example, Ireland has a tax rate of 12.5% and the United States a 35% rate, so that ending deferral (absent behavioral changes) would only collect the excess of the U.S. tax over the Irish tax on shifted revenues, or about two-thirds of lost revenue.

The Administration's estimates for ending deferral are slightly larger, over $14 billion.[51] Altshuler and Grubert estimate for 2002 that the corporate tax could be cut to 28% if deferral were ended, and based on corporate revenue in that year the gain is about $11 billion.[52] That year was at a low point because of the recession; if the share remained the same, the gain would be around $13 billion for 2004 and $26 billion for 2007. All of these estimates are based on tax data.

Researchers have looked at differences in pretax returns and estimated the revenue gain if returns were equated. This approach should provide some estimates of the magnitude of overall profit- shifting for multinationals, whether through transfer pricing, leveraging, or some other technique. Martin Sullivan, using Commerce Department data, estimates that, based on differences in pretax returns, the cost for 2004 was between $10 billion and $20 billion. Sullivan subsequently reports an estimated $17 billion increase in revenue loss from profit shifting between 1999 and 2004, which suggests that earlier number may be too small.[53] Sullivan suggests that the growth in profit shifting may be due to check-the-box.

Christian and Schultz, using rate of return on assets data from tax returns, estimated $87 billion was shifted in 2001, which, at a 35% tax rate, would imply a revenue loss of about $30 billion.[54] As a guide for potential revenue loss from avoidance, these estimates suffer from two limits. The first is the inability to determine how much was shifted out of high-tax foreign jurisdictions rather than the United States, which leads to a range of estimates. At the same time, if capital is mobile, economic theory indicates that the returns should be lower, the lower the tax rate. Thus the results could also understate the overall profit shifting and the revenue loss to the United States.

Pak and Zdanowicz examined export and import prices, and estimated that lost revenue due to transfer pricing of goods alone was $53 billion in 2001.[55] This estimate should cover both U.S. multinationals and U.S. subsidiaries of foreign parents, but is limited to one technique. Clausing, using regression techniques on cross-country data, which estimated profits reported as a function of tax rates, estimated that revenues of over $60 billion are lost for 2004 by applying a 35% tax rate to an estimated $180 billion in corporate profits shifted out of the United States.[56] She estimates that the profit shifting effects are twice as large as the effects from shifts in actual economic activity. This methodological approach differs from others which involve direct calculations based on returns or prices and is subject to the econometric limitations with cross- country panel regressions. In theory, however, it had an overall of coverage of shifting (that is both outbound by U.S. parents of foreign corporations and inbound by foreign parents of U.S. corporations and covering all techniques).

Clausing and Avi-Yonah estimate the revenue gain from moving to a formula apportionment based on sales that is on the order of $50 billion per year because the fraction of worldwide income in the United States is smaller than the fraction of worldwide sales.[57] While this estimate is not an estimate of the loss from profit shifting (since sales and income could differ for other reasons) it is suggestive of the magnitude of total effects from profit shifting. A similar result was found by another study that applied formula apportionment based on an equal weight of assets, payroll, and sales.[58]

It is very difficult to develop a separate estimate for U.S. subsidiaries of foreign multinational companies because there is no way to observe the parent firm and its other subsidiaries. Several studies have documented that these firms have lower taxable income and that some have higher debt to asset ratios than domestic firms. There are many other potential explanations these differing characteristics, however, and domestic firms that are used as comparisons also have incentives to shift profits when they have foreign operations. No quantitative estimate has been made.[59] However some evidence of earnings stripping for inverted firms was found. [60]

Importance of Different Profit Shifting Techniques

Some studies have attempted to identify the importance of techniques used for profit shifting. Grubert has estimated that about half of income shifting was due to transfer pricing of intangibles and most of the remainder to shifting of debt.[61] In a subsequent study, Altshuler and Grubert find that multinationals saved $7 billion more between 1997 and 2002 due to check the box rules.[62] Some of this gain may have been at the cost of high-tax host countries rather than the United States, however.

Some of the estimates discussed here conflict with respect to the source of profit shifting. The Pak and Zdanowich estimates suggest that transfer pricing of goods is an important mechanism of tax avoidance, while Grubert suggests that the main methods of profit shifting are due to leverage and intangibles. The estimates for pricing of goods may, however, reflect errors, or money laundering motives rather than tax motives. Much of the shifting was associated with trade with high-tax countries; for example, Japan, Canada, and Germany accounted for 18% of the total.[63] At the same time, about 14% of the estimate reflected transactions with countries that appear on tax haven lists: the Netherlands, Taiwan, Singapore, Hong Kong, and Ireland.

Some evidence that points to the importance of intangibles and the associated profits in tax haven countries can be developed by examining the sources of dividends repatriated during the "repatriation holiday" enacted in 2004.[64] This provision allowed, for a temporary period, dividends to be repatriated with an 85% deduction, leading to a tax rate of 5.25%. The pharmaceutical and medicine industry accounted for $99 billion in repatriations or 32% of the total. The computer and electronic equipment industry accounted for $58 billion or 18% of the total. Thus these two industries, which are high tech firms, accounted for half of the repatriations. The benefits were also highly concentrated in a few firms. According to a recent study, five firms (Pfizer, Merck, Hewlett-Packard, Johnson & Johnson, and IBM) are responsible for $88 billion, over a quarter (28%) of total repatriations.[65] The top 10 firms (adding Schering-Plough, Du Pont, Bristol-Myers Squibb, Eli Lilly, and PepsiCo) accounted for 42%. The top 15 (adding Procter and Gamble, Intel, Coca-Cola, Altria, and Motorola) accounted for over half (5 2%). These are firms that tend to, in most cases, have intangibles either in technology or brand names.

Finally, as shown in Table 5, which lists all countries accounting for at least 1% of the total of eligible dividends (and accounting for 87% of the total), most of the dividends were repatriated from countries that appear on tax haven lists.

Table 5. Source of Dividends from "Repatriation Holiday": Countries Accounting for At Least 1% of Dividends

Country	Percentage of Total
Netherlands	28.8
Switzerland	10.4
Bermuda	10.2
Ireland	8.2
Luxembourg	7.5
Canada	5.9
Cayman Islands	5.9
United Kingdom	5.1
Hong Kong	1.7
Singapore	1.7
Malaysia	1.2

Source: Internal Revenue Service.

METHODS OF AVOIDANCE AND EVASION BY INDIVIDUALS

Individual evasion of taxes may take different forms, and they are all facilitated by the growing international financial globalization and ease of making transactions on the Internet. Individuals can purchase foreign investments directly (outside the United States), such as stocks and bonds, or put money in foreign bank accounts and simply not report the income (although it is subject to tax under U.S. tax law). There is little or no withholding information on individual taxpayers for this type of action. They can also use structures such as trusts or shell corporations to evade tax on investments, including investments made in the United States, which may take advantage of U.S. tax laws that exempt interest income and capital gains of non-residents from U.S. tax. Rather than using withholding or information collection the United States largely relies on the Qualified Intermediary (QI) program where beneficial owners are not revealed. To the extent any information gathering from other countries is done it is through bilateral information exchanges rather than multilateral information sharing. The European Union has developed a multilateral agreement but the United States does not participate.

Tax Provisions Affecting the Treatment of Income by Individuals

The ability of U.S. persons (whether firms or individuals) to avoid tax on U.S. source income that they would normally be subject to arises from U.S. rules that do not impose withholding taxes on many sources of income. In general interest and capital gains are not subject to withholding. Dividends, non-portfolio interest (such as interest payments by a U.S. subsidiary to its parent), capital gains connected with a trade or business, and certain rents are subject to tax, although treaty arrangements widely reduce or eliminate the tax on dividends. In addition, even when dividends are potentially subject to a withholding tax, new techniques have developed to transform, through derivatives, those assets into exempt interest.[66]

The elimination of tax on interest income was unilaterally initiated by the United States in 1984, and other countries began to follow suit.[67] Currently, fears of capital flight are likely to keep countries from changing this treatment. However, it has been accompanied with a lack of information reporting and lack of information sharing that allows U.S. citizens, who are liable for these taxes, to avoid them whether on income invested abroad or income invested in the United States channeled through shell corporations and trusts. Citizens of foreign countries can also evade the tax, and the U.S. practice of not collecting information contributes to the problem.

Based on actual tax cases, Guttenberg and Avi-Yonah describe a typical way that U.S. individuals can easily evade tax on domestic income through a Cayman Islands operation using current technology with little expense with current technology. The individual, using the Internet, can open a bank account in the name of a Cayman corporation that can be set up for a minimal fee. Money can be electronically transferred without any reporting to tax authorities, and investments can be made in the United States or abroad. Investments by non-residents in interest bearing assets and most capital gains are not subject to a withholding tax in the United States.[68]

In addition to corporations, foreign trusts can be used to accomplish the same approach. Trusts may involve a trust protector who is an intermediary between the grantor and the trustees, but whose purpose may actually be to carry out the desires of the grantor. Some taxpayers argue that these trusts are legal but in either case they can be used to protect income from taxes, including those invested in the United States, from tax, while retaining control over and use of the funds.

Limited Information Reporting between Jurisdictions

In general, the international taxation of passive portfolio income by individuals is easily subject to evasion because there is no multilateral reporting of interest income. Even in those cases where bilateral information sharing treaties, referred to as Tax Information Exchange Agreements (TIEAs) are in place, they have limits. As pointed out by Avi-Yonah most of these agreements are restricted to criminal matters, which are a minor part of the revenues involved and pose difficult issues of evidence. Also, these agreements sometimes require that the activities related to the information being sought constitute crimes in both countries which can be a substantial hurdle in cases of tax evasion. The OECD has adopted a model agreement with the "dual criminality" requirements.[69] TIEAs usually allow for information only upon request, requiring the United States and other countries to identify the potential tax evaders in advance and they do not override bank secrecy laws.

In some cases the countries themselves have little or no information of value. One article, for example, discussing the possibility of an information exchange agreement with the British Virgin Islands, a country with more than 400,000 registered corporations, where laws require no identification of shareholders or directors, and require no financial records, noted: "Even if the BVI signs an information exchange agreement, it is not clear what information could be exchanged."[70]

U.S. Collection of Information on U.S. Income and Qualified Intermediaries

Under the QI program the United States itself does not require U.S. financial institutions to identify the true beneficiaries of interest and exempt dividends. The IRS has set up a QI program in 2001, under which foreign banks that received payments certify the nationality of their depositors and reveal the identity of any U.S. citizens.[71] However, although QIs are supposed to certify nationality,[72] apparently some rely on self certification.[73] They are also subject to audit. However, UBS, the Swiss bank involved in a tax abuse scandal that helped clients set up offshore plans, was a QI, and that event has raised some questions about the QI program.

A non-qualified intermediary must disclose the identity of its customers to obtain the exemption for passive income such as interest and or the reduced rates arising from tax treaties, but there are also questions about the accuracy of disclosures.

The HIRE Act, P.L. 111-147, included some provisions strengthening the rules affecting qualified intermediaries, although the projected revenue gain was quite small (less than $1 billion per year) relative to projected costs (discussed below).

European Union Savings Directive

The European Union, in its savings directive, has developed among its members an option of either information reporting or a withholding tax. The reporting or withholding option covers the member countries as well as some other countries. Three states, Austria, Belgium, and Luxembourg, have elected the withholding tax. While this multilateral agreement aids these countries' tax administration, the United States is not a participant.

ESTIMATES OF THE REVENUE COST OF INDIVIDUAL TAX EVASION

A number of different approaches have been used to estimate corporate tax avoidance, however, all of these approaches rely on data reported on assets and income. For individual evasion, estimates are much more difficult because the initial basis of the estimate is the amount of assets held abroad whose income is not reported to the tax authorities. In addition to this estimate, the expected rate of return and tax rate are needed to estimate the revenue cost.

Guttentag and Avi-Yonah estimate a value of $50 billion in individual tax evasion, based on an estimate of holdings by high net worth individuals invested outside the United States at $1.5 trillion.[74] Using a rate of return of 10% and a tax rate of approximately one-third, they obtain an estimate of $50 billion. They also summarize two other estimates in 2002 of $40 billion for the international tax gap by the IRS and $70 billion by an IRS consultant.

To the extent that the earnings are interest, the 10% rate of return may be too high, while if it is dividends and capital gains, the tax rate is too high. Using a tax rate of 15% (currently applicable to capital gains and dividends) would lead to about $23 billion. In the case of equity investments, if a third of the return is in dividends and half of capital gains is never realized, the tax rate would be 10% or about $15 billion assuming the 10% return. During 2002 and beginning in 2011, however, the tax rate on capital gains and dividends is 20%, indicating a loss of $20 billion rather than $15 billion. For interest, since investors can earn tax free returns in the neighborhood of 4% to 5% on domestic state and local bonds, to yield a 5% after-tax return at a 35% tax rates would require a pre-tax yield of about 7.7%. The estimate would then be $40 billion.

The Tax Justice Network has estimated a worldwide revenue loss for all countries of $255 billion from individual tax evasion, basically using a 7.5% return and a 30% tax rate.[75] These assumptions would be consistent with a $33 billion loss for the United States using the $1.5 trillion figure.

ALTERNATIVE POLICY OPTIONS TO ADDRESS CORPORATE PROFIT SHIFTING

Because much of the corporate tax revenue loss arises from activities that either are legal or appear to be so, it is difficult to address these issues other than with changes in the tax law. Outcomes would likely be better if there is international cooperation. Currently, the possibilities for international cooperation appear to play a bigger role in options for dealing with individual evasion than with corporate avoidance.

Broad Changes to International Tax Rules

The first set of provisions would introduce broad changes in international tax rules, and include significant restrictions in deferral or allocation of income and capital.

Repeal Deferral

One approach to mitigate the rewards of profit shifting is to repeal deferral, or to institute true worldwide taxation of foreign source income. Firms would be subject to current tax on the income of their foreign subsidiaries, although they would continue to be able to take foreign tax credits. According to estimates cited above, this change currently would raise from $11 billion to $14 billion per year.

Many of the issues surrounding the repeal of deferral have focused on the real effects of repeal on the allocation of capital. Traditionally, economic analysis has suggested that eliminating deferral would increase economic efficiency, although recently some have argued that this gain would be offset by the loss of production of some efficient firms from high-tax countries. Some have also argued for retaining the current system or moving in the other direction to a territorial tax. These economic issues are discussed in detail in another CRS report.[76]

Repeal of deferral would largely eliminate the value of the planning techniques discussed in this report. There are concerns, however, that firms could avoid the effects of repeal by having their parent incorporate in other countries that continue to allow deferral. The most direct and beneficial to reducing firms' tax liabilities of these planning approaches, inversion, has been addressed by legislation in 2004.[77] Mergers would be another method to counter the implementation of deferral, although mergers involve real changes in organization that would not likely be undertaken to gain a small tax benefit. Another possibility is that more direct portfolio investment (i.e., buying shares of stock by individual investors) in foreign corporations will occur. There has been a significant growth in this direct investment, although the evidence suggests this investment has been due to portfolio diversification and not tax avoidance.[78]

S. 3018, a broad tax reform bill introduced by Senators Wyden and Gregg, would eliminate deferral.

Targeted or Partial Elimination of Deferral

More narrow proposals to address deferral and tax avoidance would tax income in tax havens currently, or tax some additional income of foreign subsidiaries. They include

- eliminating deferral for specified tax havens,
- eliminating deferral in countries with tax rates that are below the U.S. rate by a specified proportion,
- eliminating deferral for income on the production of goods that are in turn imported into the United States,

- eliminate deferral for income on the production of goods that are exported, and
- requiring a minimum payout share.

Restricting current taxation to tax havens would likely address some of the problems associated with transfer pricing and leveraging, without ending deferral entirely. Defining a tax haven under those circumstances would be crucial. A bill introduced in the 110th Congress, S. 396, which defined as a U.S. firm any U.S. subsidiary in a tax haven not engaged in an active business, had a list of countries that was the same as the original OECD tax haven list, except for the U.S. Virgin Islands. Some countries that are often considered tax havens, would not be subject to such provisions, leaving some scope for corporate tax avoidance. In addition, firms could shift some operations to other lower tax countries and increase the amount of foreign tax credits available, which would be a loss to U.S. revenue. Some concerns have also been expressed that listing specific tax haven countries would make cooperative approaches, such as tax information sharing treaties, more difficult.

An alternative, which would not require identifying particular countries, would be to restrict deferral based on a tax rate that is lower than the U.S. rate by a specified amount. For example, the French, who generally have a territorial tax, tax income earned in jurisdictions with tax rates one-third lower than the French rate. For the United States, whose tax rate is similar to the French rate, this ratio would indicate a tax rate lower than 24%.

Another proposal directed to "runaway" plans would eliminate deferral for investments abroad that produce exports into the United States. S. 1284, also in the 110th Congress, would impose current taxation on such activities by expanding Subpart F income to include income attributable to imports into the United States of goods produced by foreign subsidiaries of U.S. firms. The main problem with this proposal is administering it, which would include tracing selling to a third party for resale.

A somewhat different and more restrictive proposal was made by Senator Kerry during the 2004 presidential campaign. He proposed to eliminate deferral except in the case where income is produced and sold in the controlled foreign corporation's (CFC's) jurisdiction. This approach would, like deferral in general, be likely to significantly restrict opportunities for artificial profit shifting, since most of the income in tax haven or low-tax jurisdictions do not arise from real activity; indeed, these jurisdictions are too small in many cases to provide a market. As with the previous proposal, however, the administration of such a plan would be difficult.

A final option that would not go as far as eliminating deferral altogether would be to require some minimum share to be paid out.

Allocation of Deductions and Credits with Respect to Deferred Income/Restrictions on Cross Crediting

A proposal that does not end deferral but makes the shifting of profits from high-tax countries less attractive is a provision to allocate deductions and credits, so as to deny those benefits until income is repatriated. This approach was included in a tax reform bill introduced by Chairman Rangel of the Ways and Means Committee in 2007 (H.R. 3970) and is included in the current proposals by President Obama. Under this proposal, a portion of certain overall deductions, such as interest or overhead, that reflects the share of foreign deferred income, would be disallowed. The foreign tax credit allocation rule would allow credits for the share of foreign taxes paid that is equal to the share of foreign source income repatriated. Disallowed deductions and credits would be carried forward. (President Obama's proposal does not allocate research and experimental expenses.)

The allocation-of-deductions provision would decrease the tax benefits of sheltering income in low-tax jurisdictions and encourage repatriation of income relative to current law and presumably reduce profit shifting, as well as decreasing benefits of real investment abroad. The foreign tax credit allocation rule could have a variety of effects. It would make foreign investment abroad less attractive because it would increase the tax on income when eventually repatriated, it would discourage investment in low-tax jurisdictions that could no longer be sheltered by foreign tax credits, and it would discourage repatriation of earnings on existing activities because of the potential tax to be collected.

The allocation of credits accomplishes some of the restrictions on cross crediting that could also be achieved by increasing the number of baskets. As discussed below, one possible separate basket would be for active royalties. Another possibility would be to impose a per country limit with a separate basket for each country (and baskets within each for passive, active, etc., income). S. 3018, a broad tax reform bill introduced by Senators Wyden and Gregg, would provide for a per country limit.

Formula Apportionment

Another approach to addressing income shifting is through formula apportionment, which would be a major change in the international tax system. With formula apportionment, income would be allocated to different jurisdictions based on their shares of some combination of sales, assets, and employment. This approach is used by many states in the United States and by the Canadian provinces to allocate income. (In the past, a three factor apportionment was used, but some states have moved to a sales based system.) Studies have estimated a significant increase in taxes from adopting formula apportionment. Slemrod and Shackleford estimate a 38% revenue increase from an equally weighted three-factor system.[79] A sales-based formula has been proposed by Avi-Yonah and Clausing that they estimate would raise about 35% of additional corporate revenue, or $50 billion annually over the 200 1-2004 period.[80]

The ability of a formula apportionment system to address some of the problems of shifting income becomes problematic with intangible assets.[81] If all capital were tangible capital, such as buildings and equipment, a formula apportionment system based on capital would at least lead to the same rate of return for tax purposes across high-tax and low-tax jurisdictions. Real distortions in the allocation of capital would remain, since capital would still flow to low-tax jurisdictions, but paper profits could not be shifted. An allocation system based on assets becomes more difficult when intangible assets are involved. It is probably as difficult to estimate the stock of intangible investment (given lack of information on the future pattern of profitability) as it is to allocate it under arms-length pricing. In the case of an allocation based on sales, profits that might appropriately be associated with domestic income as they arise from domestic investment in R&D would be allocated abroad. Moreover, new avenues of tax planning, such as selling to an intermediary in a low-tax country for resale, would complicate the administration of such a plan. Whether the benefits are greater than the costs is in some dispute.

One problem is that if the Untied States adopted the system there could be double taxation of some income and no taxation of other income unless there were a multinational plan. The European Union has been considering a formula apportionment, based on property, gross receipts, number of employees and cost of employment. This proposal and the consequences for different countries are discussed by Devereux and Loretz.[82] If the European Union adopted such a plan it would be easier for the United States to adopt a similar apportionment formula without as much risk of double or no taxation with respect to its major trading partners.

Eliminate Check the Box, Hybrid Entities, and Hybrid Instruments; Foreign Tax Credit Splitting from Income

A number of proposals have been made to eliminate check the box, and in general to adopt rules that would require that legal entities be characterized in a consistent manner by the United States and the country where the entity is established. This proposal has been made by McIntyre.[83] In general rules to require that legal entities be characterized in a consistent manner by the United States and by the country where established and that tax benefits that arise from inconsistent treatment of instruments be denied would address this particular class of provisions that undermine Subpart F and the matching of credits and deductions with income. President Obama's proposal includes a provision that disallows a subsidiary to treat a subsidiary chartered in another country as a disregarded entity. It also includes a provision to prevent foreign tax credits without the associated income, which can currently be accomplished with reverse hybrids. This provision is included in H.R. 4213, the American Jobs and Closing Loopholes Act, passed by the House.

Narrower Provisions Affecting Multinational Profit Shifting

A number of more narrow provisions could be considered that would be more focused on preventing abuses and have fewer consequences for the overall structure of international corporate taxation.

Tighten Earnings Stripping Rules

In the American Jobs Creation Act a further restriction on earnings stripping rules was considered as an alternative to the anti-inversion measure. These provisions were not enacted, but were to be studied in a Treasury report. The 2004 House proposal would have raised revenue by dropping the debt to asset share test and lowering the interest share standard to 25% for ordinary debt, 50% for guaranteed debt, and 30% overall. In general, further restrictions on earnings stripping could be considered to address shifting through debt for U.S. subsidiaries of foreign parents.

President Obama's plan includes dropping the asset test and lowering the interest share standard to 25% for inverted firms, with respect to related party non-guaranteed debt.

Foreign Tax Credits: Source Royalties as Domestic Income for Purposes of the Foreign Tax Credit Limit, Or Create Separate Basket; Eliminate Title Passage Rule; Restrict Credits for Taxes Producing an Economic Benefit; Address Specific Techniques for Enhancing Foreign Tax Credits

As noted above, one of the issues surrounding the cross-crediting of the foreign tax credit is the use of excess credits to shield royalties from U.S. tax on income that could be considered U.S. source income. Two options might be considered to address that issue: sourcing these royalties as domestic income for purposes of the credit or putting them into a separate foreign tax credit basket.[84] The same issue applies to the provision that allows half of the income from exports to be allocated to the country in which the title passes. President Obama's proposal includes a provision to restrict the crediting of taxes that are in exchange for an economic benefit (such as payments that are the equivalent of royalties).

H.R. 4213, the American Jobs and Closing Loopholes Act, passed by the House, would address a number of specialized techniques for increasing foreign tax credits.

Transfer pricing

Michael McIntyre has suggested some other proposals to deal with transfer pricing, which include making transfer pricing penalties nearly automatic for taxpayers who have not kept contemporaneous records. He also suggests use of some type of formula apportionment plan as a default for transfer pricing for non-complying taxpayers so the IRS does not have to conduct a detailed transaction by transaction assessment for the court.

President Obama's proposals would address some of the transfer pricing issues associated with the transfer of intangibles by clarifying that intangibles include workforce in place, goodwill, and going concern value and that they are valued at their highest and best use. The plan would allow the IRS Commissioner to aggregate intangibles if that leads to a more appropriate value.

These proposals would likely have small effects. Any significant solution to the transfer pricing problem, especially for intangibles, is difficult to entertain short of an elimination of deferral.

The President's FY2011 budget proposal included a plan to treat excess returns on intangibles in a low-tax country as Subpart F income (and therefore not subject to deferral) and to place it in a separate foreign tax-credit basket. If such an approach could be successfully implemented it might have important consequences for transfer pricing using intangibles.

Codify Economic Substance Doctrine (Enacted Provision)

The economic substance doctrine was recently adopted in the health reform legislation, P.L. 111- 148. This provision is relevant to international tax evasion and avoidance. Firms that enter into tax savings arrangements that are found not to have economic substance can have their tax benefits disallowed by the courts under what has become known as the economic substance doctrine. The doctrine is sometimes interpreted differently by different courts and recent legislative proposals have sought to make the doctrine more uniform through statute. Generally these proposals would require a transaction to meet both an objective test (profit was made) and a subjective test (profit was intended). Penalties are also imposed. Supporters argue that the stricter test will not only reduce tax avoidance but also make treatment more consistent across the courts. Some tax attorneys are concerned that more specific rules might provide a roadmap to structuring arrangements that will pass the test. The provision adopted in P.L. 111-148 included a two-part statutory standard.

Prevent Dividend Repatriation through Reorganizations (Boot within Gain)

President Obama's plan would revise the rule on reorganizations when property as well as stock is received to treat distributions as dividends in the case of cross-border transactions, and this provision is included in H.R. 4213, the American Jobs and Closing Loopholes Act, passed by the House.

OPTIONS TO ADDRESS INDIVIDUAL EVASION

Most of the options for addressing individual evasion involve more information reporting and additional enforcement. There are options that would involve fundamental changes in the law, such as shifting from a residence to a source basis for passive income. That is, the United States would tax this passive income earned in its borders, just as is the case for corporate and other active income. This change involves, however, many other economic and efficiency effects that are probably not desirable. The remainder of the proposals discussed here do not involve any fundamental changes in the tax itself, but rather focus on administration and enforcement.

The options discussed below are drawn from many sources, including academics and practitioners, organizations, and the Internal Revenue Service, and contained in legislative proposals; citations to these sources are provided at this point and legislative proposals are summarized in the next section.[85]

Some of the options discussed in this section are included in the HIRE Act, P.L. 111-147, and that inclusion will be noted.

Information Reporting

Expanded information reporting can involve multilateral efforts, changes in the current bilateral treaties, or unilateral changes.

Multilateral Information Sharing or Withholding; International Cooperation

The option that appears likely to recover most of the revenues would be to join in the European Union Directive, which would require information reporting on all income paid to foreign entities by U.S. banks and other institutions. If the beneficial owner cannot be identified, withholding could be imposed (a refund would be allowed if evidence of reporting to the home country could be shown). This approach has been proposed by the Tax Justice Network, which also suggests expanding the treaty to other tax havens. If the European Union is receptive, it would benefit other countries by reporting income paid to foreign nationals and benefit the United States by achieving third party information reporting on foreign investments of U.S. citizens.

Avi-Yonah and Avi-Yonah and Guttentag have suggested that current Treasury policy is to focus on bilateral agreements to achieve information exchange, but that the United States should also focus on cooperation with the OECD and G-20 and other appropriate organizations to improve information and persuade tax havens to enter into exchanges based on the OECD model. Shay suggests this approach as well and particularly references electronic information exchange.

The Tax Justice Network has proposed that the United Nations develop a global tax cooperation standard, set up a panel to determine compliant states, and deny recognition to non-compliant jurisdictions. They have also suggested that the IMF and World Bank country assessments address tax compliance.

Expanding Bilateral Information Exchange

A number of commentators have suggested an increase in the scope of bilateral information treaties to provide for regular and automatic exchanges of information. This would require the U.S. banks to increase their collection of information.

Avi-Yonah and Avid-Yonah and Guttentag suggest adopting the model OECD bilateral Tax Information Exchange Agreement (TIEA). This information exchange would relate to civil as well as criminal issues, it would not require suspicion of a crime other than tax evasion, and would override tax haven bank secrecy laws. Non-tax havens could be induced to make such agreements to obtain information, and thus, such a change would require collection of information on interest payments by banks and financial institutions. Treasury has proposed only 16 countries, but Avi-Yonah and Guttenberg suggest no reason to restrict the provision in this way. Treasury could use existing authority not to exchange information that might be misused by non-democratic foreign governments.

Martin Sullivan suggests that automatic information exchange might be the only way to stop evasion, which would require renegotiating existing agreements and a major policy change. He notes that that the proposed Stop Tax Haven Abuse Act (S. 506, H.R. 1265) requires automatic information exchange for a country to stay off the tax haven list.

Unilateral Approaches: Withholding/Refund Approach; Increased Information Reporting Requirements

This step is one that the United States could undertake without multilateral or bilateral cooperation, namely imposing withholding taxes on interest income and other exempt income received from U.S. sources by foreign intermediaries and providing a refund upon proof that the beneficial recipient was eligible. Avi-Yonah suggests this change with the hope that it would be adopted multilaterally.

A variation of this approach would be to require disclosure of the names of customers including beneficial owners, with withholding imposed if disclosure was not forthcoming. Such a proposal has been made by Michael McIntyre, and has been included, for accounts identified as U.S. beneficiaries in the HIRE Act, P.L. 111-147. The Stop Tax haven Abuse Act and President Obama's budget proposals addressed these issues as well. S. 3018, the Wyden-Gregg tax reform act, requires withholding on all accounts unless information on the beneficial owner is supplied, without an initial determination by the institute that the account has a U.S. owner.

President Obama's proposals also include provisions to require information reporting by U.S. financial intermediaries and qualified intermediaries on transfers of funds and by U.S. persons and qualified intermediaries on the formation or acquisition of a foreign entity.

The proposed Stop Tax Haven Abuse Act would also require reporting by U.S. shareholders and persons forming, sending, or receiving assets from Passive Foreign Investment Corporations (PFICs), and this provision was included in the HIRE Act, P.L. 111-147.

Other Measures That Might Improve Compliance

Incentives/Sanctions for Tax Havens

Avi-Yonah and Avi-Yonah and Guttenberg suggest a carrot and stick approach to tax havens. They argue that little of the benefit of tax havens flows to their sometimes needy residents, but rather to the professionals providing banking and legal services, who often live elsewhere. They suggest transitional aid to move away from these offshore activities. For non-cooperating tax havens, they suggest the Treasury use its existing authority to deny benefits of the interest exemption. They suggest that tax havens cannot continue to exist unless the wealthy countries permit it, because funds are not productive in tax havens.

The proposed Stop Tax Haven Abuse Act would extend to tax enforcement the sanctions of the Patriot Act used to impose penalties for money laundering and terrorist financing. Sanctions vary in severity and range from increased reporting on transactions to prohibitions. Sullivan points out that the U.S. government has used the Patriot Act sparingly, however, and questions whether this change would be a credible threat.

Blessing suggests that sanctions should be multilateral rather than unilateral.

Revise and Strengthen the Qualified Intermediary (QI)Program

Several proposals relating to the QI program, which were discussed by witnesses at a Ways and Means Committee hearing on March 31, 2009, were reported by Sullivan. Some of these provisions are also included in the proposed Stop Tax Haven Abuse Act. If enough effective revisions could be made in the QI program, a great deal of potential information about U.S. taxpayers' income would be obtained. These proposals include the following. QIs would be required to inquire about and independently verify the ownership of foreign corporations and similar entities, information that they already must acquire to deal with money laundering. QIs would also be required to report any non-U.S. income of U.S. taxpayers. QIs would be required to submit information electronically, and IRS would be given resources to handle and use this information. The current exemption from withholding rules for bearer bonds (where no registration occurs) would be eliminated. Another possible change is to require QIs to share information about foreign customers to U.S. treaty partners (although one witness warned that this might be too severe a requirement). Finally, external audits of QIs would be strengthened by requiring QIs to promptly notify the IRS of any material failure in oversight, improve the evaluation of risk of circumvention of U.S. taxes by U.S. persons, and require audit oversight by a U.S. auditor.

Blum emphasizes the problem of accepting a shell corporation as the beneficial owner, and says this loophole in the law should be closed. He also suggests that penalties for failure to enforce should include withholding of capital gains as well as interest and dividends.

McIntyre stresses that audits of the QIs should be done by firms that do not at the same time sell tax shelters. Avi-Yonah and Avi-Yonah and Guttentag also suggest that IRS should require U.S. payors to issue form 1099s when they know or have reason to suspect the beneficial owner is a U.S. citizen (rather than the W8-BEN which provides evidence of foreign status).

President Obama's proposals would revise the treatment of non-qualified intermediaries. As noted above, the proposal includes a withholding/refund mechanism for non-qualified intermediaries. It would require that QIs can qualify only if all of their affiliates are QIs and, as noted above, increase information reporting by QIs.

The HIRE Act, P.L. 111-147, discussed below, contains some modifications in this area.

Placing the Burden of Proof on the Taxpayer

An important part of the Stop Tax Haven Abuse proposal is to place the burden of proof in court on the taxpayer; this approach was also suggested by Blum. As noted above, there is also a shift in the burden of proof for accounts with non-qualified intermediaries for filing an FBAR (Foreign Bank and Financial Account Report).

President Obama's proposal would create a presumption that the funds in foreign accounts are large enough to require an FBAR, which is required when amounts exceed $10,000. It would treat failure to file for amounts in excess of $200,000 as willful, which permits criminal penalties and larger civil penalties.

The HIRE Act (P.L. 111-147) would assume that, when adequate information is not provided, foreign accounts exceed the $50,000 minimum that requires reporting (under other provisions) on the tax return for purposes of assessing penalties.

Treat Shell Corporations as U.S. Firms

The Stop Tax Haven Abuse Act includes a provision to treat any firm that is publicly traded or has assets over $50 million as a U.S. corporation. This provision would include hedge funds but would not affect subsidiaries of multinational firms because decisions are made by the parent firm. Sullivan argues that such a provision would have a devastating effect on the U.S. hedge fund industry, where offshore firms generally attract tax exempt U.S. investors and foreigners who wish to avoid filing tax returns, as well as U.S. tax evaders, and that legislative relief for U.S. tax exempt investors (pension funds, university endowments) would be likely.

Impose Restrictions on Foreign Trusts

The proposed Stop Tax Haven Abuse Acts would impose further restrictions on foreign trusts, by providing that any powers held by trust protectors would be attributed to the trust grantor, providing that any U.S. person who benefits from the trust will be treated as a formal beneficiary even if not named, providing that a future or contingent beneficiary be treated as a current one, and treating loans of assets and property as distributions. The Senate Finance Committee draft would expand the definition of contributions to include items such as art and jewelry. The HIRE Act (P.L. 111-147) includes these provisions.

Treat Dividend Equivalents as Dividends

As noted earlier, the withholding tax on dividends has been avoided with the use of derivatives and other arrangements to re-characterize them as interest. The proposed Stop Tax Haven Abuse Act would treat dividend equivalents as dividends. Proposals for change in this area were also made by Avi-Yonah. President Obama's plan treats equity swaps as dividends. The HIRE Act (P.L. 111-147) includes this provision.

Extend the Statute of Limitations

Extensions in the statute of limitations are said by some to be needed due to the complexity of the international cases and difficulty of obtaining information. Extension has been proposed by numerous commentators, is supported by the IRS officials and is included in the proposed Stop Tax Haven Abuse Act , proposals discussed by the Senate Finance Committee, and proposals made by President Obama. These legislative proposals would extend the statute of limitations from three years to six years, but Blum also suggests the possibility of 10 years. The HIRE Act (P.L. 111-147) extends the statute of limitations to six years.

Greater Resources for the Internal Revenue Service to Focus on Offshore

Numerous suggestions have been made to expand IRS resources for combating overseas tax abuses. President Obama's proposal, for example, has proposed to fund 800 new positions to combat international abuses.

Blum says that agents should not be pressured to give up difficult cases because of short-term performance goals based on closing cases and collecting revenues.

Make Civil Cases Public as a Deterrent

Blum suggests all settlements involving offshore schemes in excess of $1 million should be excluded from the restrictions of Section 6103 that require settled civil cases to be confidential. He argues that no one knows about these cases and thus taxpayers think the possibility of being caught is small.

Revise Rules for FBAR (Foreign Bank Account Report)

Blum argues that language in the FBAR should be clarified to make it easier for the Justice Department to pursue cases; the proposed Stop Tax Haven Abuse Act would change the disclosure rules to make this information easier to use. The FBAR report on foreign bank accounts is filed separately from the tax return; individuals must check a box to indicate whether or not they have these accounts. It is possible that a reporting requirement on the tax return would increase the visibility and force of this requirement. The Senate Finance Committee would require this report to be filed with the tax return and require due diligence on the part of tax preparers to determine if it should be filed. (Note also, as discussed below, that some of the strengthened penalties relate to FBAR.) President Obama's FY20 10 plan would require the information from the FBAR to also be reported on the tax return and any transfer of funds that sums to more than $10,000 would also be reported. His FY20 11 plan increases the minimum to $50,000, and this provision is included in the HIRE Act (P.L. 111-147).

John Doe Summons

A provision in the proposed Stop Tax Haven Abuse Act would make it easier to issue John Doe summons where the IRS does not know the names of taxpayers and now must ask courts for permission to serve the summons. This section provides that in any case involving offshore secret accounts, the court is to presume tax compliance is at issue, to relieve the IRS of the obligation when the only records sought are U.S. bank records, and to issue John Doe summons for large investigative projects without addressing each set of summons separately.

Strengthening of Penalties

Increased penalties are included in the proposed Stop Tax Haven Abuse Act, the Finance Committee Draft and President Obama's proposals. Among the penalty provisions in various proposals are increased penalties for failure to file FBARs; basing the FBAR penalty on the highest amount in period rather than on a particular day; and increased penalties on abusive tax shelters, failure to file information on foreign trusts, and certain offshore transactions. President Obama's proposals would double accuracy-related penalties for foreign transactions and increase penalties for trusts and permit them to be imposed if the amount in the trust cannot be established; this provision was included in The HIRE Act (P.L. 111-147).

The proposed Stop Tax Haven Abuse Act also includes a provision that legal opinions that take the position that a transaction is more likely than not to prevail for tax purposes will no longer shield taxpayers from penalties.

S. 386, the Fraud Recovery and Investment Act. would introduce criminal penalties. Some tax attorneys have questioned whether these proposals are too harsh or might undermine amnesty or voluntary compliance. [86]

Address Tax Shelters; Codify Economic Substance Doctrine

The proposed Stop Tax Haven Abuse Act would make a number of additional changes addressing tax shelters, including prohibiting the patenting of tax shelters, developing an examination procedure so that bank regulators could detect questionable tax activities, disallowing fees contingent on tax savings, removing communication barriers between enforcement agencies, codifying regulations, making it clear that prohibition of disclosure by tax preparers does not prevent congressional subpoenas, and providing standards for tax shelter opinion letters.

It would also codify the economic substance doctrine. This proposal is discussed among options for reducing corporate tax avoidance, but would also be applicable to individual evasion issues. The health reform legislation (P.L. 111-148) codified the economic substance doctrine.

Regulate the Rules Used by States to Permit Incorporation

Blum suggests that all U.S. Limited Liability Companies (LLCs) have a taxpayer ID number, a requirement not imposed in Delaware and other states that keep no records of ownership. S. 569 would tighten regulations to require record-keeping and identification of beneficial owners of corporations and LLCs and commission a study of partnerships and trusts.

Make Suspicious Activity Reports Available to Civil Side of IRS

The proposal that information on suspicious activity reports filed by financial institutions under anti-money laundering acts be made available to the civil side of IRS was made by Blum, who indicated that agency policy at the top levels had prohibited this information sharing. It is included in a provision in the Stop Tax Haven Abuse Act.

SUMMARY OF ENACTED LEGISLATION

Two bills contain provisions relating to international compliance, the HIRE Act and the health reform legislation.

The Hiring Incentives to Restore Employment (HIRE) Act (P.L. 111-147)

The foreign provisions in this act are projected to have a relatively small effect, $8.7 billion over 10 years, when compared with estimated costs of international evasion of around $40 billion a year.

Reporting on Foreign Accounts

This provision would institute withholding on payments, at a 30% rate, to foreign financial institutions and other institutions unless certain requirements are met. Although the provision allows considerable regulatory scope, the requirements include providing specific details on U.S. beneficial owners. The institution determines U.S. beneficial owners, with oversight by the Treasury.

Deduction of Interest for Bearer (Non-Registered) Bonds

Non-registered bonds (with some exceptions, including those issued by natural persons, not for public sale, or of maturities of less than a year) are subject to restrictions, including an excise tax and denial of interest deductions; there is an exception for foreign targeted bonds. Foreign- targeted bonds are designed to be sold to non-U.S. persons, payable outside of the United States, and containing a statement that any bond held by a U.S. person will be subject to U.S. tax laws. This provision would repeal the foreign targeted bond exception for purposes of interest deductibility. Non-registered state and local bond interest for these bonds are also not eligible for tax exclusion.

Additional Information Reported on Tax Returns

Individuals who are required to file an FBAR (Foreign Bank and Financial Account Report) would also be required to report this information on the tax return if the amount in the account is $50,000 or more. For purposes of this report on the tax return, interests in foreign trusts would also be included. A presumption will be made that the amount of the account is at least $50,000 when no detailed information is provided.

Penalties

The 20% accuracy-related penalty that already applies would be increased to 40% for transactions involving foreign accounts where the taxpayer failed to disclose reportable information. A reasonable cause exception would not be available. In the case of failure to report or underreporting foreign trusts, the initial penalty is 35% of the trust amount (5% in certain cases). If the failure to report continues for 90 days, an additional penalty of $10,000 is imposed for each 30-day period, but the total cannot exceed the amount of the trust. This provision would change the initial penalty from 35% (5%) of the trust amount a minimum of $10,000. The $10,000 for each 30-day period would be continued indefinitely, with a refund of any excess when the taxpayer does report. This proposal addresses the problem of the IRS not being able to assess a penalty because it cannot determine the amount in the account.

Statute of Limitations

The statute of limitations for cross-border transactions is extended from three to six years in instances where more than $5,000 of income is omitted.

Reporting on Foreign Passive Investment Companies

The legislation addresses reporting by passive foreign investment companies (PFICs) by codifying proposed regulations requiring shareholders to file annual information reports. The Secretary of the Treasury has regulatory authority over the type of information and can also provide for regulations that address duplicate reporting from other provisions in the legislation.

Electronic Filing

Electronic filing is required of persons who file at least 250 returns (including information returns). This legislation requires electronic filing for financial institutions regardless of whether the institution provides 250 returns, which would generally be relevant to foreign financial institutions.

Trusts

The legislation would further restrict foreign trusts by treating the grantor as the owner if there is a future contingency for a U.S. beneficiary or an agreement the grantor is involved in that might provide for a U.S. beneficiary. It also places the burden of proof on the grantor, treats a loan or use of property without appropriate compensation as a benefit, and requires information reporting.

Treat Equity Swaps as Dividends

This provision addresses the problem of disguising dividends that are subject to taxation as interest that is not. This provision, which would generally treat equity swaps as dividends, would raise $1.1 billion for FY20 11 -FY2020 according to the President's proposals.

Economic Substance Doctrine: The Patient Protection and Affordable Care Act, P.L. 111-148

The health reform included the codification of the economic substance doctrine, requiring both a subjective (profit intended) and objective (profit achieved) test. This provision has been enacted as part of the revenue offsets and, although not specifically targeted to foreign transactions, would have a potential impact.

The Act: P.L. 111-226

On May 20, 2010, the Ways and Means Committee Chairman Levin and Senate Finance Committee Baucus released a plan for combining Senate and House proposals for extending temporary tax benefits and providing for spending increases.[87] Among the revenue raisers were several foreign provisions largely relating to the foreign tax credit, which were developed jointly with the Treasury Department. Some are also included in the President's 2011 budget proposals. They would raise $14.451 billion over 10 years. These provisions were adopted as part of H.R. 4213 on May 28, 2010.

Some of these issues arise from the overall limit on the foreign tax credit, which allows aggregate foreign taxes paid abroad to be credited against U.S. tax on aggregate foreign earnings. Under these rules, firms are either in excess credit positions (they have foreign taxes that cannot be used because aggregate foreign taxes exceed aggregate U.S. tax on foreign source income) or in an excess limit position (they don't have enough foreign taxes to offset U.S. tax on foreign source income). In the former case, any technique that increases the amount of their income that is considered foreign source reduces overall tax because it increases the limit on foreign tax credits; in the latter case, any technique that allows recognition of foreign taxes without the accompanying income reduces taxes.

H.R. 4213 was not enacted, but a smaller spending bill using H.R. 1586 as a vehicle included most of the foreign provisions in H.R. 4213. H.R. 1586 provided money to the states for education and Medicaid funding, with costs paid for in part by these foreign revisions. It was signed into law on August 10, 2010. The provisions are summarized below.

Preventing Splitting Foreign Tax Credits from Income

This provision would address the issue of reverse hybrids and mechanisms that allow firms to recognize and take credits for foreign taxes paid without reporting the income that gave rise to the foreign taxes (discussed earlier in this report), thus using those credits to offset tax on unrelated income. The proposal would implement a matching rule so that foreign tax credits would not be recognized until the income is taken into account. This proposal is estimated to raise $6.325 billion over 10 years.

Denial of Foreign Tax credits for Covered Asset Acquisitions

Taxpayers can acquire a firm by purchasing stock or by purchasing the underlying assets. In the latter case, assets are valued at current market value, which generally increases depreciation deductions. Certain U.S. tax rules allow a stock acquisition to be treated as an asset acquisition. Foreign governments may not apply a similar rule. As a result, depreciation deductions under the foreign rules are smaller than under the U.S. rules, and income and foreign taxes paid are higher. The excess of foreign taxes over U.S. taxes on this transaction can be used to offset U.S. tax on unrelated foreign income under the overall foreign tax credit limitation. Such an outcome can also occur when taxpayers acquire entities that are partnerships for U.S. purposes and corporations for foreign tax purposes. The proposal would prevent firms from obtaining credits for these excess taxes. This proposal is estimated to raise $4.025 billion over 10 years.

Separate Foreign Tax Credit Limit for Items Resourced Under Treaties

Current tax treaties provide that some income that would normally be considered U.S. source income can be resourced in foreign countries. For example, interest paid on U.S. securities to a firm's foreign subsidiary would normally be U.S. source income, but under a treaty may be sourced in the foreign country. The foreign country may tax net interest (interest income less interest paid), but the entire gross interest payment would be considered foreign source and eligible for offsetting foreign tax credits. This increase in foreign source income could, absent other provisions, lead to tax reductions from excess foreign taxes on other income. Current law places this operation in a separate foreign tax credit basket when the foreign firm is a subsidiary of a U.S. firm incorporated abroad. This provision extends the treatment to branch operations and disregarded entities (that are treated the same as branches under check the box rules). The provision would apply to taxable years beginning after the date of enactment. This proposal is estimated to raise $253 million over 10 years.

Limitation on the Use of Section 956 (the "Hopscotch" Rule)

The hopscotch rules issue arises from the combination of two different tax provisions. The first is the treatment of dividends from foreign subsidiaries when there are multiple tiers of these subsidiaries. For example, a U.S. parent might have a subsidiary (tier 1), which in turn has a subsidiary (tier 2). If a tier 2 firm wants to pay a dividend to the parent, it would first be paid to the tier 1 subsidiary, which would in turn pay it to the parent. The foreign tax credit allowed would be a blend of the tax rate in the tier one subsidiary and the tier 2 subsidiary. For example, if one-half of the income of the tier 1 subsidiary was its own and the tax rate was 10% and one-half was from the payment from the tier 2 firm with a 50% tax rate, and dividend paid by the tier 1 subsidiary to the U.S. parent would have a 30% rate. These deemed taxes paid could be used for foreign tax credits against any U.S. tax on foreign source income. The second provision is Section 956, which was designed to prevent firms from returning income to the U. S. parent without paying tax, but using methods such as lending to the parent or buying property from the parent. A payment made in this fashion is construed as a dividend. Therefore, if the tier 2 subsidiary made a transaction that fell into the Section 956 rules, it could "hopscotch" over the tier 1 subsidiary and receive a full 50% tax rate: two-thirds larger than the 30% rate allowed under the blended credit rule. This provision preserves the blended rate in the case of Section 956 transactions. This proposal is estimated to raise $1.010 billion over 10 years.

Special Rule for Certain Redemptions by Foreign Subsidiaries

This issue relates to circumstances where a foreign multinational company owns a U.S. firm, which in turn owns a foreign subsidiary, and the foreign subsidiary purchases stock in the U.S. firm from the foreign multinational with cash. The cash payment can be considered a direct dividend payment to the foreign multinational up to the earnings and profits of the foreign subsidiary and thus bypasses the U.S. tax system. (If earnings and profits of the subsidiary are exhausted the payment comes from earnings and profits of the U.S. company and are subject to dividend withholding taxes unless exempted by treaty.) The earnings and profits of the foreign subsidiary are reduced by the amount of the payment so that they are not available for future taxation. If the foreign subsidiary had paid a dividend directly to the U.S. parent, it would have been subject to tax at the firm level and to a withholding tax on the dividend (unless exempted by treaty). This provisions would not allow earnings and profits of the foreign subsidiary to be taken into account if more than 50% of the dividend would bypass the U.S. tax system. This proposal is estimated to raise $255 million over 10 years.

Modification of Affiliation Rules for Allocating Interest Expense

Foreign tax credits are limited to the U.S. tax that would be due on foreign source income if taxed in the United States. In determining foreign source income, a share of the interest paid by the U.S. parent and related U.S. affiliates is assigned to foreign income based on the share of total assets that are foreign. The more interest that is assigned to foreign sources, the smaller the foreign source income and the lower the foreign tax credit limit. Although the affiliate rules generally exclude foreign corporations, a special provision applies to foreign affiliates that are 80% owned and where 50% of earnings are effectively connected to U.S. business to prevent firms from hiding their interest in these types of affiliates. If the effectively connected earnings are greater than 80%, all interest and assets are taken into account. If the effectively connected earnings are between 50% and 80%, only the effectively connected assets and earnings are included. This provision provides that all assets and interest are included as long as effectively connected earnings are 50% or more. This proposal is estimated to raise $405 million over 10 years.

Repeal of 80/20 Rules

Under current law, dividends and interest paid by a domestic corporation are generally U.S. source income and subject to gross basis withholding if paid to a foreign person. (As discussed earlier in this report, portfolio interest and bank deposit interest paid to foreigners is exempt.) Interest and dividends paid by a firm with a least 80% of its gross income foreign source and due to an active foreign business are not subject to withholding. This interest can also increase foreign source income and the foreign tax credit limit. The determination of eligibility is made during the previous three-year period. The bill would repeal the 80/20 company rules (and also the 80/20 rules for resident alien individuals). The proposal would grandfather existing 80/20 companies if they also meet a new test (that combines the company with its existing subsidiaries) and if it does not add a new substantial line of business. It also excludes payment of interest on existing obligations. This provision is estimated to raise $153 million over 10 years.

Technical Correction to the HIRE Act

The bill would make a technical correction to the foreign compliance provisions of the Hiring Incentives to Restore Employment Act (P.L. 111-147) to clarify the statute of limitations.

Summary of Legislative Proposals

This section summarizes current legislative proposals that are designed to address or have consequences for international tax evasion and avoidance.

American Jobs and Closing Loopholes Act (H.R. 4213)

As noted above, most foreign provisions in H.R. 4213 were included in the act, P.L. 111-226. Below are two provisions, one specifically a foreign provision and one related to foreign tax issues, that were not included.

Source Rules on Guarantees

Dividends and interest are generally sourced depending on the residence of the payor, whereas payments for services are sourced to the country where the service is performed. The treatment of guarantee fees is unclear, depending on whether compared to interest or services. Sourcing these payments like services allows U.S. subsidiaries of foreign firms to make deductible payments that reduce U.S. income without paying the withholding tax (as they would with interest). This provision treats these fees the same as interest: sourced to the residence of the payor. Payments by foreign persons are also U.S. source if allocable to income effectively connected with U.S. business. Treasury is to identify other transactions that are in the nature of guarantees. This proposal is estimated to raise $2.025 billion over 10 years.

Boot-Within-Gain

The boot-within-gain revisions are generally applicable to domestic as well as foreign activities, but have implications for international transactions. When a person or firm sells stock and uses the proceeds to purchase other stocks, capital gain is recognized to the extent that the sales price of the stock exceeds the basis of that stock (typically what was originally paid for it). In general, a gain is not recognized in exchanges of stock in corporate reorganizations. If the exchange includes cash or property ("boot"), gain is recognized to the extent of the boot. If the boot is more than the gain, all of the boot will not be taxed. However, if the boot is considered equivalent to a dividend, it will be taxed in full. One of the rules that allows the payment not to be considered as a dividend is a termination of interest (liquidation). Check-the-box rules permit a transaction to be considered a liquidation for U.S. purposes (i.e., a disregarded entity), but not for foreign purposes. Thus one foreign subsidiary of a U.S. firm can pay cash to the U.S. parent for stock in another foreign subsidiary of the U.S. firm without the transactions being viewed as a dividend repatriation, thereby potentially reducing U.S. tax. In addition, two U.S. subsidiaries of a foreign parent can engage in a similar transaction without generated a U.S. withholding tax on the dividend. If the foreign parent does not have a treaty eliminating the tax, this treatment reduces U.S. taxes. This revision would treat payments in these cases as a dividend.

President Obama's International Tax Proposals[88]

President Obama's international proposals include several proposals that relate to multinational corporations: allocation of deductions and credits, a restriction on use of foreign tax credits when associated income is not recognized, and a restriction on check-the-box. They also include proposals addressing individual tax evasion. Overall these provisions are projected to raise $210 billion for FY2010-FY2019 as presented in the 2010 budget and $122 billion for FY2011-FY2020 as presented in the FY2011 budget. The provisions are discussed in the order in which they are presented unless otherwise noted, since revenue effects depend on that order. Note also that the budget proposes additional resources for the IRS for international enforcement.

Some of the President's proposals have been adopted. Two provisions relating to foreign tax credits were enacted in P.L. 111-226, and are noted. The HIRE Act (P.L. 111-147) included a provision treating equity swaps and other dividend equivalent payments as dividends; the other foreign compliance provisions were, in most cases, also in the President's FY20 10 or FY20 11 proposals. These provisions are not listed. The health reform legislation also included the economic substance doctrine which, although not specifically part of the international provisions in the budget proposals, is relevant to foreign enforcement.

Provisions Affecting Multinational Corporations and Other Tax Law Changes

Hybrid Entities and Check-the Box

The most significant provision in the FY2010 budget, based on revenue gain, is a revision directed at hybrid entities and check-the-box. This provision requires that a corporation cannot disregard a subsidiary corporation unless it is incorporated in the same jurisdiction. This rule does not apply to the parent and its first level subsidiary. Thus, a U.S. parent with a subsidiary in a low tax country could treat that subsidiary as a branch (disregard it as a separate entity). The subsidiary in the low-tax country, however, could not treat its own high-tax country subsidiary as a disregarded entity. This provision was included in the FY2010 proposals, where it was projected to raise $86.5 billion for FY2010-FY2019.[89] It was not included in the FY20 11 budget.

Allocation of Deductions and Credits

Two of these proposals would allocate deductions and credits, so as to deny those benefits until income is repatriated. This approach was included in a tax reform bill introduced by Chairman Rangel of the Ways and Means Committee in 2007 (H.R. 3970). A portion of overall deductions, such as interest, that reflects the share of foreign deferred income, would be disallowed until the income is repatriated. The foreign tax credit allocation rule would allow credits for the share of foreign taxes paid that is equal to the share of foreign source income repatriated, a provision the discussion of the proposals refers to as pooling. Disallowed deductions and credits would be carried forward. The proposal specifically excludes deductions for research and experimentation from the allocation rule. The FY20 11 budget proposal was narrower, and it was limited to interest deductions; it also includes a different set of allocation rules.

The revenue gain for FY2019-FY2020 was $25.6 billion for the limit on interest deductions and $32.0 billion for the foreign tax credit pooling. The FY2010-FY2019 budget proposal was $60.1 billion for the deduction allocation and $24.5 billion for the foreign tax credit pooling in the FY2010 budget.

Limiting the Foreign Tax Credit; Reverse Hybrids (Enacted in P.L. 111-226)

Another provision aimed at multinational corporations would disallow foreign tax credits when the associated income is not received, as can occur with reverse hybrids. A matching rule would apply. This provision is estimated to raise $27.4 billion for FY20 1 1-FY2020. (Note that a similar proposal was included in H.R. 4213, but was scored at only $6 billion).

Taxing Excess Returns on Intangibles

This provision, which appears only in the 2011 budget proposal, would treat excess returns in a low-tax country on intangibles transferred to it from the United States as Subpart F income (subject to current taxation) and in a separate foreign tax credit basket (so that other foreign taxes could not offset U.S. taxes due on the excess returns). This provision is scored at $15.5 billion for FY2011-FY2020.

Transfer Pricing of Intangibles

The proposal would clarify several rules that are relevant to the transfer of intangibles. First, it would clarify that intangibles include workforce in place, goodwill, and going concern value. Second, it would allow the IRS commission to aggregate intangibles if that leads to a more appropriate value. Finally, it would clarify that intangibles are to valued at their highest and best as it would be by a willing buyer and seller with reasonable knowledge of the relevant facts. This provision is projected to raise $1.2 billion for FY2011 -FY2020.

Disallow Deductions for Reinsurance Premiums to Foreign Affiliates

U.S. insurance companies can reduce taxes by purchasing reinsurance from foreign affiliates, with a deduction of the premiums by the U.S. firm but no tax on the income of the foreign affiliate. This provision would disallow these deductions for reinsurance premiums when they are more than 50% of the basic premiums received. This provision is contained only in the FY20 11 budget and is projected to raise $519 billion in revenue from 2011-2020.

Earnings Stripping by Inverted Firms

The proposal would apply the provisions on earnings stripping discussed in 2004 to inverted firms. For these firms the debt-to-equity safe harbor would be eliminated and non-guaranteed related party debt would not be deductible when debt exceeded the 25% threshold. Carryforwards of disallowed interest would be limited. This provision is projected to raise $3.6 billion for FY20 1 1-FY2020. The FY20 11 provision appears broader than the FY20 10 provision because it covers debt paid to unrelated parties but guaranteed by a related party.

Prevent Repatriation of Earnings in Cross-Border Transactions (Boot-Within Gain)

The plan includes a proposal to require that distributions that are characterized as reorganizations but are in the nature of a dividend repatriation are subject to tax. This issue arises within the framework of an exchange of stock on the one hand for stock and property (called "boot") and rules that provide the minimum of gain be based on the boot or overall gain. This proposal is projected to raise $297 million from FY2010 to FY2019. The 2011 budget includes a broader provision regarding to boot in gain that covers domestic transactions as well, and such a provision is also included in H.R. 4213.

Repeal 80/20 Rules (Enacted in P.L. 111-226)

This provision is related to dividends and affects individuals. Under current law, withholding is applied to interest and dividends paid by corporations, but there is an exception for firms who have 80% of their income from active foreign operations. This provision would repeal that exception, raising projected revenues of $1.2 billion for FY20 11 -FY2020.

Foreign Tax Credits for Dual Capacity Taxpayers

This provision would disallow a foreign tax credit for taxes paid where there is an income tax that is paid in part to receive a benefit (i.e., the firm is paying a tax in a dual capacity) unless the income tax is generally imposed on the country's own residents as well as foreign persons. The current rule does not require the tax to be imposed on the country's residents. This provision typically relates to taxes being substituted for royalties in oil producing countries; there is a provision that it will not abrogate any existing treaties. This provision was projected to raise $4.5 billion for FY2010-FY2019. The FY2011 budget has a slightly different provision that restricts the tax credit to the amount that would be paid if the taxpayer were not a dual capacity taxpayer. The FY2011-FY2020 revenue loss was $8.5 billion.

Provisions Relating to Individual Tax Evasion, Not Enacted in the HIRE Act

The President's proposals included a number of provisions relating to individual evasion, including reporting of information, withholding, and various penalties. Overall these provisions were projected to raise revenues of $8.7 billion from FY2010 to FY2019 in the FY2010 budget and $5.4 billion from FY2011 -FY2029 in the FY2011 budget. Most of these provisions, or some version of them, were adopted in the HIRE Act, including increased reporting on foreign accounts (withholding and information on U.S. beneficial owners). The remaining provisions are summarized below.

Reporting on Transfers

U.S. persons financial intermediaries and qualified intermediaries would be required to report financial transfers. U.S. persons and qualified intermediaries would be required to report the formation or establishment of a foreign entity. The floor is $10,000 in the FY2010 budget proposal, but $50,000 in the FY2011 proposal.

Additional Information Reported on Tax Returns: Lower Floor

The HIRE Act required individuals who are required to file an FBAR (Foreign Bank and Financial Account Reports) to report t his information on the tax return if the amount in the account is $50,000 or more, a provision similar to the FY20 11 budget proposal. The FY20 10 proposal had a lower floor of $10,000.

Burden of Proof and Presumption Provisions

The FY2010 proposal contains a number of provisions that provide evidentiary presumptions (shifts in the burden of proof) in civil and administrative cases. If an individual has a foreign account it is presumed to be large enough to require filing an FBAR. If a person has an account of over $200,000 it is presumed that failure to file is willful (which opens the possibility of criminal as well as higher civil penalties). If a payment subject to withholding is made to a foreign person on an FDAP, the presumption is that that person is not eligible for withholding.

Statute of Limitation: No Floor

The statute of limitations for cross-border transactions is extended from three to six years with no floor in the FY2010 budget proposal; in the HIRE Act and the FY2011 budget, it applies to instances where more than $5,000 of income is omitted.

Stop Tax Haven Abuse Act, S. 506 and H.R. 1265[90]

This bill has been introduced in the Senate by Senator Carl Levin and in the House by Representative Lloyd Doggett. As with the President's proposals, some of these provisions or related provisions were included in the HIRE Act. Provisions in the Stop Tax Haven Abuse that are addressed in the HIRE Act (P.L. 11 1-147)include burden of proof (Section 101), statute of limitations (Section 104), information reporting on U.S. beneficiaries of foreign accounts (Section 105), trust abuses (Section 106), treatment of dividend equivalents (Section 108), and PFICs (Section 109). Also, the health reform legislation included the economic substance doctrine. The bill is summarized as introduced, including the provisions that have been enacted.

Section 101 would provide a burden of proof change. It would require the taxpayer involved in offshore secrecy jurisdictions to produce evidence, based on the presumption that the taxpayer is in control, that funds or other property are not taxable income, and that the account is not large enough to trigger a reporting threshold. (The bill also addresses securities law issues.) This section also contains the list of 34 tax haven jurisdictions taken from IRS court filings, and provides Treasury with the authority to add or remove jurisdictions. An important standard for being excluded from the list is an effective, and automatic, exchange of information.

Section 102 would expand the provisions in the Patriot Act of 2001, which gave Treasury the authority to require domestic financial institutions to take special measures (including providing information and prohibiting transactions) with respect to foreign jurisdictions relating to money laundering to cover instances of impeding U.S. tax enforcement.

Section 103 would require a publicly traded corporation or one with gross assets of $50 million or more whose management and control occurs primarily in the United States to be treated as a U.S. company. This provision is directed at shell corporations, including hedge funds and investment management businesses, set up in jurisdictions such as the Cayman Islands. It would not apply to subsidiaries of U.S. corporations simply because some decisions are made at the parent headquarters, but would still apply to shell subsidiaries.

Section 104 would extend the limit on audit periods from three years to six years for offshore jurisdictions with secrecy laws.

Section 105 would require U.S. financial institutions and brokers to file 1099 forms for any foreign account when they know the beneficial owner is a U.S. person. It would also require these institutions to report to the IRS when they set up offshore accounts and entities.

Section 106 addresses potential trust abuses. Foreign trusts have employed liaisons called trust protectors as a way for shielding U.S. taxpayers exercising control over the trust; the legislation provides that any powers held by a trust protector would be attributed to the trust grantor. It also provides that any U.S. person benefitting from a trust is treated as a beneficiary even if not named in the trust instrument, that future or contingent beneficiaries are treated as current ones, and that loans of assets and property as well as cash or security are treated as trust distributions.

Section 107 addresses legal opinions, stating that an activity is more likely than not to survive challenge by the IRS, which are used to shield taxpayers from large penalties. The legislation provides that a legal opinion of this nature would not apply in an offshore secrecy jurisdiction, providing exceptions to protect legitimate operations.

Section 108 would prevent dividend equivalents from escaping the dividend withholding tax.

Section 109 addresses reporting by passive foreign investment corporations (PFICs) by codifying proposed regulations regarding PFIC reporting by direct or indirect shareholders who are U.S. persons, and also requiring reporting by U.S. persons who directly or indirectly cause the PFIC to be formed or sent or receive assets.

Some of the sections of title II of the bill affect securities law rather than tax issues. Some provisions are tax-related, however.

Section 204 addresses an IRS John Doe summons where the IRS does not know the names of taxpayers and now must ask courts for permission to serve the summons. This section provides that in any case involving offshore secret accounts, the court is to presume tax compliance is at issue, to relieve the IRS of the obligation when the only records sought are U.S. bank records, and to allow them to issue John Doe summonses for large investigative projects without addressing each set of summonses separately.

Section 205 would address issues relating to the Foreign Bank and Financial Account Report (FBAR) requirement for a person controlling a foreign financial account of over $10,000. This is a additional rule from the requirement to report this information on the tax return, and IRS is now charged with enforcing this FBAR requirement. This provision would amend tax disclosure rules to more easily permit IRS to use tax data, change the penalty to refer to the highest average in the account during a year (and not on a specific day), and allow IRS access to information on Suspicious Activity Reports (SAR).

The last title of the bill relates to abusive tax shelters, and contains several provisions. It would strengthen penalties, prohibit the patenting of tax shelters, require development of an examination procedure so that bank regulators could detect questionable tax activities, disallow fees contingent on tax savings for tax shelters, remove communication barriers between enforcement agencies, codify regulations and make it clear that prohibition of disclosure by tax preparers does not prevent congressional subpoenas, and provide standards for tax shelter opinion letters. It would also codify the economic substance doctrine, to require both an objective and subjective test for economic substance.

Finance Committee Proposal

A draft of this proposal was circulated on March 12 and has been discussed by Sullivan.[91] Several of its proposals were included in the HIRE Act (statute of limitations, requiring FBAR information to be filed with the tax return, increasing trust penalties to a minimum of $10,000, expanding the definition of distributions, and increasing the penalties for underpayments associated with foreign accounts).

- It would require entities transferring funds offshore to report to the IRS the amount, destination, and account information. Publicly traded companies would be excluded.
- The statute of limitations would be extended from three to six years for tax returns that report or should have reported certain international transactions.
- It would require the foreign bank and financial account report (FBAR) to be filed with the tax returns.
- Tax preparers would be required to ask due diligence questions to determine whether an FBAR should be filed.
- The foreign trust failure-to-file penalty would be increased to a $10,000 minimum and the definition of property considered to be a distribution for foreign trusts would be expanded, and would include artwork and jewelry.
- Fines and penalties on payments attributable to certain offshore transactions would be doubled.
- A provision in the Heroes Earnings Assistance and Relief Tax Act of 2008 (P.L. 110-245) would be modified to require offshore entities that hire workers under a government contract be treated as American employers by establishing a rule that any individual who performs at least 100 hours of service a month is an employee and not an independent contractor.

Fraud Enforcement and Recovery Act, S. 386

This proposal, introduced by the Chairman Leahy of the Senate Judiciary Committee, includes a provision to apply the international money laundering statute to tax evasion, and set aside funds for the Justice Department to pursue financial fraud, including funds to the tax division. It has been passed by the Senate. The House version of the bill, H.R. 1748, does not include the tax provision but does include additional funds.

Incorporation Transparency and Law Enforcement Assistance Act, S. 569

This proposal would establish uniform requirements for states relating to the disclosure of beneficial owners of corporations and limited liability companies, including updating and maintenance of information after terminating, imposing additional requirements for those not U.S. citizens or permanent residents, providing penalties, and updating of such disclosures. It also authorizes a study of requirements of partnerships, trusts, and other legal entities. This bill is relevant, among other things, to issues raised about the use of states as international tax havens.

The Bipartisan Tax Fairness and Simplification Act, S. 3018

This general tax reform proposal introduced by Senators Wyden and Gregg would, among other changes, lower the corporate tax rate from 35% to 24%. Among the base broadening provisions is a repeal of deferral and imposition of a per country foreign tax credit limit. The latter proposal would prevent cross-crediting across different countries. The bill also includes withholding on all foreign accounts, regardless of whether the account is considered by the foreign institution to have a U.S. beneficiary, unless there is full information reporting.

End Notes

[1] See U.S. Senate Subcommittee on Investigations, *Staff Report on Dividend Tax Abuse*, September 11, 2008.

[2] Joseph Guttentag and Reven Avi-Yonah, "Closing the International Tax Gap, In Max B. Sawicky, ed. *Bridging the Tax Gap: Addressing the Crisis in Federal Tax Administration*, Washington, DC, Economic Policy Institute, 2005.

[3] For a chronology, see Martin Sullivan, "Proposals to Fight Offshore Tax Evasion, Part 3," *Tax Notes* May 4, 2009, p. 517.

[4] Organization for Economic Development and Cooperation, *Harmful Tax Competition: An Emerging Global Issue*, 1998, p. 23.

[5] J.R. Hines and E.M. Rice, "Fiscal Paradise: Foreign Tax havens and American Business," *Quarterly Journal of Economics*, vol. 109, February 1994, pp. 149-182.

[6] Government Accountability Office, International Taxation: Large U.S. Corporations and Federal Contractors with Subsidiaries in Jurisdictions Listed as Tax Havens or Financial Privacy Jurisdictions, GAO-op-157, December 2008.

[7] J. C. Sharman, *Havens in a Storm, The Struggle for Global Tax Regulation*, Cornell University Press, Ithaca, New York, 2006; Martin A. Sullivan, "Lessons From the Last War on Tax Havens," *Tax Notes*, July 30, 2007, pp. 327-337.

[8] David Spencer and J.C. Sharman, International Tax Cooperation, *Journal of International Taxation*, published in three parts in December 2007, pp. 35-49, January 2008, pp. 27-44, 64, February 2008, pp. 39-58.

[9] For a discussion of these cases see Joint Committee on Taxation *Tax Compliance and Enforcement Issues With Respect to Offshore Entities and Accounts*, JCX-23-09, March 30, 2009. The discussion of UBS begins on p. 31 and the discussion of LGT begins on p. 40. This document also discusses the inquiries of the Permanent Subcommittee on Investigations of the Senate Homeland Security Committee relating to these cases.

[10] Anthony Faiola and Mary Jordan, "Tax-Haven Blacklist Stirs Nations: After G-20 Issues mandate, Many Rush to Get Off Roll," *Washington Post*, April 4, p. A7.

[11] This announcement by the OECD was posted at http://www.oecd.org/document/0/ 0,3343,en_2649_ 34487_42521280_1_1_1_1,00.html.

[12] David D. Stewart, "G-20 Declares End to Bank Secrecy as OECD Issues Tiered List," *Tax Notes*, April 6, 2009, pp. 3 8-39.

[13] Organization for Economic Development and Cooperation, http://www.oecd.org/dataoecd/50/0/43606256.pdf.

[14] See, for example, Micheil van Dijk, Francix Weyzig, and Richard Murphy, *The Netherlands: A Tax Haven?* SOMO (Centre for Research on Multinational Corporations), Amersterdam, 2007 and Rosanne Altshuler and Harry Grubert, "Governments and Multinational Corporations in the Race to the Bottom, Tax Notes, February 27, 2009, pp. 979-992.

[15] Fergal O'Brien, "Bono, Preacher on Poverty, Tarnishes Halo Irish Tax Move," October 15, 2006, Bloomberg.com, http://bloomberg.com/apps/news?pid=20601109&refer=home&sid=aef6sR60oDgM#.

[16] Charles Gnaedinger, "Luxembourg P.M Calls out U.S. States as Tax Havens" *Tax Notes International*, April 6, 2009, p. 13.

[17] http://www.offshore-fox.com/offshore-corporations/offshore_corporations_0401.html.

[18] Another offshore website lists in addition to the countries in Table 1 Austria, Campione d'Italia, Denmark, Hungary, Iceland, Madeira, Russian Federation, United Kingdom, Brunei, Dubai, Lebanon, Canada, Puerto Rico, South Africa, New Zealand, Labuan, Uruguay, and the United States. See http://www.mydeltaquest.com/english/.

[19] http://www.offshore-manual.com/taxhavens/.

[20] "Haven Hypocrisy," *The Economist*, March 26, 2008.

[21] Michael McIntyre, "A Program for International Tax Reform," *Tax Notes*, February 23, 2009, pp. 102 1-1026.

[22] Charles Gnaedinger, "U. S.,Cayman Islands Debate Tax Haven Status," *Tax Notes*, May 4, 2009, p. 548-545.

[23] http://www.oecd.org/document/60/0,3343,en_2649_34897_1942460_1_1_1_1,00.html.

[24] For tax rates see http://www.worldwide

[25] Tax Justice Network, *Tax Us if You Can*, September, 2005.

[26] Effects on economic activity are addressed in CRS Report RL341 15, *Reform of U.S. International Taxation: Alternatives*, by Jane G. Gravelle.

[27] Harry Grubert, "Intangible Income, Intercompany Transactions, Income Shifting and the Choice of Locations," *National Tax Journal*, vol. 56, March 2003, Part II, pp. 22 1-242.

[28] Simon J. Pak and John S. Zdanowicz, *U.S. Trade With the World, An Estimate of 2001 Lost U.S. Federal Income Tax Revenues Due to Over-Invoiced Imports and Under-Invoiced Exports*, October 31, 2002.

[29] CRS Report R40 178, *Tax Cuts on Repatriation Earnings as Economic Stimulus: An Economic Analysis*, by Donald J. Marples and Jane G. Gravelle.

[30] In 2004 the interest allocation rules were changed to allocate worldwide interest, but the implementation of that provision was delayed and has not yet taken place. See CRS Report RL34494, *The Foreign Tax Credit's Interest Allocation Rules*, by Jane G. Gravelle and Donald J. Marples.

[31] See CRS Report RL34249, The Tax Reduction and Reform Act of 2007: An Overview, by Jane G. Gravelle.

[32] U.S. Department of Treasury, *Report to Congress on Earnings Stripping, Transfer Pricing and U.S. Income Tax Treaties*, November 2007.

[33] The Treasury Department recently issued new proposed regulations relating to cost sharing arrangements. See Treasury Decision 9441, Federal Register, vol. 74, No. 2, January 5, 2009, pp. 340-391. These rules include a periodic adjustment which would, among other aspects, examine outcomes. See "Cost Sharing Periodic Payments Not Automatic, Officials Say," *Tax Notes*, February 23, 2009, p. 955.

[34] Michael McDonald, "Income Shifting from Transfer Pricing: Further Evidence from Tax Return Data," U.S. Department of the Treasury, Office of Tax Analysis, OTA Technical Working Paper 2, July 2008.

[35] See for example William W. Chip, "'Manufacturing' Foreign Base Company Sales Income," *Tax Notes*, November 19, 2007, p. 803-808.

[36] See David R. Sicular, "The New Look-Through Rule: W(h)ither Subpart F? *Tax Notes*, April 23, 2007, pp. 349-378 for a discussion of the look-through rules under Section 954(c)(6).

[37] For a discussion of reverse hybrids see Joseph M. Calianno and J. Michael Cornett, "Guardian Revision: Proposed Regulations Attach Guardian and Reverse Hybrids," *Tax Notes International*, October 2006, pp. 305-316.

[38] See Sean Foley, "U.S. Outbound: Cross border Hybrid Instrument Transactions to gain Increased Scrutiny During IRS Audit," http://www.internationaltaxreview.com/?Page=10&PUBID=35&ISS=24101&SID=697834&TYPE=20. Andrei Kraymal, International Hybrid Instruments: Jurisdiction Dependent Characterization, *Houston Business and Tax Law Journal*, 2005, http://www.hbtlj.org/v05/v05Krahmalar.pdf.

[39] Government Accountability Office, U.S. Multinational Corporations: Effective Tax Rates are Correlated With Where Income is Reported, GAO-08-950, August 2008.

[40] Harry Grubert, "Tax Credits, Source Rules, Trade and electronic Commerce: Behavioral Margins and the Design of International Tax Systems. *Tax Law Review*, vol. 58, January 2005; also issued as a CESIFO Working Paper (No. 1366), December 2004.; Harry Grubert and Rosanne Altshuler, "Corporate Taxes in a World Economy: Reforming the Taxation of Cross-Border Income," in John W. Diamond and George Zodrow, eds., *Fundamental Tax Reform: Issues, Choices and Implications*, Cambridge, MIT Press, 2008.

[41] Data on earnings and profits of controlled foreign corporations are taken from Lee Mahoney and Randy Miller, Controlled Foreign Corporations 2004, Internal Revenue Service *Statistics of Income Bulletin*, Summer 2008, http://www.irs.ustreas.gov/pub/irs-soi/04coconfor.pdf. Data on GDP from Central Intelligence Agency, *The World Factbook*, https://www.cia.gov/library/publications/the-world-factbook. Most GDP data are for 2008 and based on the exchange rate but for some countries earlier years and data based on purchasing power parity were the only data available.

[42] One offshore website points out that Canada can be desirable as a place to establish a holding company; see Shelter Offshore,http://www.shelteroffshore.com/index.php/offshore/more/canada_offshore.

[43] Harry Grubert and Rosanne Altshuler, "Corporate Taxes in a World Economy: Reforming the Taxation of Cross-Border Income," in John W. Diamond and George Zodrow, eds., *Fundamental Tax Reform: Issues, Choices and Implications*, Cambridge, MIT Press, 2008.

[44] Government Accountability Office, *U.S. Multinational Corporations: Effective Tax Rates are Correlated With Where Income is Reported*, GAO-08-950, August 2008.

[45] Martin Sullivan, U.S. Citizens Hide Hundreds of Billions in the Caymans, *Tax Notes,* May 24, 2004, p. 96.

[46] Martin Sullivan, "Extraordinary Profitability in Low-Tax Countries," *Tax Notes*, August 25, 2008, pp. 724-727. Note that the effective tax rates for some countries differ considerably depending on the source of data; the Netherlands would be classified as a low tax country based on data controlled foreign corporations but high tax based on BEA data. See Government Accountability Office, *U.S. Multinational Corporations: Effective Tax Rates are Correlated With Where Income is Reported*, GAO-08-950, August 2008.

[47] See James R. Hines, Jr., "Lessons from Behavioral Responses to International Taxation," *National Tax Journal*, vol. 52 (June 1999): 3 05-322, and Joint Committee on Taxation, *Economic Efficiency and Structural Analyses of Alternative U.S. Tax Policies for Foreign Direct Investment,* JCX-55-08, June 25, 2008 for reviews. Studies are also discussed in U.S. Department of Treasury, *The Deferral of Income of Earned Through Controlled Foreign Corporation,* May, 2000, http://www.treas.gov/offices/tax-policy

[48] This point is made by The Treasury Inspector General for Tax administration, "A Combination of Legislative Actions and Increased IRS Capability and Capacity are Required to Reduce the Multi-billion Dollar U.S. International Tax Gap," January 27 2009, 2009-I-R001.

[49] U.S. Department of the Treasury, IRS, Report on the Application and Administration of Section 482, 1999.

[50] Joint Committee on Taxation, *Estimates of Federal Tax Expenditures for 2008-2012*, October 31, 2008.

[51] Budget for FY20 10, *Analytical Perspectives*, p. 293.

[52] Harry Grubert and Rosanne Altshuler, "Corporate Taxes in the World Economy," in *Fundamental Tax Reform: Issues, Choices, and Implications* ed. John W. Diamond and George R. Zodrow, Cambridge, MIT Press, 2008.

[53] "Shifting Profits Offshore Costs U.S. Treasury $10 Billion or More," *Tax Notes*, September 27, 2004, pp. 1477-148 1; "U.S. Multinationals Shifting Profits Out of the United States," *Tax Notes*, March 10, 2008, pp. 1078-1082. $75 billion in profits is artificially shifted abroad. If all of that income were subject to U.S. tax, it would result in a gain of $26 billion for 2004. Sullivan acknowledges that there are many difficulties in determining the revenue gain. Some of this income might already be taxed under Subpart F, some might be absorbed by excess foreign tax credits, and the effective tax rate may be lower than the statutory rate. Sullivan concludes that an estimate of between $10 billion and $20 billion is appropriate. Altshuler and Grubert suggest that Sullivan's methodology may involve some double counting; however, their own analysis finds that multinationals saved $7 billion more between 1997 and 2002 due to check the box rules. Some of this gain may have been at the cost of high-tax host countries rather than the United States, however. See Rosanne Altshuler and Harry Grubert, "Governments and Multinational Corporations in the Race to the Bottom," *Tax Notes International*, February 2006, pp. 459-474.

[54] Charles W. Christian and Thomas D. Schultz, ROA-Based Estimates of Income Shifting by Multinational Corporations, *IRS Research Bulletin*, 2005 http://www.irs.gov/pub/irs-soi/05christian.pdf.

[55] Simon J. Pak and John S. Zdanowicz, *U.S. Trade With the World, An Estimate of 2001 Lost U.S. Federal Income Tax Revenues Due to Over-Invoiced Imports and Under-Invoiced Exports,* October 31, 2002.

[56] Kimberly Clausing , Multinational Firm Tax Avoidance and Tax Policy, *National Tax Journal*, vol. 62, December 2009, pp. 703-725, Working Paper, March 2008. Her method involved estimating the profit differentials as a function of tax rate differentials over the period 1982-2004 and then applying that coefficient to current earnings.

[57] Kimberly A. Clausing and Reuven S. Avi-Yonah, *Reforming Corporate Taxation in a Global Economy: A Proposal to Adopt Formulary Apportionment*, Brookings Institution: The Hamilton Project, Discussion paper 2007-2008, June 2007.

[58] Douglas Shackelford and Joel Slemrod, "The Revenue Consequences of Using Formula apportionment to Calculate U.S. and Foreign Source Income: A Firm Level Analysis," *International Tax and Public Finance*, vol. 5, no. 1, 1998, pp. 41-57.

[59] These studies are discussed and new research presented in U.S. Department of Treasury, *Report to Congress on Earnings Stripping, Transfer Pricing and U.S. Income Tax Treaties*, November 2007. One study used a different approach, examining taxes of firms before and after acquisition by foreign versus domestic acquirers, but the problem of comparison remains and the sample was very small; that study found no differences. See Jennifer L. Blouin, Julie H. Collins, and Douglas A. Shackelford, "Does Acquisition by Non-U.S. Shareholders Cause U.S. firms to Pay Less Tax?" *Journal of the American Taxation Association*, Spring 2008, pp. 25-3 8. Harry Grubert, *Debt and the Profitability of Foreign Controlled Domestic Corporations in the United States*, Office of Tax Analysis Technical Working Paper No. 1, July 2008, http://www.ustreas.gov/offices/tax-policy

[60] In addition to the 2007 Treasury study cited above, see Jim A. Seida and William F. Wempe, "Effective Tax Rate Changes and Earnings Stripping Following Corporate Inversion," *National Tax Journal*, vol. 57, December 2007, pp. 805-828. They estimated $0.7 billion of revenue loss from four firms that inverted. Inverted firms may, however, behave differently from foreign firms with U.S. subsidiaries.

[61] Harry Grubert, "Intangible Income, Intercompany Transactions, Income Shifting, and the Choice of Location," *National Tax Journal*, Vo. 56,March 2003, Part 2.

[62] Rosanne Altshuler and Harry Grubert, "Governments and Multinational Corporations in the Race to the Bottom," *Tax Notes International*, February 2006, pp. 459-474.

[63] Data are presented in "Who's Watching our Back Door?" *Business Accents*, Florida International University, Fall 2004, pp. 26-29.

[64] Data are taken from Melissa Redmiles, "The One-Time Dividends-Received Deduction," Internal Revenue Service *Statistics of Income Bulletin*, Spring 2008, http://www.irs.ustreas.gov/pub/irs-soi/08codivdeductbul.pdf.

[65] Rodney P. Mock and Andreas Simon, "Permanently Reinvested Earnings: Priceless," *Tax Notes*, November 17, 2008, pp. 83 5-848.

[66] See Joint Committee on *Taxation Tax Compliance and Enforcement Issues With Respect to Offshore Entities and Accounts*, JCX-23-09, March 30, 2009, p. 6 for a discussion.

[67] This history is described by Reuven Avi-Yonah in testimony before the Committee on Select Revenue Measures of the Ways and Means Committee, March 5, 2008.

[68] Joseph Guttentag and Reven Avi-Yonah, "Closing the International Tax Gap," in Max B. Sawicky, ed. *Bridging the Tax Gap: Addressing the Crisis in Federal Tax Administration*, Washington, D.C., Economic Policy Institute, 2005.

[69] Testimony of Reuven Avi-Yonah, Subcommittee on Select Revenue Measures, Ways and Means Committee, March 31, 2009.

[70] "Brown Pushes U.K. Tax havens On OECD Standards" *Tax Notes International*, April 20, 2009, pp. 180-181.

[71] A very clear and brief explanation of the origin of the QI program and of the requirements can be found in Martin Sullivan, "Proposals to Fight Offshore Tax Evasion," *Tax Notes*, April 20, 2009, pp. 264-268.

[72] For additional discussion of the QI program, see Joint Committee on Taxation, *Tax Compliance and Enforcement Issues With Respect to Offshore Entities and Accounts*, JCX-23-09, March 30, 2009.

[73] Martin A. Sullivan, "Proposals to Fight Offshore Tax Evasion," *Tax Notes*, April 20, 2009.

[74] Joseph Guttentag and Reven Avi-Yonah, "Closing the International Tax Gap," in Max B. Sawicky, ed. *Bridging the Tax Gap: Addressing the Crisis in Federal Tax Administration*, Washington, D.C., Economic Policy Institute, 2005.

[75] Tax Justice Network, *Tax Us If You Can,* September, 2005.

[76] CRS Report RL341 15, *Reform of U.S. International Taxation: Alternatives*, by Jane G. Gravelle.

[77] Firms with 80% continuity of ownership would be treated as U.S. firms and firms with at least 60% continuity of ownership would be subject to tax on the transfer of assets for the next 10 years.

[78] See CRS Report RL341 15, *Reform of U.S. International Taxation: Alternatives*, by Jane G. Gravelle. See also International Corporate Tax Reform Proposals: Issues and Proposals, Forthcoming, *Florida Tax Review*, by Jane G. Gravelle.

[79] Douglas Shackelford and Joel Slemrod, "The Revenue Consequences of Using Formula apportionment to Calculate U.S. and Foreign Source Income: A Firm Level Analysis," *International Tax and Public Finance*, vol. 5, no. 1, 1998, pp. 41-57.

[80] Kimberly A. Clausing and Reuven A. Avi-Yonah, *Reforming Corporate Taxation in a Global Economy : A Proposal to Adopt Formulary Apportionment*, Brookings Institution: The Hamilton Project, Discussion paper 2007-08, June 2007.

[81] These and other issues are discussed by Rosanne Altshuler and Harry Grubert, "Formula Apportionment: Is it Better than the Current System and Are There Better Alternatives?" Oxford University Centre for Business Taxation, Working paper 09/0 1.

[82] Michael P. Devereux and Simon Loretz, "The Effects of EU formula Apportionment on Corporate Tax Revenues," *Fiscal Studies*, Vol. 29, no. 1, pp. 1-33. http://www3.interscience.wiley.com/cgi-bin/fulltext/119399105/PDFSTART? CRETRY=1&SRETRY=0.

[83] Michael McIntyre, "A Program for International Tax Reform," *Tax Notes*, February 23, 2009, pp. 102 1-1026.

[84] Harry Grubert, "Tax Credits, Source Rules, Trade and Electronic Commerce: Behavioral Margins and the Design of International Tax Systems," *Tax Law Review*, vol. 58, January 2005; also issued as a CESIFO Working Paper (No. 1366), December 2004.; Harry Grubert and Rosanne Altshuler, "Corporate Taxes in a World Economy: Reforming the Taxation of Cross-Border Income," in John W. Diamond and George Zodrow, eds., *Fundamental Tax Reform: Issues, Choices and Implications*, Cambridge, MIT Press, 2008.

[85] For discussions of various proposals listed see Tax Justice Network, "Ending the Offshore Secrecy System," March 2009, http ://www.taxjustice.net/cms/upload/pdf/TJN _0903 _Action _Plan _for _G-20.pdf ; testimony of Reuven AviYonah , Peter Blessing, Stephen Shay, and Douglas Shulman before the Subcommittee on Select Revenue Measures of the Ways and Means Committee, March 31, 2009; Martin Sullivan, "Proposals to Fight Offshore Tax Evasion," *Tax Notes*, part 1, April 20, 2009, pp. 264-268; part 2: April 27, 2009, pp. 371-373; part 3, May 4, 2009, pp. 516-520; Reuven Avi-Yonah, Testimony before the Committee on Select Revenue Measures of the Ways and Means Committee, March 5, 2008; Testimony of Jack A. Blum and , Testimony on the Cayman Islands and Offshore Tax Issues before the Senate finance Committee, July 24, 2008; Michael McIntyre, "A Program for International Tax Reform," *Tax Notes*, February 23, 2009, pp. 102 1-1026.

[86] See Jeremiah Coder, "Proposed offshore Crime Legislation Worries Defense Bar," *Tax Notes Today*, March 23, 2009. The attorneys are concerned that money laundering charges would not have to be approved through the Department of Justice's tax division, that penalties of up to 20 years gives prosecutors too much power, that the provisions may trap taxpayers who want to participate in IRS voluntary disclosure, and that they would also discourage the "quiet disclosure" where taxpayers simply report past information.

[87] Press release at http://waysandmeans.house.gov/press/PRArticle.aspx?NewsID=11191; summary at http://waysandmeans.house.gov/media

[88] A summary was posted at http://www.whitehouse.gov/the_press_office/LEVELING-THE-PLAYING-FIELD-CURBING-TAX-HAVENS-AND-REMOVING-TAX-INCENTIVES-FOR-SHIFTING-JOBS-OVERSEAS/.

[89] A discussion of these provisions and revenue estimates can be found in the Treasury's Green Book, General Explanations of the Administration's Fiscal Year 2010 Revenue Proposals, http://www.treas.gov/offices/tax-policy library/grnbk09.pdf and General Explanations of the Administrations Fiscal Year 2011 Revenue Proposals, http://www.treas.gov/offices/tax-policy/library/greenbk10.pdf.

[90] For a more detailed explanation of the bill see Senator Levin's Introductory Remarks, March 3, 2009. This proposal has also been discussed by Martin Sullivan, "Proposals to Fight Offshore Tax Evasion, Part 3," *Tax Notes*, May 4, 2009, pp. 5 16-520.

[91] See Committee on Finance News Release, March 12, 2009, http://finance.senate.gov/press/Bpress/2009press/prb03 1209b.pdf; See also Martin A. Sullivan, "Proposals to fight Offshore Tax Evasion, Part 2," *Tax Notes*, April 27, 2009, pp. 371-373.

In: Corporate and International Taxation
Editor: Allison S. Garner and Daniel C. Murphy

ISBN: 978-1-61324-616-0

Chapter 6

TAXES AND INTERNATIONAL COMPETITIVENESS

Donald J. Marples

SUMMARY

The term "international competitiveness" has long been an important part of tax policy debates and most recently has been prominent in discussions about fundamental U.S. tax reform. For example, in Executive Order 13369, President Bush stated that one goal of reform should be to "strengthen the competitiveness of the United States in the global market place." And in July 2007, the U.S. Treasury Department hosted a conference on business tax policy to explore ways in which the U.S. tax system might be reformed to enhance competitiveness. Yet despite its prominent use, the meaning of "competitiveness" is often vague, with its definition frequently depending on the perspective of the user. This report looks at competitiveness from three different perspectives: that of individual domestic firms, that of multinational corporations, and that of domestic labor. In each case, the report then applies economic analysis to the competitiveness concept, which adds clarity by identifying the specific ways in which taxes affect international trade and investment. With trade, tax burdens can affect what is traded, its overall level, and who benefits from trade, but they do not directly affect the trade balance. Further, it is the pattern of relative U.S. taxes within the domestic economy that matters for trade, not how a firm's taxes compare with those of its foreign competitors. With investment, taxes can affect the extent to which U.S. firms establish operations abroad and can affect economic efficiency and welfare as well as the distribution of income within the domestic economy and between the United States and foreign countries. This report was originally written by David L. Brumbaugh, Specialist in Public Finance. It explains basic economic principles.

Taxes and International Trade: Competitiveness from theIndividual Firm's Perspective

One perspective on competitiveness is that of the individual U.S. firm with exclusively domestic operations. For such a firm, the focus of competitiveness is trade. The company and its components—its owners, managers, employees, and perhaps even the community in which it is situated—likely define competitiveness as the firm's ability to compete for market share against imports from abroad or to compete with foreign firms in overseas export markets. From this perspective, the impact of taxes on competitiveness likely seems straightforward: taxes are an item of cost, and so how the U.S. firm's own taxes compare with those of its foreign competitors likely appears to be of critical importance. And from the firm's perspective, targeted tax relief probably seems an obvious way to improve the firm's competitive position. For example, foreign governments may appear to be subsidizing the U.S. firm's foreign competitors; consequently, a tax benefit for exports or perhaps a tax credit or accelerated depreciation allowance may seem like useful ways to "level the playing field."[1]

The focus here is on trade, but although economic theory agrees that taxes can affect trade, they do so in ways that are frequently at odds with the results that may seem intuitive at the firm level. The reason for the diverging views is differences in perspective: economics points out that the impact of particular tax policies reverberates throughout the economy, causing adjustments that offset effects that may seem obvious at the firm level. As a result, to see the impact of taxes on trade accurately, the perspective must move beyond that of the individual firm to that of the economy as a whole.

In shifting to the economic perspective, we look first at the economy's trade balance, perhaps what is popularly viewed as how U.S. firms in the aggregate fare against their foreign competitors. Here, the economic conclusion appears almost counterintuitive: taxes on export income or on import-competing goods have no direct bearing on the balance of trade.[2] The reason is exchange-rate adjustments, which act to neutralize the impact of tax policies targeted at trade. An example may prove helpful. Suppose a country implements a tax benefit for exporting that is designed to offset foreign subsidies, real or perceived. Economics indicates that if foreign consumers are to buy more of the exports, they will require more of the domestic currency (i.e., dollars). The increased demand will drive up the exchange rate, making dollars more expensive for foreign buyers. The increased price of dollars will make exports more expensive for foreign buyers and imports of foreign goods less expensive for domestic buyers. Some or all of any initial expansion in exports will be offset by the adjustments, and imports will expand. After the adjustments, there will have been no change in the country's trade balance.

In short, taxes on trade do not directly affect the trade balance. Although this conclusion may seem counter intuition, its explanation is more easily understood when we look at the nature of the trade balance itself. An economy's trade balance—either a deficit or a surplus—is simply the amount by which the goods and services a country uses differs from the amount of goods and services it actually produces. A trade deficit is the excess of a country's current use of goods and services over what it produces; a trade surplus is the value of its production minus the value of what it keeps for itself. The intuition is this: just as an individual cannot consume more than he earns in a given period unless he borrows, a country cannot run a trade [illegible] unless it, in effect, borrows by importing capital from foreign countries to finance the

A country's trade balance, in short, is mirrored by its balance on capital account. For example, a country's trade deficit is necessarily mirrored by the excess of its imports of investment over investment outflows. Thus, the capital- and current-account balances move in lock-step; the trade balance can change only if capital flows change at the same time. Under the particular institutional framework of the current international economy, flexible exchange rates maintain the relation between the trade balance (the "current account") and the investment balance (the "balance on capital account"). In short, if a tax cut does not change the balance on capital account, the trade balance does not change.

If taxes do not affect the trade balance, what is their impact? Standard economic analysis relies on one of the basic foundations of international trade theory: Ricardo's theory of comparative advantage. Without presenting a comprehensive treatment of the theory, its essence holds that countries trade, in effect, in order to specialize in the production of those goods and services they produce most efficiently. Thus, it is the economy's own internal pattern of costs that matter rather than how its overall cost of production compares with those of foreign economies.

According to the theory of comparative advantage, taxes do not alter the *balance* of trade, but they can potentially alter the *composition* of trade. For example, if a country's taxes apply unevenly across its various industries, they will likely alter the particular mix of products the country imports and exports. Building on the above illustration where a tax credit or accelerated depreciation is targeted at an industry threatened by foreign competition, this analysis indicates that the targeted industry may well see its exports or import-competing sales increase as the targeted tax benefit alters the pattern of relative costs across the economy. At the same time, the international position of that country's less favored industries will decline as a part of the impact of taxes on the mix of goods that are exported and imported.

Economic analysis also indicates that tax policy towards trade can alter how economic welfare is distributed *within* the economy. For example, a targeted tax benefit designed to boost the competitiveness of one sector may in the short run benefit the owners and employees of the favored sector; at the same time, however, it will likely reduce economic welfare in sectors of the economy that do not receive the benefit. Again, however, economics emphasizes an economy- wide perspective. Here, it generally concludes that a tax policy that applies unevenly across sectors of the economy distorts the allocation of resources and diverts them from their most productive uses. Thus, although an uneven tax policy may produce "winners" in some sectors and "losers" in others, on balance the economy registers a reduction in economic welfare because of the reduction in economic efficiency. An uneven, distorting tax policy that is meant to improve trade performance likely means that the economy will specialize in the production of items it is not particularly good at making, to the detriment of overall economic welfare.

According to trade theory, each country that is a partner to trade obtains benefits from that trade; trading partners are not competing such that one country's gain is the other's loss. Rather, there are mutual gains from trade because trade allows countries to specialize in activities they do best and trade for products they make less efficiently. Under certain conditions, tax policy can alter how the gains from trade are shared among countries, but in ways that are, again, counterintuitive. For example, to the extent that an export subsidy is passed on to foreign consumers as lower prices, the subsidy shifts economic welfare from the subsidizing country to the foreign consumers of its exports. (In economic parlance, the subsidizing country's "terms of trade" are worsened.) Or, if a country has market power such that the burden of taxes on some goods is borne by foreign consumers, a judiciously applied tax policy could improve the terms of trade. However, even setting aside the international legality of such a policy and the possibility of retaliation, identifying the product areas where this might occur is problematic.

Taxes and Overseas Investment: Competitiveness andMultinational Corporations

Another perspective on competitiveness is that of a U.S. multinational corporation—a firm that is based in the United States but that has production facilities abroad (what economists term "foreign direct investment").[3] Such a firm likely defines competitiveness as the ability of its overseas operations to compete for market share with firms from foreign host countries or firms from third countries. With respect to taxes, the firm is likely to focus on how its own taxes compare with those of its foreign competitors. From this perspective, a policy that helps competitiveness is one that reduces the multinationals' taxes vis-a-vis foreign firms; multinationals have traditionally argued that a policy that exempts foreign operations from home- country (i.e., U.S.) tax ensures that U.S. multinationals are not at a competitive disadvantage with foreign firms.

The focus of this view of competitiveness is investment rather than trade. As with trade, however, economic theory's conclusions about the impact of taxes on investment differs from that of the firm. Economics agrees that home-country taxes can affect the attractiveness of overseas investment, and thus alter the extent to which U.S. firms undertake foreign direct investment. According to theory, however, the important comparison is not how foreign firms' taxes compare with those of the U.S. multinationals. Instead, the crucial comparison is between taxes on overseas investment—both U.S. taxes and any foreign taxes that apply—and the U.S. tax burden that would apply to alternative investment in the domestic economy. Where taxes on overseas investment are lower than taxes on domestic investment, firms undertake more foreign investment than they otherwise would; hence, this tax policy increases foreign investment. Where taxes on foreign investment are high, foreign investment is discouraged, and where taxes are the same in either location, tax policy does not alter the extent of foreign investment.

Theory acknowledges that a home-country exemption for foreign income may well maximize the competitiveness of the home country's multinationals. Again, however, economics indicates that a broader perspective produces different results. First, theory holds that, if left to their own devices, profit-maximizing firms will employ their investments in the most productive locations possible—a result that maximizes the economic welfare produced by the investment. Taxes, in turn, will not distort firms' investment decisions if tax burdens on domestic and foreign investment are equal. In short, although a tax exemption for foreign investment might maximize the competitive position of the home country's multinationals, a tax policy that equalizes tax burdens at home and abroad maximizes world economic welfare. In contrast, an exemption policy—one that maximizes multinational competitiveness—would likely distort the location of investment, resulting in more investment where foreign taxes are lower than taxes in the United States, and lower investment when foreign taxes are higher. The economics literature has developed labels for the different policies, as follows:

"competitive neutrality," or "capital import neutrality," is an exemption policy that maximizes the competitive position of a country's firms; "capital export neutrality" is a policy that produces equal tax burdens at home and abroad and that (as a result) maximizes world economic welfare because investment flows to its most efficient global location.

Economics also concludes that the perspective of multinationals' home country may differ from that of the foreign host countries. World economic welfare—that is, the welfare of the home and foreign countries combined—is maximized when capital is allocated to its most productive location. But if a country is capital-rich, as is the United States, the capital exporting country's economic welfare is maximized when tax policy to some extent discourages overseas investment. In such cases, foreign labor bears part of the burden of the export-discouraging tax, and policy increases the tax-inclusive return to the foreign investment that does occur. (Countries with less capital lack sufficient market power to pass on the burden of their taxes.) A tax policy of this nature, termed "national neutrality," would apply a higher tax burden to foreign operations than to domestic investment, thus damping the flow of capital abroad. As discussed further below, although a policy of national neutrality maximizes the capital exporting country's welfare, it also alters the division of income between capital and labor, shifting income towards labor and away from capital. Because national neutrality distorts the location of investment, it produces an inefficient "deadweight" reduction in world economic welfare.

It is beyond the scope of this report to describe how current U.S. tax policy affects foreign investment. Here, we simply note that U.S. policy varies widely, depending on the situation of the investing firm and the particular country where investment occurs. Different features of the system are consistent with different principles. For example, the ability of U.S. multinationals to in some cases indefinitely defer U.S. tax on foreign income is consistent with competitive neutrality. Other provisions (e.g., the foreign tax credit and Subpart F's limit of deferral) are consistent with capital export neutrality. The foreign tax credit itself is limited, however, a feature consistent with national neutrality.

International Taxation and Employment: Labor's Perspective

A third perspective on competitiveness is that of domestic labor in general.[4] As described in the first section's discussion of competitiveness from the individual firm's perspective, an individual firm's employees are likely to share concerns about trade with the firm's other "stakeholders." Like the firm's owners and managers, a trading firm's employees are likely to define competitiveness in trade as the firm's ability to compete against foreign firms in export markets or in markets within the United States. Labor's policy prescriptions are likely to be in accord with those of the firm's owners: targeted tax relief.

In contrast, labor's perspective on competitiveness and international investment generally diverges from that of a multinational firm's owners. Rather than viewing itself as being in competition with foreign multinationals (as U.S. multinationals often do), domestic labor frequently views the competition as being between investment sites; labor tends to view competitiveness as the ability of the United States to compete with foreign countries as a location for what it views as job-creating business investment. The tax policy prescription that results is in accordance with this view: domestic labor has tended to support tax polices that act to discourage overseas investment, in some cases supporting tax measures explicitly designed to penalize "runaway plants"—broadly, plants that shut down operations in the United States and shift production abroad.

What does economic theory say about labor and international investment? Here again, theory reaches certain conclusions that counter intuition. First, economic analysis is skeptical about the ability of international investment flows to affect the total level of employment in economy. In the short run, the closure of a domestic factory and its movement abroad will doubtless cause unemployment in the closed factory's location. In the long run, however, the economy tends to absorb much of the labor released when a firm shuts down or simply goes out of business. The economy as a whole, moreover, always has a certain amount of such transitional unemployment that occurs when firms alter their operations by, for example, shutting down operations in one location and moving to another, either at home or abroad.

The economic change behind such transitional employment is the result of a variety of factors, ranging from technological progress, to exogenous shocks, to changes in institutional policies. Theory suggests, however, that a permanent policy of discouraging the movement of U.S. firms abroad would not appreciably alter the economy's overall level of employment; economists generally believe that monetary and fiscal policy are the most effective methods of addressing spikes in unemployment, and that adjustment assistance is the most effective policy prescription for short-run, local job loss.

Although investment flows do not alter aggregate employment, theory does indicate that capital flows do affect the distribution of incomes within the domestic economy; this result was briefly noted in the previous section's discussion of national neutrality. The shift occurs because labor is more productive the more capital it has to work with. As a result, wages are generally higher and labor receives a larger share of income (and capital a smaller share) the higher is the domestic economy's capital/labor ratio. Thus, it is not surprising that labor views the flow of capital abroad with distrust, notwithstanding its tendency to see its results in terms of their impact on employment.

End Notes

[1] For an example of this perspective, see U.S. Congress, House, Committee on Small Business, *The WTO 's Challenge to FSC/ETI Rules and the Effects on America's Small Business Owners*, hearing, 108th Cong., 1st sess., May 14, 2003 (Washington: GPO, 2003), pp. 17-18.

[2] This sets aside the impact tax revenues may have on the trade balance through their effect on the government's budget deficit. For example, a tax cut that reduces government revenue may increase the budget deficit, placing upward pressure on real interest rates. The higher interest rates, in turn, may attract greater inflows of foreign capital. The exchange rate adjustments that result may increase the trade deficit.

[3] For an example of this perspective, see U.S. Congress, Senate, Committee on Finance, *An Examination of U.S. Tax Policy and Its Effect on the International Competitiveness of U.S.-Owned Foreign Operations*, hearing, 108th Cong., 1st sess., July 15, 2003 (Washington: GPO, 2003), p. 59.

[4] For an example of this perspective, see the testimony of AFL-CIO official Thea Lea, in U.S. Congress, House, Committee on Small Business, *The WTO 's Challenge to FSC/ETI Rules and the Effects on America's Small Business Owners*, p. 15.

Chapter Sources

The following chapters have been previously published:

Chapter 1 – This is an edited reformatted and augmented version of a Congressional Research Service publication, reportRL34115, dated December 17, 2010.
Chapter 2 – This is an edited reformatted and augmented version of a Congressional Research Service publication, report R40178, dated December 17, 2010.
Chapter 3 – This is an edited reformatted and augmented version of a Congressional Research Service publication, report RL34229, dated May 25, 2010.
Chapter 4 – This is an edited reformatted and augmented version of a Congressional Research Service publication, report RL31444. dated March 5, 2010.
Chapter 5 – This is an edited reformatted and augmented version of a Congressional Research Service publication, report R40623, dated September 3, 2010.
Chapter 6 – This is an edited reformatted and augmented version of a Congressional Research Service publication, report RS22445, dated March 11, 2008

INDEX

D

E

F

G

H

I

O

P

R

S

T

U

V

W

Y